Critter Woods Islay 19

Celebrate Good Times with Special-Occasion Recipes

WHETHER you're hosting a special holiday dinner for relatives or a more casual get-together for friends, you likely begin by planning a palate-pleasing menu. After all, a spread of home-cooked foods makes every occasion more memorable.

That's why we're pleased to present *Taste of Home's Holiday & Celebrations 2004*. This all-new photo-filled treasury features 274 mouth-watering recipes to make your Christmas, Thanksgiving, Easter and other celebrations throughout the year unforgettable. Like the previous three editions, we offer menu options and provide timetables to minimize last-minute fuss. Entertaining has never been so easy or enjoyable!

'Tis the Season. There are plenty of opportunities to gather with family and friends at Christmastime. Take the worry out of every holiday happening with a merry array of 124 dazzling dishes, including Appetizer Artichoke Bread, Beef Wellington, Swiss Potato Bake, Squash Pan Rolls, Lemon Cream Cheese Spritz and Chocolate-Macadamia Freezer Pie. If you're looking to host a sit-down dinner, you'll find two tasty menus—one casual chili dinner and one more formal meal. Or head to the kitchen and make yummy Yuletide treats to package in pretty ways and share with others.

Giving Thanks. Are you hoping to spice up your Thanksgiving menus but think you'll be met with some resistance? We guarantee your family will fall for Mandarin Goose, Golden Corn Muffins, Cranberry Dressing, Chunky Apple Pumpkin Bread, Ginger Pear Pie and many more of the 33 splendid dishes in this chapter.

Easter Gatherings. Early-day entertaining is a snap with a bounty of brunch recipes like Banana Hotcakes, Twice-Baked Cheese Souffles, Potatoes Olé and Dessert Corn Crepes. There will be many compliments for the cook when you serve a tried-and-true ham dinner. Round out these springtime menus with a selection of seasonal breads.

Special Celebrations. We also offer 86 family-favorite recipes for a host of other gatherings throughout the year. To keep winter blues at bay, celebrate the Chinese New Year, treat your sweetie to a fireside Valentine's Day dinner or plan a teddy bear birthday party for your child. Come summer, soak up the warm sunshine with a Memorial Day get-together, beach picnic or gathering in the garden. Then in autumn, root for your favorite football team at a winning tailgate party.

Can-Do Decorating Ideas. There are dozens of ideas for stunning table toppers (turn to page 118 for a splendid Sugared Fruit Centerpiece), quick and easy decorations (like the naturally dyed Easter eggs shown on page 155) and eye-catching napkin folds (see page 193 for a Heart-Shaped Napkin).

With unforgettable fare, simple decorating ideas and perfect party menus, *Taste of Home's Holiday & Celebrations Cookbook 2004* will help you make magical memories at every gathering with family and friends throughout the year.

WOULD YOU like to see one of your family-favorite recipes featured in a future edition of this timeless treasury? See page 256 for details!

HOLIDAY & Celebrations COOKBOOK 2004

Editor: Julie Schnittka
Senior Art Director: Linda Dzik
Food Editor: Janaan Cunningham
Craft Editor: Jane Craig
Associate Editors: Jean Steiner, Heidi Reuter Lloyd
Associate Food Editor: Coleen Martin
Assistant Food Editor: Karen Wright
Senior Recipe Editor: Sue A. Jurack
Recipe Editor: Janet Briggs
Test Kitchen Director: Karen Johnson
Test Kitchen Home Economists: Sue Draheim,
Tamra Duncan, Peggy Fleming, Wendy Stenman
Test Kitchen Assistants: Rita Krajcir, Megan Taylor
Food Stylists: Kristin Arnett, Joylyn Trickel
Food Photography: Rob Hagen, Dan Roberts
Senior Food Photography Artist: Stephanie Marchese
Food Photography Artist: Julie Ferron
Photo Studio Manager: Anne Schimmel
Graphic Art Associates: Ellen Lloyd, Catherine Fletcher
Chairman and Founder: Roy Reiman

Taste of Home Books
©2004 Reiman Media Group, Inc.
5400 S. 60th St., Greendale WI 53129
International Standard Book Number: 0-89821-414-9
International Standard Serial Number: 1535-2781
All rights reserved.
Printed in U.S.A.

For additional copies of this book, write *Taste of Home* Books, P.O.
Box 908, Greendale WI 53129. Or to order by credit card, call
toll-free 1-800/344-2560 or visit our Web site at
www.reimanpub.com.

PICTURED ON THE COVER: Mandarin Goose with Roasted
Autumn Vegetables (p. 116) and Cran-Apple Pie (p. 117).

'TIS THE
Season

The Christmas season presents ample opportunities to
get together with family and friends. We offer two
sit-down dinner choices—one casual chili supper and
one more formal affair. Perhaps hosting a party
with a table decked out in just desserts or
appetizers works better with your busy schedule.
We have all of your holiday happenings covered with
a merry array of dishes. We even offer ideas for making
(and creatively packaging!) gifts from the kitchen.

Chili Adds Spark to Christmas Eve Supper

WHEN there's a nip in the air on Christmas Eve, your dinner guests will warm up to the idea of a comfortable, low-key supper showcasing steaming pots of chili.

The delicious recipes featured here prove that a simple spread can be just as inviting as something more elaborate.

With its lovely red tomato base, Zippy Sausage Chili is the perfect color for Christmas.

As a tasty twist, encourage family and friends to ladle up hearty helpings of White Chili with Hominy. Then round out the homey meal by passing Herbed Breadsticks. (All recipes shown at right.)

This chapter also includes other merry main course ideas, a selection of salads and done-in-a-dash desserts.

KETTLE CREATIONS
White Chili with Hominy (p. 9)

Zippy Sausage Chili (p. 8)

Herbed Breadsticks (p. 8)

Zippy Sausage Chili

(Pictured on page 6)

Our family loves Mexican food, but I wasn't happy with any chili recipes I came across.
So I decided to make up my own. It's a winner with everyone who tries it.
—Laura Squier, Montrose, Pennsylvania

1-1/2 pounds bulk pork sausage
1 medium carrot, chopped
1/2 cup chopped green pepper
1 celery rib, chopped
1 can (28 ounces) stewed tomatoes
1 can (16 ounces) kidney beans, rinsed and drained
1 can (15-1/2 ounces) chili beans, undrained
1 can (15 ounces) pinto beans, rinsed and drained
1 can (5-1/2 ounces) V8 juice
3 tablespoons dried minced onion
1 teaspoon garlic powder
1 teaspoon pepper
1/4 teaspoon salt

In a large saucepan or soup kettle, cook the sausage, carrot, green pepper and celery over medium heat until meat is no longer pink; drain. Stir in the remaining ingredients. Bring to a boil. Reduce heat; cover and simmer for 45 minutes or until heated through. **Yield:** 8-10 servings.

Herbed Breadsticks

(Pictured on page 6)

Parmesan and a blend of seasonings flavor every bite of these cornmeal breadsticks that were
developed in our Test Kitchen. The dough is easy to roll out and cut into strips.

3-1/2 to 4 cups all-purpose flour
1 cup cornmeal
2 packages (1/4 ounce *each*) active dry yeast
2 teaspoons garlic salt
2 teaspoons Italian seasoning
1/2 teaspoon onion powder
1-1/3 cups milk
1/2 cup butter, cubed
4 eggs
1-1/2 cups shredded Parmesan cheese
Melted butter and additional Parmesan cheese

In a large mixing bowl, combine 2 cups flour, cornmeal, yeast, garlic salt, Italian seasoning and onion powder. In a small saucepan, heat milk and butter to 120°-130°. Add to dry ingredients; beat just until moistened. Add eggs; beat until smooth. Stir in the Parmesan cheese and enough remaining flour to form a soft dough. Do not knead (dough will be sticky). Cover and let rest for 15 minutes.

Divide dough in half. On a lightly floured surface, roll each portion into a 10-in. square. Cut into 1-in. strips. Place 2 in. apart on greased baking sheets. Cover and let rise in a warm place for 30 minutes.

Bake at 375° for 13-15 minutes or until golden brown. Brush with melted butter; sprinkle with additional Parmesan cheese. Serve warm. **Yield:** 20 breadsticks.

White Chili With Hominy

(Pictured at right and on page 6)

To make this chili a day ahead, cool, cover and chill after removing from the heat. The next day, reheat over low heat; add the sour cream, half-and-half and cilantro just before serving.

1 **pound boneless skinless chicken breasts, cut into 1/2-inch cubes**
1 **medium onion, chopped**
1 **tablespoon vegetable oil**
1 **can (15-1/2 ounces) white hominy, drained**
1 **can (15 ounces) white kidney *or* cannellini beans, rinsed and drained**
1 **can (14-1/2 ounces) chicken broth**
2 **cans (4 ounces *each*) chopped green chilies**
1 **teaspoon garlic salt**
1 **teaspoon dried basil**
1 **teaspoon ground cumin**
1/4 **teaspoon white pepper**
1/8 **to 1/4 teaspoon cayenne pepper**
1 **cup (8 ounces) sour cream**
1/3 **cup half-and-half cream**
2 **tablespoons minced fresh cilantro, *divided***

In a large saucepan, saute the chicken and onion in oil until chicken is no longer pink. Add the hominy, beans, broth, chilies and seasonings. Bring to a boil. Reduce heat; simmer, uncovered, for 30 minutes. Remove from the heat; stir in the sour cream, half-and-half and 1 tablespoon cilantro. Garnish with remaining cilantro. **Yield:** 6 servings.

Family Traditions

A few years ago, my mom invited everyone over for a chili dinner before the church service on Christmas Eve. Because my mom's chili isn't my favorite, I volunteered to make my own. I've been hosting the Christmas Eve chili dinner for our growing family ever since!
—Scott Craig
Big Bend, Wisconsin

Chow Mein Turkey Salad

Friends and family tease that I'm welcome at any gathering as long as I have this crunchy salad in tow! Soy sauce and chow mein noodles give it a slightly Asian flavor.
—*Cynthia Sweeney, Kapaau, Hawaii*

2 cups cubed cooked turkey *or* chicken
2 celery ribs, chopped
1 cup frozen peas, thawed
1/4 cup thinly sliced green onions
3/4 cup mayonnaise
1 tablespoon lemon juice
1 tablespoon soy sauce
1-1/2 teaspoons garlic powder
1 teaspoon Worcestershire sauce
1/4 teaspoon ground mustard
1 cup chow mein noodles
1/2 cup slivered almonds, toasted

In a bowl, combine the turkey, celery, peas and onions. In a small bowl, combine the mayonnaise, lemon juice, soy sauce, garlic powder, Worcestershire sauce and mustard. Add to turkey mixture and stir to coat. Cover and refrigerate for at least 3 hours. Just before serving, stir in chow mein noodles and almonds. **Yield:** 4 servings.

Broccoli-Cheese Stuffed Pizza

After eating stuffed pizza at various Italian restaurants, I decided to come up with my own version. The filling is very rich and resembles broccoli lasagna.
—*Gloria Vallieres, Shortsville, New York*

2 packages (1/4 ounce *each*) active dry yeast
1-1/2 cups warm water (110° to 115°)
5 tablespoons vegetable oil, *divided*
2 teaspoons salt
4-1/2 to 5 cups all-purpose flour
1 carton (15 ounces) ricotta cheese
1/2 teaspoon garlic powder
1/2 teaspoon dried oregano
2 cups (8 ounces) shredded mozzarella cheese
1 package (10 ounces) frozen broccoli florets, cooked and drained
1 can (4 ounces) sliced mushrooms, drained

In a mixing bowl, dissolve yeast in warm water. Add 4 tablespoons oil, salt and enough flour to form a soft dough. Turn onto a floured surface; knead until smooth and elastic, about 6-8 minutes. Place in a greased bowl, turning once to grease top. Cover and let rise in a warm place until doubled, about 1 hour.

Punch dough down. Turn onto a lightly floured surface; knead for 10 minutes. Divide in half. Roll each portion into a 15-in. x 10-in. rectangle; transfer each to a greased 15-in. x 10-in. x 1-in. baking pan. Cover and let rise until doubled, about 30 minutes.

Brush one rectangle with remaining oil. Spread with ricotta cheese. Sprinkle with garlic powder and oregano. Layer with mozzarella cheese, broccoli and mushrooms. Invert remaining rectangle over filling; pinch edges to seal. Bake at 400° for 20-30 minutes or until golden brown. **Yield:** 12-16 servings.

Italian Meatballs

(Pictured at right)

Grandma "Sini" would make these meatballs for our traditional spaghetti dinner every Sunday. They freeze well, so bake an extra batch when time allows. Then combine with your favorite homemade or purchased sauce and serve over pasta.
—Adele Pansini
Huntington Beach, California

    4 slices day-old French bread
       (1/2 inch thick)
    1 cup milk
    2 eggs
 1/3 cup grated Parmesan cheese
 1/4 cup minced fresh parsley
    4 garlic cloves, peeled
    1 tablespoon olive oil
    2 teaspoons salt
 1/2 teaspoon pepper
 1/4 teaspoon ground allspice
    2 pounds ground beef
 1/2 pound bulk Italian sausage
Marinara sauce
Hot cooked pasta

Soak bread in milk for 10 minutes; drain and squeeze bread. In a blender or food processor, combine the bread, eggs, Parmesan cheese, parsley, garlic, oil, salt, pepper and allspice; cover and process until smooth.

In a large bowl, combine the beef and sausage. Add bread mixture; mix well. Shape into 2-in. balls. Place in an ungreased 15-in. x 10-in. x 1-in. baking pan. Bake, uncovered, at 400° for 20-25 minutes or until the meatballs are no longer pink. In a large saucepan, heat marinara sauce; add the meatballs and heat through. Serve over pasta. **Yield:** 6-8 servings.

Mocha Angel Food Torte

*Our Test Kitchen home economists dress up purchased angel food cake with
an easy-to-make coffee-flavored frosting.*

2 tablespoons instant coffee
   granules
3 tablespoons boiling water
1 cup butter, softened
2 tablespoons baking cocoa
4 cups confectioners' sugar
1 prepared angel food cake
   (8 to 10 inches)
Chocolate sprinkles, optional

For frosting, in a small bowl, dissolve coffee granules in water; set aside. In a mixing bowl, cream butter until light and fluffy. Beat in cocoa. Gradually beat in confectioners' sugar and coffee until smooth.

Cut cake into three horizontal layers. Place bottom layer on a serving plate; spread with frosting. Repeat with middle cake layer. Top with remaining cake layer; frost top and sides of cake. Garnish with chocolate sprinkles if desired. **Yield:** 10-12 servings.

CUTTING A CAKE INTO THREE LAYERS

TO CUT A CAKE into three layers, first measure the height of the cake with a ruler. Divide the number by three to determine the height of each layer. (It's okay if each layer's height isn't exactly the same…make them as close as possible.)

With the ruler, mark the height of the bottom layer with a toothpick. From that toothpick, measure the height of the middle layer and mark with a toothpick. Continue measuring around the cake, inserting toothpicks every few inches.

Using the highest set of toothpicks as guides, cut off the top layer of the cake with a long serrated knife. Carefully set aside. Using the remaining toothpicks as guides, cut off the middle layer; carefully set aside. Discard toothpicks. Frost as directed.

Frosted Cranberry Salad

*Covered with a fluffy white topping, squares of this
fruity gelatin salad can be served as a side dish or dessert.*
—Lila June Bungard, Moundsville, West Virginia

1 can (8 ounces) crushed
   pineapple
1 package (6 ounces) lemon
   gelatin
1 cup ginger ale, chilled
1 can (16 ounces) jellied
   cranberry sauce

1/2 cup chopped peeled tart apple
1/2 cup chopped celery
  1 package (8 ounces) cream cheese, softened
1/4 cup sugar
  1 envelope whipped topping mix
1/2 cup chopped pecans, toasted

Drain pineapple, reserving juice; set pineapple aside. Add enough water to juice to measure 1 cup. Pour into a small saucepan; bring to a boil. Carefully pour into a large bowl; stir in gelatin until dissolved. Add ginger ale. Refrigerate until syrupy, about 45 minutes.

Combine the cranberry sauce, apple, celery and reserved pineapple; fold into gelatin mixture. Transfer to a 9-in. square dish. Refrigerate until firm.

In a small mixing bowl, beat cream cheese and sugar until fluffy. Prepare whipped topping mix according to package directions; fold into cream cheese mixture. Spread over gelatin. Sprinkle with pecans. **Yield:** 9-12 servings.

Layered Brownie Dessert

(Pictured at right)

A tasty brownie is the base for cream cheese and chocolate pudding layers in this make-ahead dessert.
—*Muriel Ledeboer, Oostburg, Wisconsin*

1 cup butter, softened
2 cups sugar
2 eggs
1 teaspoon vanilla extract
2 cups all-purpose flour
1/2 cup baking cocoa
1/2 teaspoon salt
1/2 teaspoon baking powder
1 cup chopped walnuts
FILLING:
  2 packages (one 8 ounces, one 3 ounces) cream cheese, softened
  2 cups confectioners' sugar
  2 cups whipped topping
TOPPING:
  2 cups cold milk
  1 package (3.9 ounces) instant chocolate pudding mix
Whipped topping and chopped walnuts

In a large mixing bowl, cream butter and sugar. Add eggs, one at a time, beating well after each addition. Add vanilla. Combine the flour, cocoa, salt and baking powder; add to creamed mixture just until moistened. Stir in nuts. Transfer to a greased 13-in. x 9-in. x 2-in. baking pan. Bake at 350° for 20-25 minutes or until a toothpick inserted near the center comes out clean. Cool completely on a wire rack.

In a small mixing bowl, beat cream cheese and confectioners' sugar until smooth. Fold in whipped topping; spread over brownies. In a bowl, whisk milk and pudding mix for 2 minutes. Let stand for 2 minutes or until soft-set. Spread over filling. Refrigerate for 1 hour or until serving. Cut into squares; garnish with whipped topping and nuts. **Yield:** 12-15 servings.

Sweet 'n' Sour Polish Sausage

Since my sister, Evelyn Brower, shared this recipe with me, I've made it for many gatherings.
It can be cooked in a skillet, then transferred to a slow cooker to keep warm.
—Elaine Hair, Stedman, North Carolina

1 **pound fully cooked Polish sausage *or* kielbasa, cut into 1/2-inch slices**
1 **medium onion, diced**
1 **small green pepper, diced**
1 **celery rib, diced**
1 **tablespoon butter**
1 **cup packed brown sugar**
3/4 **cup ketchup**
1/2 **cup cider vinegar**
1 **teaspoon salt**
1 **can (20 ounces) pineapple chunks**
3 **tablespoons cornstarch**
1/4 **cup cold water**
Hot cooked rice

In a large skillet, saute the sausage, onion, green pepper and celery in butter over medium heat until meat is no longer pink and vegetables are tender; remove with a slotted spoon and set aside.

In the same skillet, combine the brown sugar, ketchup, vinegar and salt. Drain pineapple, reserving juice; set pineapple aside. Add juice to skillet; bring to a boil. Return sausage mixture to pan. Combine the cornstarch and water until smooth; stir into skillet. Bring to a boil; cook and stir for 2 minutes or until thickened. Stir in reserved pineapple; heat through. Serve over rice. **Yield:** 6 servings.

BEAN POT CENTERPIECES

TO PLAY upon the ingredients in the chili featured in our Christmas Eve supper, we concocted individual Bean Pot Centerpieces.

Simply fill small cast-iron pots (or any other small sturdy containers) with an assortment of dried beans. Place a candle in the center. Set a bean-filled pot in the middle of the table between each place setting.

If you prefer one large centerpiece, use a bigger pot and several candles of varying heights. Place in the middle of the table.

A Cozy Table for Christmas

(Pictured above)

WHEN hosting a casual dinner at Christmastime, select table coverings that suggest a more informal setting.

Instead of turning to your most luxurious linens, get creative and blanket the table with a clean flannel, fleece or wool throw. Even a smooth cotton quilt is an eye-catching alternative. (For easy cleanup, look for a covering that can easily be washed before and after use.)

We relied on a red and green plaid flannel stadium blanket. But any festive color or winter pattern will do. Use one large throw—or several throws—to cover the entire table.

Next round up inexpensive fleece scarves. Although we used only solid green scarves, feel free to mix and match colors and patterns that go with your table covering.

At each place setting, lay a scarf across the width of the table, draping over the edges. Set out your dishes and flatware on these innovative place mats.

If you don't have any scarves that work, head to the fabric store and have some colorful felt cut to size.

Then place Bean Pot Centerpieces (see page 14) in the middle of the scarves between each place setting.

Christmas Dinner Has Touch of Class

THE mouth-watering Christmas Day dinner highlighted here takes tried-and-true foods and gives them a tasty twist.

Ordinary pork tenderloins become extra-special when filled with a stuffing in Cranberry-Apricot Pork Tenderloins.

A side dish like Twice-as-Nice Mashed Potatoes is doubly delicious because it features both red and sweet potatoes.

Grapefruit, oranges and avocados put a new spin on simple salad greens in Citrus Avocado Salad.

Maple Praline Cheesecake teams maple syrup and toffee bits. (All recipes shown at right.)

Appetizer Blue Cheese Logs and Marvelous Mushroom Soup round out this yummy Yuletide dinner.

MERRY CHRISTMAS MENU
(Clockwise from top)

Citrus Avocado Salad (p. 19)

Twice-as-Nice Mashed Potatoes (p. 20)

Cranberry-Apricot Pork Tenderloins (p. 20)

Maple Praline Cheesecake (p. 22)

CHRISTMAS DINNER MENU PLANNER

A Few Weeks Before:
- Prepare two grocery lists—one for non-perishable items to purchase now and one for perishable items to purchase a few days before Christmas Day.

Two Days Before:
- Set the table.
- Buy remaining grocery items, including those for the Hurricane Lamp Centerpiece (see page 23). Fill hurricane with nuts and kumquats. Make Clove-Studded Oranges.
- Bake Maple Praline Cheesecake, refrigerate and remove sides of pan as directed. Do not top with maple syrup-flavored whipped topping. Return to the refrigerator.
- Roast garlic bulb for Twice-as-Nice Mashed Potatoes; reserve oil and peel cloves. Place garlic and oil in an airtight container; chill.
- Chop the onions for Marvelous Mushroom Soup. Refrigerate in a resealable plastic bag.

Christmas Eve:
- Make the fruit stuffing for Cranberry-Apricot Pork Tenderloins. Transfer to a covered container; chill. Flatten the pork tenderloins and place on a baking sheet. Cover and refrigerate.
- Assemble the Twice-as-Nice Mashed Potatoes; cover and refrigerate.

- For Citrus Avocado Salad, wash and tear the salad greens; chill in a resealable plastic bag. Peel and section or slice the grapefruit, oranges and onion; refrigerate in separate resealable plastic bags. Make and chill the dressing.
- Assemble Appetizer Blue Cheese Logs; cover and refrigerate.

Christmas Day:
- In the morning, assemble the Cranberry-Apricot Pork Tenderloins; place on a rack in a shallow roasting pan. Cover and refrigerate until ready to bake.
- Make Marvelous Mushroom Soup; cool. Cover and refrigerate. Reheat just before serving.
- Finish making the centerpiece by setting evergreen and holly branches and Clove-Studded Oranges around it.
- Just before guests arrive, set out crackers and Appetizer Blue Cheese Logs.
- Remove Twice-as-Nice Mashed Potatoes from the refrigerator 30 minutes before baking as directed.
- After removing pork tenderloins from the oven, peel and slice avocados for the salad; combine with remaining salad ingredients. Shake dressing; drizzle over salad and toss to coat.
- For the Maple Praline Cheesecake, combine whipped topping and maple syrup. Spread over the top and serve.

Citrus Avocado Salad

(Pictured at right and on page 17)

This recipe nicely showcases grapefruit and oranges, which are at their peak around the holidays. Citrus fruits pair well with a sweet dressing.
—Sonia Candler, Edmonton, Alberta

12 cups torn salad greens
2 medium grapefruit, peeled and sectioned
2 medium navel oranges, peeled and sectioned
2 medium ripe avocados, peeled and sliced
1 small red onion, thinly sliced and separated into rings

DRESSING:
1/2 cup vegetable oil
1/4 cup sugar
3 tablespoons lemon juice
1-1/2 teaspoons poppy seeds
1/2 teaspoon salt
1/4 teaspoon ground mustard
1/4 teaspoon grated onion

In a large salad bowl, gently toss the greens, grapefruit, oranges, avocados and red onion. In a jar with a tight-fitting lid, combine the dressing ingredients; shake well. Drizzle over salad and toss to coat. **Yield:** 12 servings.

PEELING AND SECTIONING GRAPEFRUIT

WHEN peeling and sectioning grapefruit to use in salads, it's sometimes difficult to remove the bitter white pith.

An easy solution is to bring water to a boil in a saucepan; place the whole grapefruit in the water. Remove from the heat; let stand for about 5 minutes. With a tongs, remove the grapefruit from the water. When cool enough to handle, easily peel away the skin and pith.

Cranberry-Apricot Pork Tenderloins

(Pictured on page 16)

A cranberry and apricot stuffing wonderfully complements pork tenderloin.
This is an elegant entree that you can pull together in no time.
—Joann Brown, Los Alamos, New Mexico

1 cup dried cranberries
1 cup chopped dried apricots
3 tablespoons water
2 teaspoons dried rosemary, crushed
1/2 teaspoon salt
1/4 teaspoon pepper
2 pork tenderloins (1 pound *each*)
Additional salt and pepper, optional

In a saucepan, combine the cranberries, apricots, water, rosemary, salt and pepper. Bring to a boil. Reduce heat; cover and simmer for 10 minutes or until fruit is softened. Cool.

Cut a lengthwise slit down the center of each tenderloin to within 1/2 in. of bottom. Open tenderloins so they lie flat; cover with plastic wrap. Flatten to 3/4-in. thickness; remove plastic. Spread fruit mixture to within 1/2 in. of ends. Close tenderloins; tie several times with kitchen string and secure with toothpicks.

Place on a rack in a shallow roasting pan. Sprinkle with additional salt and pepper if desired. Bake, uncovered, at 400° for 30-35 minutes or until a meat thermometer reads 160°. **Yield:** 6-8 servings.

Twice-as-Nice Mashed Potatoes

(Pictured on page 17)

If you can't decide what kind of potatoes to serve, reach for this recipe, which blends both
red and sweet potatoes. It will quickly become a staple at all of your holiday dinners.
—Kerry Schroeppel, Springfield, Missouri

1 large whole garlic bulb
2 tablespoons olive oil
1-1/2 pounds red potatoes, peeled and cubed
1-1/2 pounds sweet potatoes, peeled and cubed
1/2 cup milk
1/4 cup butter, softened
1/2 teaspoon dried rosemary, crushed
1/3 cup grated Parmesan cheese
Salt and pepper to taste

Remove papery outer skin from garlic (do not peel or separate cloves). Brush with oil. Wrap bulb in heavy-duty foil. Bake at 425° for 30-35 minutes or until softened. Cool for 10-15 minutes; peel garlic and reserve oil. Reduce heat to 400°.

Place red and sweet potatoes in separate saucepans; cover with water. Bring to a boil. Reduce heat; cover and cook for 15-20 minutes or until very tender. Drain.

Place both potatoes in a large mixing bowl. Add the milk, butter, rosemary, roasted garlic and reserved oil. Stir in Parmesan cheese, salt and pepper. Transfer to a greased 1-1/2-qt. baking dish. Cover and bake for 25-30 minutes or until heated through. **Yield:** 6-8 servings.

Marvelous Mushroom Soup

(Pictured at right)

Some mushroom soups seem to have more broth than mushrooms. That's why I love this version brimming with superb "shrooms"!
—Laura Mahaffey
Annapolis, Maryland

    3 medium onions, chopped
    2 garlic cloves, minced
1/4 cup butter
    2 pounds fresh mushrooms,
      chopped
    2 cups heavy whipping cream
    2 cups beef broth
1/2 teaspoon salt
1/2 teaspoon pepper
**Grated Parmesan cheese and
  minced fresh parsley, optional**

In a large saucepan, cook onions and garlic in butter over medium-low heat until tender. Reduce heat to low; add the mushrooms. Cook for 8-10 minutes or until tender, stirring occasionally.

Add the cream, broth, salt and pepper; cook and stir over low heat until heated through. Garnish with Parmesan cheese and parsley if desired. **Yield:** 9 servings (about 2 quarts).

Maple Praline Cheesecake

(Pictured on page 16)

Our Test Kitchen home economists created this cheesecake filled with maple syrup and toffee bits.

1-1/2 cups finely chopped pecans
1/2 cup flaked coconut
1/3 cup all-purpose flour
2 tablespoons brown sugar
1/4 cup butter, melted
FILLING:
4 packages (8 ounces *each*)
cream cheese, softened
3/4 cup packed brown sugar
1/4 cup all-purpose flour
3/4 cup half-and-half cream
1/4 cup maple syrup
2 teaspoons vanilla extract
1/4 teaspoon salt
3 eggs, lightly beaten
1/2 cup English toffee bits *or*
almond brickle chips
TOPPING:
2 tablespoons maple syrup
2 cups whipped topping

1/4 cup English toffee bits *or* almond brickle chips

In a bowl, combine the pecans, coconut, flour and brown sugar; stir in butter. Press onto the bottom of a 10-in. springform pan. Place on a baking sheet. Bake at 350° for 10 minutes. Place pan on a wire rack (leave oven on).

In a large mixing bowl, beat cream cheese until smooth. Combine brown sugar and flour; add to cream cheese. Add the cream, syrup, vanilla and salt; beat until smooth. Beat in the eggs just until combined. Stir in toffee bits. Pour over crust. Return pan to baking sheet.

Bake for 50-55 minutes or until center is almost set. Cool on a wire rack for 10 minutes. Carefully run a knife around edge of pan to loosen; cool 1 hour longer. Refrigerate overnight.

Remove sides of pan. In a small bowl, combine the syrup and whipped topping; carefully spread over cheesecake. Sprinkle with toffee bits. Refrigerate leftovers. **Yield:** 16 servings.

Appetizer Blue Cheese Logs

Three kinds of cheese and some curry powder make this cheese log a little more lively than most.
—Ethel Johnson, North Saanich, British Columbia

1 package (8 ounces) cream
cheese, softened
1 cup (4 ounces) shredded
sharp cheddar cheese
1/2 cup crumbled blue cheese
1-1/2 teaspoons curry powder
1 tablespoon butter
1/2 cup finely chopped pecans
2 tablespoons minced fresh
parsley
Assorted crackers

In a mixing bowl, beat the cream cheese. Fold in cheddar cheese and blue cheese. Cover and refrigerate for at least 2 hours.

In a small skillet, saute curry powder in butter for 1-2 minutes. Stir in pecans; cook and stir for 1 minute. Stir in parsley. Cool slightly. Roll cheese mixture into two logs, about 5 in. long. Roll in pecan mixture. Cover and refrigerate until serving. Serve with crackers. **Yield:** 2 cheese logs.

Hurricane Lamp Centerpiece

(Pictured at right and on page 17)

CELEBRATE the Yuletide season by fashioning this centerpiece, which showcases mixed nuts, oranges and pine branches.

Start with a tall clear glass hurricane with an enclosed bottom. Apply a little candle tack to the bottom of a taper candle. Center the candle in the bottom of the hurricane.

Carefully arrange mixed nuts around the candle. We also tucked in some fresh kumquats. These small yellow-orange citrus fruits break up the brown tones of the nuts. Position the filled hurricane on the table.

Place several short fresh evergreen and holly branches around the base of the hurricane. Set Clove-Studded Oranges (see below) on the branches.

The contents of the hurricane and the Clove-Studded Oranges can be assembled several days in advance. On

Christmas morning, set the branches around the hurricane, then top with the oranges.

CLOVE-STUDDED ORANGES

FOR CENTURIES, people have used clove-studded fruits, called pomanders, to naturally add fragrance to their homes, especially at Christmastime.

Traditional pomanders are studded with cloves, covered with a special spice mix and allowed to dry. For the easy-to-prepare pomanders shown here, use a metal skewer or nail to create a spiral design on the oranges. Insert whole cloves into each hole. Position oranges on the branches for the Hurricane Lamp Centerpiece (above). The pomanders can also be displayed in a clear glass bowl.

Holiday Appetizers A Tasteful Tone

Crab Spread

IF PLANNING a sit-down holiday dinner for your close friends isn't in tune with your busy schedule, a table topped with elegant appetizers will be music to your ears!

That's because many of the recipes featured here have make-ahead qualities that strike a chord with time-conscious cooks.

Your party won't have a single sour note if you pour Cherry Jubilee Splash, then present hearty Pork Pinwheels and Shrimp with Roasted Peppers.

Oven-fresh snacks like Crab Spread and Feta Artichoke Bites will have hungry guests singing your praises. (All recipes are shown at right.)

Turn the page for a mouth-watering melody of more hot and cold appetizers.

Cherry Jubilee Splash

Shrimp with Roasted Peppers

Feta Artichoke Bites

Pork Pinwheels

A SYMPHONY OF SNACKS
(Clockwise from top left)

Crab Spread (p. 28)

Shrimp with Roasted Peppers (p. 27)

Cherry Jubilee Splash (p. 26)

Feta Artichoke Bites (p. 30)

Pork Pinwheels (p. 26)

Pork Pinwheels

(Pictured on page 24)

A flavorful filling peeks out from the swirled slices of pork.
This make-ahead appetizer is enhanced with garlic mayonnaise.
—Mary Lou Wayman, Salt Lake City, Utah

GARLIC MAYONNAISE:
- 1 large whole garlic bulb
- 2 teaspoons olive oil
- 1/2 cup mayonnaise
- 1 to 3 teaspoons milk, optional

STUFFING:
- 3 medium leeks (white portion only), thinly sliced
- 4 tablespoons olive oil, *divided*
- 1 cup minced fresh parsley
- 1/4 cup grated Parmesan cheese
- 1 tablespoon minced fresh thyme *or* 1 teaspoon dried thyme
- 1/4 teaspoon salt
- 1/4 teaspoon pepper
- 1/4 cup chopped walnuts
- 2 pork tenderloins (3/4 pound *each*)

Remove the papery outer skin from garlic (do not peel or separate cloves). Cut top off garlic bulb. Brush with oil. Wrap bulb in heavy-duty foil. Bake at 425° for 30-35 minutes or until softened. Cool for 10-15 minutes. Squeeze softened garlic into a small bowl; mash until smooth. Stir in mayonnaise and milk if needed to achieve a creamy consistency. Cover and chill for at least 3 hours.

In a skillet, saute leeks in 1 tablespoon oil until tender; remove from the heat. In a blender or food processor, combine the parsley, Parmesan cheese, thyme, salt and pepper. Gradually add the remaining oil; process until creamy. Add walnuts and leek mixture; coarsely chop. Set aside.

Make a lengthwise slit in each tenderloin to within 1/2 in. of the opposite side. Open tenderloins so they lie flat; cover with plastic wrap. Flatten to 3/4-in. thickness; remove plastic wrap. Spread leek mixture to within 1 in. of edges. Roll up from a long side; tie with kitchen string to secure.

Place tenderloins seam side down on a rack in a shallow roasting pan. Bake, uncovered, at 325° for 45-55 minutes or until a meat thermometer reads 160°. Let stand for 15 minutes. Cover and chill. Discard string; cut pork into 1/2-in. slices. Serve with garlic mayonnaise. **Yield:** about 2-1/2 dozen.

Cherry Jubilee Splash

(Pictured on page 25)

When entertaining, it's nice to rely on recipes like this that go together quickly.
—Karen Ann Bland, Gove, Kansas

- 4 cups orange juice
- 4 cups ginger ale, chilled
- 1 cup maraschino cherry juice
- 4 cups ice cubes

Maraschino cherries with stems and fresh mint

In a large pitcher, combine the orange juice, ginger ale and cherry juice. Pour into eight tall glasses filled with ice. Garnish with cherries and mint. **Yield:** 8 servings.

Shrimp with Roasted Peppers

(Pictured at right and on page 25)

Our Test Kitchen home economists came up with this flavor-packed variation of shrimp cocktail.

2 large sweet red peppers
2 large sweet yellow peppers
1 can (15 ounces) black beans, rinsed and drained
1 cup chopped seeded tomatoes
2/3 cup chopped red onion
1/4 cup minced fresh cilantro
1 jalapeno pepper, seeded and chopped*
MARINADE:
3/4 cup lemon juice
1/4 cup olive oil
1 tablespoon crushed red pepper flakes
1/2 teaspoon salt
1/2 teaspoon ground cumin
1 pound uncooked large shrimp, peeled and deveined
AVOCADO DRESSING:
2/3 cup olive oil
1/4 cup white wine vinegar
1 tablespoon lemon juice
1 tablespoon minced fresh cilantro
1/2 teaspoon salt
Dash cayenne pepper
1 medium ripe avocado, peeled and sliced
Lemon slices and cilantro leaves

Cut peppers in half; remove stems and seeds. Broil skin side up 4 in. from the heat until skins are blistered and black-ened. Immediately place peppers in a bowl; cover and let stand for 15-20 minutes. Meanwhile, combine the beans, tomatoes, onion, cilantro and jalapeno in a large bowl. Peel off and discard charred skin from peppers. Cut into thin 1-in. strips; add to tomato mixture and set aside.

In a large resealable plastic bag, combine the lemon juice, oil, pepper flakes, salt and cumin; add shrimp. Seal bag and turn to coat; refrigerate for 30 minutes.

For dressing, combine the oil, vinegar, lemon juice, cilantro, salt and cayenne in a blender; cover and process until smooth. Add avocado; cover and pulse just until blended.

Drain and discard marinade from shrimp. In a large skillet, saute shrimp for 3-5 minutes or until shrimp turn pink. Add to pepper mixture. Add 1/2 cup avocado dress-ing; toss to coat. Spoon into serving glasses or bowls; gar-nish with lemon and cilantro. Serve with remaining avoca-do dressing. **Yield:** 6 servings.

*Editor's Note: When cutting or seeding hot peppers, use rubber or plastic gloves to protect your hands. Avoid touch-ing your face.

APPETIZER STEMWARE SERVERS

WITH the assortment of hors d'oeuvres at your ap-petizer buffet, guests will likely have their plates piled high! Instead of having them juggle to add Shrimp with Roasted Peppers to their already-full plates, use stemware to dish out single-serving por-tions, as shown in the photo above.

ORCHESTRATE AN APPETIZER PARTY WITH EASE

HOSTING an appetizer buffet with no set seating is easy on the host. But to make it more manageable for guests to mingle while munching, make note of these key tips:

- Think about guests who might have trouble standing for any length of time. Arrange a few groupings of two to three chairs where several people can converse.
- Position extra end tables throughout the house so guests are able to set down their beverages.
- When planning the menu, look for recipes with make-ahead aspects to prevent last-minute fuss. Have a variety of tastes, textures and colors to please your guests' palates.
- Chose a selection of snacks that can be picked up and eaten without a plate, such as cubed sausage and cheese, skewered meatballs, fruit kabobs and cut-up vegetables. Avoid foods that require a lot of cutting.
- Set out bowls of nuts and snack mixes in other rooms. Make extra napkins readily available.

- Offer guests small, sturdy plates that are easy to handle. Consider making simple-to-carry bundles of cutlery and napkins.
- Think about the traffic flow and place plates, napkins and utensils on the buffet table near the doorway where folks will walk into the room. Make sure guests can reach all of the serving platters on the table.
- To discourage lingering and congestion around the buffet, remove chairs and other tables from the room. Set up the beverage station in a different area.
- People are more inclined to eat something when they know exactly what it is. So consider labeling the appetizers on your buffet table with place cards. (See our innovative idea on page 41.)
- It's tempting to hide trash receptacles for a party, but all of the used plates, napkins, utensils and toothpicks from an appetizer buffet can look a little unsightly when they start piling up. So make wastebaskets visible in various rooms.

Crab Spread
(Pictured on page 24)

My family has fond memories of traveling to my parents' house for Christmas dinner. After a 12-hour drive, we'd be welcomed in the door with this special seafood spread.
—Barbara Biddle, Harrisburg, Pennsylvania

1 package (8 ounces) cream cheese, softened
1 can (6 ounces) crabmeat, drained, flaked and cartilage removed
2 tablespoons mayonnaise
1 teaspoon Dijon mustard
1/2 teaspoon lemon-pepper seasoning
1/4 teaspoon minced garlic
Paprika
Crackers *or* vegetables

In a small mixing bowl, combine the first six ingredients. To serve chilled, cover and refrigerate until serving. Sprinkle with paprika. To serve warm, spoon into a greased 3-cup baking dish. Bake, uncovered, at 375° for 15 minutes or until heated through. Serve with crackers or vegetables. **Yield:** 2 cups.

Salsa Cheesecake

(Pictured at right)

After receiving this recipe from a friend several years ago, I made it for our family Christmas party. It's now one of our traditional holiday foods. It's a tasty spin on taco dip.
—Glory Windham
Grand Cane, Louisiana

2 packages (8 ounces *each*) cream cheese, softened
2 cups (8 ounces) shredded Monterey Jack cheese
2 cups (16 ounces) sour cream, *divided*
3 eggs, lightly beaten
1 cup salsa
1 can (4 ounces) chopped green chilies, drained
Guacamole
1 medium tomato, diced
Tortilla chips *or* crackers

In a small mixing bowl, beat cream cheese and Monterey Jack cheese until light and fluffy. Beat in 1 cup sour cream just until combined. Add eggs; beat on low speed just until combined. Stir in the salsa and chilies. Pour into a greased 9-in. springform pan. Place pan on a baking sheet. Bake at 350° for 40-45 minutes or until center is almost set.

Remove from the oven; immediately spread with remaining sour cream. Cool on a wire rack for 10 minutes. Carefully run a knife around edge of pan to loosen; cool 1 hour longer. Refrigerate for at least 5 hours or overnight.

To serve, remove sides of pan. Garnish with guacamole and diced tomato. Serve with tortilla chips or crackers. Refrigerate leftovers. **Yield:** 20-24 servings.

Feta Artichoke Bites

(Pictured on page 25)

You can prepare the flavorful topping for this appetizer ahead of time.
Then spread onto slices of bread and broil for a fast, festive snack.
—Louise Leach, Chino, California

1 jar (7-1/2 ounces) marinated
  artichoke hearts
1 cup diced seeded tomatoes
1 cup (4 ounces) crumbled feta
  cheese
1/3 cup grated Parmesan cheese
2 green onions, thinly sliced
1 sourdough baguette (about 20
  inches long)

Drain artichokes, reserving 2 table-spoons marinade. Chop artichokes and place in a bowl. Stir in the tomatoes, cheeses, onions and reserved marinade. Cover and refrigerate for 1 hour. Cut baguette into 1/2-in. slices. Spread with artichoke mixture. Place on an ungreased baking sheet. Broil 4-6 in. from the heat for 4-5 minutes or until edges of bread are browned. Serve immediately. **Yield:** about 3 dozen.

THE HISTORY OF FETA CHEESE

FETA is a white, salty, semi-firm cheese. Traditionally it was made from sheep or goat's milk but is now also made with cow's milk. After feta is formed in a special mold, it's sliced into large pieces, salted and soaked in brine. Although feta cheese is mostly associated with Greek cooking, "feta" comes from the Italian word "fette", meaning slice of food.

Spinach Roll-Ups

These pretty pinwheels capture the classic flavor of spinach dip served in a bread bowl.
—Patti Koepp, Marquette, Michigan

1 cup mayonnaise
1/2 cup sour cream
1 package (3 ounces) cream
  cheese, softened
6 green onions, chopped
1/3 cup crumbled cooked bacon
1 envelope ranch salad
  dressing mix
2 packages (10 ounces *each*)
  frozen chopped spinach,
  thawed and squeezed dry
6 flour tortillas (8 inches)

In a bowl, combine the mayonnaise, sour cream, cream cheese, onions, bacon and salad dressing mix. Stir in spinach until well blended. Spread over tortillas; roll up tightly jelly-roll style. Wrap in plastic wrap. Refrigerate for at least 5 hours. With a serrated knife, cut into 1/2-in. slices. Refrigerate leftovers. **Yield:** 12-14 servings.

Ham and Cheese Tarts

(Pictured at right)

These savory tarts have been a family favorite for years. Make the ham mixture in advance to save time when guests arrive.
—*Delores Romyn, Stratton, Ontario*

- 2 packages (3 ounces *each*) cream cheese, softened
- 1/2 cup French onion dip
- 1 tablespoon milk
- 1/4 teaspoon ground mustard
- 1/4 teaspoon grated orange peel
- 1/2 cup finely chopped fully cooked ham
- 1 tube (12 ounces) refrigerated buttermilk biscuits
- 1/4 teaspoon paprika

In a small mixing bowl, beat the cream cheese, onion dip, milk, mustard and orange peel until blended. Stir in ham. Split each biscuit into thirds; press into lightly greased miniature muffin cups. Spoon a scant tablespoonful of ham mixture into each cup; sprinkle with paprika. Bake at 375° for 12-17 minutes or until golden brown. Serve warm. **Yield:** 2-1/2 dozen.

Party Taco Dip

My pie plate is always scraped clean whenever I make this fast and flavorful dip.
For a pretty presentation, garnish with chopped tomatoes, sliced black olives and shredded lettuce.
—*Gloria Hanefeld, Continental, Ohio*

- 1 pound ground beef
- 1 medium onion, chopped
- 1 can (16 ounces) refried beans
- 1 can (8 ounces) tomato sauce
- 1 envelope taco seasoning
- 1/2 cup sour cream
- 1/2 cup shredded cheddar cheese
- Tortilla chips

In a large skillet, cook beef and onion over medium heat until meat is no longer pink; drain. Stir in the beans, tomato sauce and taco seasoning. Spread into an ungreased 9-in. pie plate. Top with sour cream and cheese. Bake, uncovered, at 350° for 5-10 minutes or until cheese is melted. Serve with chips. **Yield:** 6 cups.

Sweet 'n' Sour Meatballs

When I serve these saucy meatballs at our Christmas Eve celebration,
I have to make four batches...and they always disappear!
—Ruth Hoke, Lee's Summit, Maryland

1 bottle (12 ounces) chili sauce
1 jar (10 ounces) sweet-and-
  sour sauce
1 cup pineapple chunks
2 tablespoons brown sugar
1 egg, beaten
2 tablespoons crushed saltines
1/2 teaspoon ground allspice
1/4 teaspoon ground nutmeg
1 pound bulk pork sausage
1 large green pepper, cut into
  1-inch pieces

In a large saucepan, combine the chili sauce, sweet-and-sour sauce, pineapple and brown sugar; bring to a boil. Reduce heat; cover and simmer for 15 minutes. Meanwhile, in a large bowl, combine the egg, cracker crumbs, all-spice and nutmeg. Crumble sausage over mixture and mix well. Shape into 1-in. balls.

Broil meatballs 6-8 in. from the heat for 6-8 minutes or until meat is no longer pink. Add green pepper and meatballs to sauce. Simmer, uncovered, for 10 minutes or until heated through. **Yield:** about 3 dozen.

MAKING MEATBALLS OF EQUAL SIZE

FOR meatballs to cook evenly, it's important to make them the same size. The easiest way to do this is by using a 1- or 1-1/2-inch cookie scoop. Scoop the meat mixture and level off the top. Gently roll into a ball.

Horseradish Ham Cubes

Horseradish and ham have always been perfect partners.
Here they combine in a zesty variation of ham roll-ups.
—Connie Tolley, Oak Hill, West Virginia

1 package (8 ounces) cream
  cheese, softened
2 tablespoons prepared
  horseradish
1 teaspoon Worcestershire
  sauce
1/2 teaspoon seasoned salt
1/8 teaspoon pepper
10 square slices deli ham

In a mixing bowl, combine the cream cheese, horseradish, Worcestershire sauce, seasoned salt and pepper. Spread about 2 tablespoons over each ham slice. Make two stacks, using five ham slices for each. Wrap each stack in plastic wrap; chill for 4 hours. Cut each stack into 1-in. cubes. **Yield:** about 5 dozen.

Appetizer Artichoke Bread

(Pictured at right)

Family and friends refer to this as "Maureen's Party Bread" and request it for many gatherings. Serve it as an appetizer or alongside soup for lunch.
—Maureen Buschko, Phoenix, Arizona

1 loaf unsliced French bread
(1 pound)
1-1/2 cups (12 ounces) sour cream
1/2 cup butter, melted
2 tablespoons sesame seeds
2 cups (8 ounces) shredded
Monterey Jack cheese
1 cup (4 ounces) shredded
cheddar cheese
1/4 cup grated Parmesan cheese
1 jar (6-1/2 ounces) marinated
artichoke hearts, drained and
chopped
4 garlic cloves, minced
2 tablespoons minced fresh
parsley
2 teaspoons lemon-pepper
seasoning

Cut bread in half lengthwise; hollow out, leaving 1/2-in. shells. Set shells aside. Place removed bread in a food processor or blender; cover and process until crumbly. In a bowl, combine the bread crumbs, sour cream, butter and sesame seeds; spread onto a baking sheet. Broil 4 in. from the heat for 8-10 minutes or until lightly browned, stirring once.

In a bowl, combine the crumb mixture, cheeses, artichokes, garlic, parsley and lemon-pepper. Spoon into bread shells. Place on a baking sheet. Bake at 350° for 25 minutes or until golden brown. Slice and serve warm. **Yield:** 12-14 servings.

Beef Turnovers

The recipe for these Russian turnovers called Piroshkis was given to me by a cousin.
Serve barbecue or sweet-and-sour sauce alongside for extra flavor.
—Dorothy Radichel, Mankato, Minnesota

1/2 pound ground beef
1 tablespoon finely chopped
  onion
2 tablespoons sour cream
1 teaspoon dill weed
1/4 teaspoon salt
1/4 teaspoon prepared mustard
1/8 teaspoon curry powder
1/8 teaspoon pepper
3 sheets refrigerated pie pastry
  (9 inches)
Barbecue *or* sweet-and-sour sauce,
  optional

In a large skillet, cook the beef and onion over medium heat until meat is no longer pink; drain. Stir in the sour cream, dill, salt, mustard, curry and pepper; remove from the heat.

Unfold pastry sheets onto a lightly floured surface; cut into 3-in. circles. Place 1-1/2 teaspoons of beef mixture in the center of each circle. Brush edge of pastry with water; fold circles in half. Place on greased baking sheets. With a fork, press edges to seal and poke holes in top. Bake at 400° for 10-12 minutes or until golden brown. Serve warm with barbecue or sweet-and-sour sauce if desired. **Yield:** 2-1/2 dozen.

Cheddar Bacon Wedges

This recipe is really great for both late-night snacks at home and appetizers at parties.
I sometimes use thinly sliced English muffin bread in place of English muffins.
—Carolyn Kyzer, Alexander, Arkansas

1 cup (4 ounces) shredded
  cheddar cheese
1/3 cup mayonnaise
4 bacon strips, cooked and
  crumbled
2 green onions, finely chopped
1/4 cup finely chopped peanuts
1/2 teaspoon Worcestershire
  sauce
1/4 teaspoon Salad Supreme
  Seasoning
1/8 teaspoon cayenne pepper
4 English muffins, split

In a bowl, combine the first eight ingredients. Spread about 3 tablespoons on each English muffin half. Place on ungreased baking sheets. Bake at 400° for 8-10 minutes or until cheese is melted. Cut each into four wedges. **Yield:** 32 appetizers.

Editor's Note: Reduced-fat or fat-free mayonnaise may not be substituted for regular mayonnaise in this recipe. Salad Supreme Seasoning can be found in the spice section of most grocery stores.

Christmas Glow Punch

(Pictured at right)

With a pretty crimson color, this sweet tropical beverage is perfect for the holidays. Have the punch base chilling in the refrigerator, then add the ginger ale and sherbet just before serving.
—Marge Hodel, Roanoke, Illinois

4-1/2 cups tropical punch
  1 cup cranberry juice
  1 can (6 ounces) pineapple juice
1/3 cup lemon juice
  2 to 3 cups chilled ginger ale
  1 pint raspberry sherbet

In a 2-qt. container, combine the punch and juices. Cover and refrigerate until chilled. Just before serving, transfer to a small punch bowl. Stir in ginger ale; top with scoops of sherbet. **Yield:** about 2 quarts.

Fried Cheese Nuggets

There's just something about cheese that folks can't resist, and these deep-fried cheese nuggets are no exception. I barely finish making a batch before they disappear!
—Pat Waymire, Yellow Springs, Ohio

1/2 cup dry bread crumbs
  1 tablespoon sesame seeds
  1 package (10 ounces) extra
    sharp cheddar cheese
  2 eggs, beaten
Oil for deep-fat frying

In a shallow bowl, combine bread crumbs and sesame seeds. Cut cheese into 3/4-in. cubes; dip in beaten eggs, then coat with crumb mixture. Refrigerate for 15 minutes or until coating is set. In an electric skillet or deep-fat fryer, heat 1 in. of oil to 375°. Fry cheese cubes for 1-2 minutes or until browned. Drain on paper towels. Serve warm. **Yield:** 2 dozen.

Cranberry-Brie Phyllo Triangles

A creamy fruit filling is tucked inside flaky phyllo dough in this special appetizer.
One big batch never lasts long at my house!
—Susan Jones, Aurora, Colorado

1 package (16 ounces, 18-inch x 14-inch sheet size) frozen phyllo dough, thawed
1 to 1-1/4 cups butter, melted
1 to 1-1/2 cups cranberry-orange sauce *or* whole-berry cranberry sauce
8 ounces Brie *or* Camembert, rind removed and cubed

Cut phyllo sheets lengthwise into 2-in. strips; cut each strip in half widthwise. Using five strips at a time, brush each strip with butter and stack on top of one another. (Keep remaining phyllo covered with waxed paper to avoid drying out.) Place 1 teaspoon cranberry sauce and one to two cheese cubes at the end of each stack. Fold into a triangle as you would fold a flag.

Place in an ungreased 15-in. x 10-in. x 1-in. baking pan; brush with butter. Bake at 400° for 10 minutes or until golden brown. Let stand for 5 minutes before serving. **Yield:** about 4-1/2 dozen.

Mexican Chicken Roll-Ups

Refrigerated crescent rolls make these hearty appetizers easy to assemble.
Keep the ingredients on hand for last-minute snacking.
—Julie McDaniel, Batesville, Indiana

2-1/2 teaspoons cornmeal, *divided*
2-1/4 cups cubed cooked chicken
1 cup (4 ounces) shredded cheddar cheese
1/2 cup sliced ripe olives
1/2 cup sour cream
1 can (4 ounces) chopped green chilies, drained
1/4 cup chopped onion
2 tubes (8 ounces *each*) refrigerated crescent rolls
1 egg white
1 tablespoon water
Salsa

Grease a baking sheet and sprinkle with 1-1/2 teaspoons cornmeal; set aside. In a large bowl, combine the chicken, cheese, olives, sour cream, chilies and onion; set aside.

Separate crescent dough into eight rectangles; firmly press perforations to seal. Spread 1/2 cup chicken mixture over each rectangle to within 1 in. of edges. Roll up, starting from a long side. Place 1 in. apart on prepared pan.

In a small mixing bowl, beat egg white and water until foamy; brush over roll-ups. Sprinkle with remaining cornmeal. Bake at 375° for 20-25 minutes or until golden brown. Serve warm with salsa. Refrigerate leftovers. **Yield:** 8 servings.

Pimiento-Olive Cheese Log

(Pictured at right)

Pimientos give great color to this soft-textured cheese log. I make it for many occasions throughout the year.
—Linda Norton, Sonora, California

1 package (8 ounces) cream
  cheese, softened
1 jar (2 ounces) diced
  pimientos, drained
2 tablespoons finely chopped
  ripe olives
1-1/2 teaspoons grated onion
1 teaspoon lemon juice
1 garlic clove, minced
1/4 teaspoon salt
1/8 teaspoon dried thyme
1/8 teaspoon ground mustard
1/8 teaspoon hot pepper sauce
Assorted crackers

In a small mixing bowl, beat the cream cheese. Stir in the next nine ingredients. Cover and refrigerate for 1 hour or until firm. Shape into a log. Cover and refrigerate for 4 hours or overnight. Serve with crackers. **Yield:** 1-1/4 cups.

Sugar-and-Spice Pecans

Curry combined with sugar, cinnamon, cloves and nutmeg fabulously flavors pecans.
—Mary Duncan, Albion, Michigan

1-1/2 cups sugar
1 teaspoon ground nutmeg
1 teaspoon ground cinnamon
1 teaspoon ground cloves
1 teaspoon curry powder
2 egg whites
2 pounds pecan *or* walnut
  halves

In a large resealable bag, combine the sugar and seasonings; set aside. In a large mixing bowl, beat egg whites until foamy; fold in the nuts. Transfer to the bag; seal and shake to coat evenly.

Place nuts in a single layer in two greased 15-in. x 10-in. x 1-in. baking pans. Bake at 250° for 1-1/2 hours, stirring every 30 minutes. Cool completely on wire racks. Store in airtight containers. **Yield:** 2-3/4 quarts.

Seafood Appetizer Balls

After sampling a similar appetizer at a local restaurant, I went home to create my own.
Family and friends like my version even better!
—*Helen McLain, Quinlan, Texas*

1 can (6 ounces) crabmeat, drained, flaked and cartilage removed
3/4 cup seasoned bread crumbs, *divided*
1/4 cup finely chopped celery
1/4 cup frozen cooked tiny shrimp, thawed
1 egg, lightly beaten
1 green onion, sliced
1 tablespoon diced sweet red pepper
1 tablespoon milk
1 teaspoon garlic powder
1/2 teaspoon dried parsley flakes
1/2 teaspoon seafood seasoning
1/2 teaspoon pepper
1 cup crushed butter-flavored crackers (about 25 crackers)
1 egg white, lightly beaten
Oil for deep-fat frying

In a large mixing bowl, combine the crab, 1/4 cup bread crumbs, celery, shrimp, egg, onion, red pepper, milk, garlic powder, parsley, seafood seasoning and pepper. Shape into 1-in. balls. Place the cracker crumbs, egg white and remaining bread crumbs in separate shallow bowls. Roll balls in bread crumbs; dip in egg white, then roll in cracker crumbs.

In an electric skillet or deep-fat fryer, heat oil to 375°. Fry a few balls at a time for 1-2 minutes on each side or until golden brown. Drain on paper towels. Serve warm. **Yield:** 1-1/2 dozen.

Cheesy Chicken Wontons

When hosting an informal get-together with close friends, enlist guests to help assemble these
savory snacks from our Test Kitchen. As a reward, they get to eat the fruits of their labor!

2 cups (8 ounces) shredded mozzarella cheese
1-1/2 cups shredded cooked chicken
3 green onions, chopped
1/3 cup chopped fresh tomato
1 tablespoon salt-free garlic and herb seasoning
1/8 teaspoon cayenne pepper
1 package (12 ounces) wonton wrappers
1 egg, beaten
Oil for deep-fat frying
Pizza *or* spaghetti sauce, warmed

In a bowl, combine the cheese, chicken, onions, tomato, herb seasoning and cayenne. Place about 2 tablespoons in the center of each wonton wrapper. Brush edges with egg; fold corner over, making a triangle. Seal seams.

In an electric skillet or deep-fat fryer, heat 1 in. of oil to 375°. Fry wontons, a few at a time, for 1 to 1–1/2 minutes on each side or until golden brown. Drain on paper towels. Serve warm with pizza or spaghetti sauce. **Yield:** about 4 dozen.

Artichoke Caprese Platter

(Pictured at right)

This classic Italian combination of mozzarella, tomatoes and basil is dressed up with marinated artichokes. It looks so lovely on a platter. Using fresh mozzarella is the key to great taste.
—Margaret Wilson, Hemet, California

2 jars (7-1/2 ounces *each*) marinated artichoke hearts
2 tablespoons red wine vinegar
2 tablespoons olive oil
6 plum tomatoes, sliced
2 balls (8 ounces *each*) fresh mozzarella cheese*, halved and sliced
2 cups loosely packed fresh basil leaves

Drain artichokes, reserving 1/2 cup marinade; cut artichokes in half. In a small bowl, whisk vinegar, oil and reserved marinade. On a large serving platter, arrange artichokes, tomatoes, mozzarella cheese and basil. Drizzle with vinaigrette. Serve immediately. **Yield:** 10-12 servings.

*Editor's Note: Fresh mozzarella can be found in the deli section of most grocery stores.

Fresh Mozzarella Facts

COMPARED to the more firm texture of most commercially produced mozzarella, fresh mozzarella is soft and moist. The flavor is mild, delicate and somewhat milky.

Fresh mozzarella is usually shaped into balls and stored in brine. After buying fresh mozzarella, it should be refrigerated in the brine and eaten within a few days.

Stuffed French Bread

If you need a hearty appetizer, look no further than this savory stuffed bread.
No dipping sauce is required for these cheesy slices.
— Elaine Damato, Menomonee Falls, Wisconsin

1 loaf unsliced French bread
   (1 pound, 20 inches long)
1 pound bulk Italian sausage
1 cup sliced fresh mushrooms
1/2 cup chopped onion
1/2 cup chopped green pepper
1 package (8 ounces) cream
   cheese, softened
1/2 cup grated Parmesan cheese
1/2 teaspoon garlic powder
1/2 teaspoon dried oregano
8 ounces sliced mozzarella
   cheese

Cut the top third off the loaf of bread; carefully hollow out top and bottom, leaving a 1-in. shell. (Discard removed bread or save for another use.) Set loaf aside.

In a large skillet, cook the sausage, mushrooms, onion and green pepper over medium heat until meat is no longer pink; drain. In a large mixing bowl, beat the cream cheese, Parmesan cheese, garlic powder and oregano. Stir in the sausage mixture.

Line the bottom bread shell with mozzarella slices; top with sausage mixture. Replace bread top; wrap in foil. Place on a baking sheet. Bake at 350° for 15-20 minutes or until heated through. Cool for 5 minutes before slicing. **Yield:** 20 slices.

Bavarian Cheese Ball

No one will guess this cheese spread features a whole can of sauerkraut!
Shredded cheese and chopped dried beef provide a little texture.
— Rita Kerr, San Antonio, Texas

1 can (14 ounces) sauerkraut,
   rinsed and drained
1 cup (4 ounces) finely
   shredded cheddar cheese
1 cup chopped dried beef
1 cup (8 ounces) sour cream
1/2 cup mayonnaise
14 saltines, broken into pieces
2 tablespoons minced fresh
   parsley
1 tablespoon chopped onion
Additional parsley
Assorted crackers

Place sauerkraut in a food processor; cover and process until creamy. Add the cheese, dried beef, sour cream, mayonnaise, saltines, parsley and onion; cover and process until blended. Transfer to a bowl; cover and refrigerate for 30 minutes. Shape into a ball; roll in additional parsley. Cover and refrigerate until serving. Serve with crackers. **Yield:** 3-1/2 cups.

Clever Candle Arrangement

(Pictured at right)

THE soft glow of candles adds instant ambiance to any gathering, especially at Christmastime.

If your holiday party has a music theme, consider creating the simple candle ensemble at right, which features festive French horns.

Look for large brass French horn ornaments at craft or discount department stores. (While you're there, you may want to pick up some smaller French horns for the buffet table food markers described below.)

Set varying heights of pillar candles on top of a cake pedestal that has a slightly raised decorative edge. Nestle some fresh evergreen branches between the candles.

Jazz up this centerpiece by leaning

three or four French horns against the candles, using the pedestal's edge to help hold the horns in place.

FRENCH HORN FOOD MARKER FOR A BUFFET

WHEN setting up a buffet table for your party, you may want to identify the featured foods so that guests are more likely to sample them.

To stay in tune with the music theme of the candle composition above, we fashioned food markers from small French horn ornaments. (See the photo at right and on pages 24 and 25.) It's so simple to do!

Purchase small French horn ornaments at a craft or discount department store. Write or type the recipe name on a piece of sturdy paper. With the horn openings pointing down, slip the paper into the place where the two bands of metal come together.

We found the horns stood up better on the table when we scrunched the tablecloth and created pockets for them to rest in.

'TIS THE *Season*

Entrees Set a New Course

DID YOU serve roast turkey at Thanksgiving? And are you now struggling with what to offer on Christmas Day?

From beef and pork to poultry and seafood, this chapter offers a merry array of main courses your guests won't be able to resist.

Meat lovers will be delighted to see impressive Garlic 'n' Pepper Prime Rib or Orange-Maple Pork Roast adorning the holiday table.

For a little more elegance, top each person's plate with their very own Spinach-Mushroom Stuffed Chicken. (All recipes shown at right.)

Whether you're hosting a casual get-together or formal sit-down dinner, you'll find a delightful main dish to suit the occasion.

HOLIDAY MENU SUGGESTIONS

TO MAKE meal planning a little easier for you during the hectic holidays, our Test Kitchen home economists offer the following five mouth-watering menus that are perfect for weekday dinners or fancy get-togethers. Each meal features a main dish from this chapter and side dishes and desserts found in other chapters of this book.

- **Fine Dining.** Impress dinner guests with mushroom-filled Beef Wellington (page 50) wrapped in a golden, flaky pastry. It makes for a festive meal when teamed with Confetti Long Grain and Wild Rice (page 65), steamed green beans and Poppy Seed Citrus Cheesecake (page 96).
- **A Tasty of Italy.** Meals don't have to be fancy to be memorable. Your guests will remember every luscious bite of Cheesy Lasagna (page 53). Easy accompaniments include Marinated Vegetable Salad (page 240), purchased breadsticks and Chocolate Caramel Tart (page 90).

- **From-the-Sea Supper.** Are you fishing for a special dinner that feeds four? You'll net many compliments with Citrus Scallops (page 46), Herbed Onion Foccacia (page 173), cooked carrots and Cranberry Mousse (page 88).
- **Revel in a Roast.** Entertaining a crowd can be easy with the right foods. Orange-Maple Pork Roast (below) has only six ingredients and bakes for hours, allowing you to visit guests. Just before eating, set out Bread Machine Crescent Rolls (page 162) and a simple green salad. For a make-ahead dessert, turn to Raspberry Vanilla Trifle (page 95).
- **Fix-It-and-Forget-It Fare.** Unwind and enjoy a down-home weekday dinner of slow-cooked Chicken Saltimbocca (page 48). For a side dish that offers both a green vegetable and potato, prepare Broccoli Potato Supreme (page 56). Ginger Pear Pie (page 140) is a fruity finale.

Orange-Maple Pork Roast

(Pictured on page 42)

A short list of ingredients makes this recipe so appealing for entertaining. Leftovers can be used in a stir-fry along with your favorite vegetables.
—*Patricia Leonetti, Burbank, Oklahoma*

1 can (11 ounces) mandarin oranges
1 boneless whole pork loin roast (about 4 pounds)
2 tablespoons olive oil
1/2 cup maple syrup
2 tablespoons minced fresh rosemary *or* 2 teaspoons dried rosemary, crushed
Sliced starfruit

Drain oranges, reserving juice; set juice and oranges aside. In a large skillet, brown roast in oil on all sides. Transfer to a rack in a shallow roasting pan. Combine syrup and reserved juice; pour over roast. Sprinkle with rosemary. Cover and bake at 325° for 1-1/2 to 2 hours or until a meat thermometer reads 160°, basting every 30 minutes.

Let stand for 10-15 minutes before slicing. Garnish with starfruit and reserved oranges. Drizzle with pan juices if desired. **Yield:** 14-16 servings.

Spinach-Mushroom Stuffed Chicken

(Pictured at right and on page 43)

A colorful spinach stuffing peeks out from the golden skin in this recipe developed in our Test Kitchen.

1 cup sliced fresh mushrooms
2 tablespoons finely chopped onion
1 garlic clove, minced
2 tablespoons butter
1 package (10 ounces) frozen chopped spinach, thawed and squeezed dry
1/4 cup julienned sweet red pepper (2-inch pieces)
1/2 cup finely shredded Swiss cheese
1/4 cup seasoned bread crumbs
1/2 teaspoon grated lemon peel
1/4 teaspoon salt
1/4 teaspoon pepper
8 bone-in chicken breast halves with skin
2 cups white wine *or* chicken broth
1 cup heavy whipping cream
1/2 teaspoon Dijon mustard

In a large skillet, saute the mushrooms, onion and garlic in butter until tender. Stir in the spinach and red pepper; cook for 3 minutes. Remove from the heat; stir in the Swiss cheese, bread crumbs, lemon peel, salt and pepper.

Carefully loosen chicken skin on one side of each chicken breast half to form a pocket; stuff with spinach mixture. Place in a greased 15-in. x 10-in. x 1-in. baking pan. Bake, uncovered, at 350° for 50-60 minutes or until juices run clear.

In a small saucepan, bring wine or broth to a boil. Reduce heat; simmer until reduced to 1 cup. Slowly whisk in cream and mustard. Bring to a boil. Reduce heat; simmer for 2 minutes. Spoon over chicken. **Yield:** 8 servings.

STUFFING CHICKEN BREASTS

1. With your hands, loosen the skin from one side of a bone-in chicken breast half. Lift it up to form a pocket.

2. Spoon stuffing into the pocket, covering with the skin as much as possible.

Garlic 'n' Pepper Prime Rib

(Pictured on page 42)

Family and friends are delighted to see this roast adorning our table at celebrations throughout the year. It's a fancy favorite that's actually fuss-free.
—Debbie Konovitz, Tonawanda, New York

1 small end beef rib roast
  (about 4 pounds)
Coarsely ground pepper
  1 large onion, chopped
  4 to 5 garlic cloves, minced
1-1/2 cups beef broth
  1/3 cup ketchup

Sprinkle roast with pepper; place rib side down in a small roasting pan. Combine onion and garlic; spread over all sides of roast. Combine broth and ketchup; spoon 3/4 cup over roast. Set remaining broth mixture aside.

Bake, uncovered, at 325° for 2 hours or until meat reaches desired doneness (for rare, a meat thermometer should read 140°; medium, 160°; well-done, 170°). Baste with pan drippings every 20 minutes, adding reserved broth mixture as needed. Let stand for 10 minutes before slicing. Stir any remaining broth mixture into pan drippings; heat through and serve with roast. **Yield:** 6-8 servings.

HAVE A BEEF WITH BONES?

THE BONES on a beef rib roast add unbeatable flavor when roasting, but they can also pose a challenge when carving.

So when ordering your roast, ask the butcher to remove the bones and tie them back onto the meat. When the roast is done baking, simply untie and discard the bones, then slice the meat.

Citrus Scallops

My husband and I like to eat seafood at least once a week.
Oranges and lemon juice give scallops a refreshing burst of flavor.
—Cheri Hawthorne, North Canton, Ohio

1 medium green *or* sweet red
  pepper, julienned
4 green onions, chopped
1 garlic clove, minced
2 tablespoons olive oil
1 pound sea scallops
1/2 teaspoon salt
1/4 teaspoon crushed red pepper
  flakes
2 tablespoons lime juice
1/2 teaspoon grated lime peel
4 medium navel oranges, peeled and sectioned
2 teaspoons minced fresh cilantro
Hot cooked rice *or* pasta

In a large skillet, saute the green pepper, onions and garlic in oil for 1 minute. Add scallops, salt and pepper flakes; cook for 4 minutes. Add lime juice and peel; cook for 1 minute. Reduce heat; add orange sections and cilantro; cook 2 minutes longer or until scallops are opaque. Serve with rice or pasta. **Yield:** 4 servings.

Greek Lemon Turkey

(Pictured at right)

Baking this bird in an oven bag keeps it moist and tender. Round out servings of meat and vegetables with the flavorful herb drippings.
—*Marjorie Perry, Las Vegas, Nevada*

1 turkey (15 to 20 pounds)
6 garlic cloves, peeled and quartered
1/2 cup dried oregano*
1/2 cup lemon juice
1 tablespoon salt
1 tablespoon pepper
1 tablespoon all-purpose flour
5 large onions, quartered
6 large potatoes, cut into 2-inch cubes
5 medium carrots, quartered

Make several deep slits in the turkey; insert a garlic slice into each slit. Combine the oregano, lemon juice, salt and pepper; rub over turkey. Place flour in a 23-1/2-in. x 19-in. oven roasting bag and shake well. Place turkey in bag and close. Refrigerate for 6 hours or overnight.

Place oven bag in a roasting pan at least 2 in. deep. Add onions, potatoes and carrots to bag. Close bag with nylon tie provided (do not allow oven bag to hang over pan). Bake, uncovered, at 325° for 3-1/2 to 4 hours or until a meat thermometer reads 180°. Remove turkey from bag. Let stand for 20 minutes before carving. Keep vegetables warm. Serve turkey and vegetables with drippings. **Yield:** 16-20 servings.

*Editor's Note: This amount of oregano is correct.

Chicken Saltimbocca

White wine dresses up cream of chicken soup to make a lovely sauce for chicken,
ham and Swiss cheese roll-ups. The tried-and-true recipe comes from my mother.
—Carol McCollough, Missoula, Montana

6 boneless skinless chicken
  breast halves
6 thin slices deli ham
6 slices Swiss cheese
1/4 cup all-purpose flour
1/4 cup grated Parmesan cheese
1/2 teaspoon salt
1/4 teaspoon pepper
2 tablespoons vegetable oil
1 can (10-3/4 ounces)
  condensed cream of chicken
  soup, undiluted

1/2 cup dry white wine *or* chicken broth
Hot cooked rice

Flatten chicken to 1/4-in. thickness. Top each piece with a slice of ham and cheese. Roll up tightly; secure with toothpicks. In a shallow bowl, combine the flour, Parmesan cheese, salt and pepper. Roll chicken in flour mixture; refrigerate for 1 hour.

  In a skillet, brown roll-ups in oil on all sides; transfer to a slow cooker. Combine the soup and wine or broth; pour over chicken. Cover and cook on low for 4-5 hours or until a meat thermometer reads 170°. Remove roll-ups and stir sauce. Serve with rice. **Yield:** 6 servings.

Chicken Sausage Jambalaya

Having a cousin who's a pork producer is a bonus when looking for great recipes.
This slightly spicy entree turns out perfectly every time.
—Nancy Horsburgh, Everett, Ontario

1/2 pound boneless skinless
  chicken breasts, cut into
  1-inch cubes
1 teaspoon salt, *divided*
3/4 teaspoon pepper, *divided*
1/4 teaspoon paprika
2 tablespoons vegetable oil
1 cup sliced green onions
1 cup sliced celery
1 cup diced green pepper
1/2 cup diced sweet red pepper
1/2 pound fully cooked smoked
  sausage, cut into 1/4-inch
  slices

1 cup uncooked long grain rice
1 garlic clove, minced
1/8 to 1/4 teaspoon cayenne pepper
2 cups chicken broth

Sprinkle chicken with 1/2 teaspoon salt, 1/2 teaspoon pepper and paprika. In a large skillet, cook chicken in oil over medium-high heat until juices run clear. Remove chicken and set aside.

  In the same pan, saute the onions, celery and peppers over medium heat for 1 minute. Stir in the sausage, rice, garlic, cayenne, chicken and remaining salt and pepper. Add broth; bring to a boil. Reduce heat; cover and simmer for 20-25 minutes or until rice is tender and liquid is absorbed. Fluff with a fork. **Yield:** 4-6 servings.

Stuffed Sirloin Roast

(Pictured at right)

Bacon on top gives this roast a slightly smoky flavor. With a colorful stuffing, slices look lovely on a platter.
—*Jackie Hannahs, Fountain, Michigan*

9 bacon strips, *divided*
1 medium onion, chopped
3/4 cup chopped celery
1 large carrot, chopped
1/3 cup dry bread crumbs
2 teaspoons dried parsley flakes
1/4 teaspoon garlic powder
1/8 teaspoon pepper
1 boneless beef sirloin tip roast
   (3 to 4 pounds)

In a large skillet, cook six bacon strips over medium heat until crisp. Remove to paper towels; drain, reserving 3 tablespoons drippings. Crumble bacon and set aside. In the drippings, saute the onion, celery and carrot until crisp-tender. Remove from the heat; stir in the bread crumbs, parsley, garlic powder, pepper and bacon. Let stand until the liquid is absorbed.

Cut a lengthwise slit down the center of the roast to within 1/2 in. of bottom. Open roast so it lies flat; cover with plastic wrap. Flatten to 1-in. thickness. Remove plastic; spread stuffing over meat to within 1 in. of edges. Close roast and tie at 1-in. intervals with kitchen string.

Place on a rack in a shallow roasting pan. Cut remaining bacon strips in half; arrange over top of roast. Bake, uncovered, at 325° for 1-1/2 to 2 hours or until meat reaches desired doneness (for rare, a meat thermometer should read 140°; medium, 160°; well-done, 170°). Let stand for 10 minutes before slicing. **Yield:** 10-14 servings.

Special Seafood Casserole

I first sampled this casserole at a baby shower and found myself going back for more!
—Angela Schwartz, Marietta, Georgia

1/2 pound sea scallops
1 small onion, finely chopped
1 celery rib, finely chopped
6 tablespoons butter, cubed
7 tablespoons all-purpose flour
1-1/2 cups half-and-half cream
1 cup (4 ounces) shredded
   sharp cheddar cheese
6 tablespoons sherry *or* apple
   juice
3/4 teaspoon salt
1/4 teaspoon cayenne pepper
1 pound cooked medium
   shrimp, peeled and deveined
1 can (6 ounces) crabmeat,
   drained, flaked and
   cartilage removed

1 can (14 ounces) water-packed artichoke hearts,
   drained, rinsed, chopped and patted dry
1 can (8 ounces) sliced water chestnuts, drained
1/2 cup sliced almonds
1/4 cup grated Parmesan cheese

In a Dutch oven or large saucepan, saute the scallops, onion and celery in butter. Stir in the flour until blended. Add cream. Bring to a boil; cook and stir for 2 minutes or until thickened. Stir in the cheddar cheese, sherry or juice, salt and cayenne. Remove from the heat; set aside.

In a greased 11-in. x 7-in. x 2-in. baking dish, layer the shrimp, crab, artichokes and water chestnuts. Top with the sauce. Sprinkle with almonds and Parmesan cheese. Bake, uncovered, at 350° for 25-30 minutes or until heated through. Let stand for 10 minutes before serving. **Yield:** 6-8 servings.

Beef Wellington

Traditional beef Wellington often calls for liver pate, but I prefer the mushroom and ham
filling in this version. This dish has replaced turkey as our standard Christmas fare.
—Martha Stine, Johnstown, Pennsylvania

3-3/4 cups all-purpose flour
1 teaspoon salt
1 cup cold butter
2 tablespoons shortening
12 to 14 tablespoons cold water
MUSHROOM FILLING:
1 pound fresh mushrooms,
   finely chopped
1/4 cup chopped green onions
1/4 cup butter, cubed
2 teaspoons all-purpose flour
1 teaspoon salt, *divided*
3/4 teaspoon pepper, *divided*

1/4 cup beef broth
1/2 cup finely chopped fully cooked ham
2 tablespoons minced fresh parsley
4 to 4-1/2 pounds whole beef tenderloin, trimmed
1 egg, beaten
2 tablespoons sesame seeds

For pastry, combine flour and salt in a large bowl. Cut in butter and shortening until mixture resembles coarse crumbs. Gradually add water, tossing with a fork until a firm ball forms. Chill for 30-60 minutes.

In a skillet, saute mushrooms and onions in butter for 18-20 minutes or until liquid has evaporated. Stir in the flour,

1/2 teaspoon salt and 1/8 teaspoon pepper until blended. Gradually stir in broth. Bring to a boil; cook and stir for 2 minutes or until thickened. In a bowl, combine ham and parsley; stir in mushroom mixture. Cover and refrigerate.

Place tenderloin on a greased rack in a shallow roasting pan. Sprinkle with remaining salt and pepper. Bake, uncovered, at 425° for 30-35 minutes. Remove from the oven; let stand 20-25 minutes. Reduce heat to 400°.

On a lightly floured surface, roll pastry into a 19-in. x 14-in. rectangle. Moisten edges. Spread filling to within 1 in. of edges. Place tenderloin in center of pastry; fold short sides of pastry over meat. Fold long sides over top; pinch seams to seal.

Place seam side down on a greased baking sheet. Add decorative cutouts if desired. Brush with egg; sprinkle with sesame seeds. Bake, uncovered, at 400° for 30-35 minutes or until pastry is golden brown and meat reaches desired doneness (for rare, a meat thermometer should read 140°; medium, 160°; well-done, 170°). Let stand for 10 minutes before slicing. **Yield:** 16-18 servings.

Braised Herb Pork Chops

(Pictured at right)

This herb-packed entree is great for entertaining because it goes together quickly and bakes for 2 hours. While visiting, my guests and I can enjoy the wonderful aroma.
—*Darci Truax, Billings, Montana*

1/4 cup dried parsley flakes
  2 teaspoons paprika
  1 teaspoon rubbed sage
  1 teaspoon dried thyme
  1 teaspoon ground mustard
  1 teaspoon pepper
1/2 teaspoon salt
1/2 teaspoon dried oregano
  7 bone-in pork loin chops
    (1/2 inch thick)
  2 tablespoons vegetable oil
  2 cups thinly sliced onions
  4 large garlic cloves, sliced
  5 medium carrots, cut into
    2-inch pieces
  2 cups chicken broth
Hot mashed potatoes

Combine the first eight ingredients; rub over both sides of pork chops. In a Dutch oven, brown chops in oil for 2-3 minutes on each side. Remove and set aside. In the same pan, saute onions and garlic for 2 minutes. Add carrots and broth. Bring to a boil; reduce heat.

Return chops to pan. Cover and bake at 325° for 1-1/2 to 2 hours or until meat and vegetables are tender. Thicken pan juices for gravy if desired. Serve with potatoes. **Yield:** 7 servings.

Steak 'n' Onion Pie

The recipe for this old-fashioned meat pie comes from my mom, who made it for me when
I was a child. No one will go away from the table hungry when this hearty dish is served.
— Bernice Bourassa, Little Chute, Wisconsin

1/2 cup all-purpose flour
1 teaspoon salt
1/2 teaspoon paprika
1/4 teaspoon pepper
1/8 teaspoon ground cloves
1/8 teaspoon ground allspice
2 pounds boneless beef round steak, cut into 1/2-inch cubes
1 large onion, halved and thinly sliced
3 tablespoons butter
3 to 4 medium potatoes, peeled and sliced

PASTRY:
1-1/2 cups all-purpose flour
1/2 teaspoon salt
1/3 cup shortening
4 to 5 tablespoons cold water

In a large resealable plastic bag, combine the first six ingredients. Add beef, a few pieces at a time, and shake to coat. In a large skillet, saute onion in butter until tender; remove and set aside. In the same skillet, brown meat on all sides. Add enough water to cover. Bring to a boil. Reduce heat; cover and simmer for 1 hour.

Add potatoes. Cover and simmer until meat is tender, adding more water if needed. Transfer meat and potato mixture to a lightly greased shallow 2-qt. baking dish. Place reserved onion slices over the top.

In a bowl, combine flour and salt. Cut in shortening until mixture resembles coarse crumbs. Sprinkle with water, 1 tablespoon at a time, tossing with a fork until dough forms a ball. On a floured surface, roll out dough to fit baking dish. Place over filling; trim and flute edges. Cut slits in top. Bake at 350° for 55-60 minutes or until golden brown. **Yield:** 6-8 servings.

Currant-Glazed Ham Balls

Of the 10 or so varieties of meatballs I make, these are by far the best.
Ham and ground beef meatballs are dotted with chopped dried cranberries.
— Kelly Thornberry, LaPorte, Indiana

1 egg, beaten
1 slice bread, crumbled
1/3 cup dried cranberries, chopped
1/4 cup finely chopped green onions
1 teaspoon dried parsley flakes
1/4 teaspoon pepper
1/2 pound ground fully cooked ham
1/2 pound ground beef

2/3 cup currant jelly
2 tablespoons prepared mustard

In a bowl, combine the first six ingredients. Crumble ham and beef over mixture and mix well. Shape into 1-in. balls. Place in an ungreased 15-in. x 10-in. x 1-in. baking pan. Bake, uncovered, at 350° for 15-18 minutes or until meatballs are no longer pink. Remove from pan; drain if needed.

In a large skillet, combine jelly and mustard. Cook and stir over low heat until jelly is melted. Add meatballs; stir to coat. **Yield:** 4-6 servings.

Cheesy Lasagna

(Pictured at right)

During the holidays, it's nice to welcome friends and family into your home for a hearty meal of lasagna. Every bite is packed with cheese, sausage and sauce.
—*Gay Barker, Chanute, Kansas*

1-1/4 cups chopped onion
   3 to 4 garlic cloves, minced
   2 teaspoons vegetable oil
   5 cups crushed tomatoes
   1 can (6 ounces) tomato paste
   1 celery rib, chopped
1/4 cup minced fresh parsley
   1 bay leaf
   1 tablespoon brown sugar
   2 teaspoons dried oregano
1-1/2 teaspoons salt
1/2 teaspoon dried thyme
   1 pound bulk Italian sausage
   6 lasagna noodles, cooked and drained
   1 carton (15 ounces) ricotta cheese
   1 pound sliced mozzarella cheese
1/2 pound sliced provolone cheese

In a large saucepan, saute onion and garlic in oil until tender. Stir in the tomatoes, tomato paste, celery, parsley, bay leaf, brown sugar, oregano, salt and thyme. Bring to a boil. Reduce heat; simmer, uncovered, for 1 hour, stirring occasionally.

Meanwhile, in a skillet, cook sausage over medium heat until no longer pink; drain. Discard bay leaf from sauce. Set 1 cup aside. Add sausage to remaining sauce. Spread reserved sauce into a greased 13-in. x 9-in. x 2-in. baking dish. Layer with three noodles, half of the sauce, ricotta, mozzarella and provolone. Repeat layers (dish will be full).

Cover and bake at 350° for 60 minutes. Uncover; bake 10-20 minutes longer or until cheese is melted and sauce is bubbly. Let stand for 15 minutes before cutting. **Yield:** 12-15 servings.

'Tis the Season

Tasty Yuletide Trimmings

WHEN planning a special-occasion menu, folks usually begin by selecting the main dish and dessert.

But great cooks know that nothing completes the meal quite like a variety of side dishes!

From vegetables, potatoes and salads to relishes, rice and more, the following pages feature an array of accompaniments that won't play second fiddle at any of your holiday dinners.

Whether served warm or cold, Chunky Cranberry Applesauce will enliven every meaty entree.

For Winter Beet Salad, start with a convenient package of greens, then toss in beets, oranges and a simple homemade dressing.

Broccoli Potato Supreme is a clever casserole that offers two vegetables in one. (All recipes shown at right.)

SUPER SIDE DISHES
(Clockwise from top)

Chunky Cranberry Applesauce (p. 58)

Winter Beet Salad (p. 57)

Broccoli Potato Supreme (p. 56)

Broccoli Potato Supreme

(Pictured on page 54)

*My family insists that this two-in-one casserole makes an appearance at
all of our special meals. Every bite is doubly delicious!*
—Jane Birch, Edison, New Jersey

3 cups hot mashed potatoes
1 package (3 ounces) cream
   cheese, softened
1/4 cup milk
1 egg
2 tablespoons butter, softened
1/2 teaspoon salt
1/4 teaspoon pepper
1 can (2.8 ounces) french-fried
   onions, *divided*
4-1/2 cups fresh broccoli florets
1 cup (4 ounces) shredded
   cheddar cheese

In a mixing bowl, combine the first seven ingredients; beat until smooth. Fold in half of the onions. Spread onto the bottom and up the sides of a greased 13-in. x 9-in. x 2-in. baking dish, forming a shell. Bake, uncovered, at 350° for 20-25 minutes or until edges are lightly browned.

Cook broccoli in a small amount of water until crisp-tender; drain. Place in the potato shell. Sprinkle with cheese and remaining onions. Bake 10 minutes longer. **Yield:** 8 servings.

Squash Pan Rolls

*These lovely rolls have been a part of my family's holiday dinners for more than 40 years.
I'm passing on the tradition by including my grandkids in the preparation.*
—Florence Hobbs, Moodus, Connecticut

2 packages (1/4 ounce *each*)
   active dry yeast
1 cup warm water (110° to
   115°), *divided*
1 teaspoon plus 3/4 cup sugar,
   divided
1 cup warm mashed cooked
   butternut squash (110° to 115°)
1/2 cup nonfat dry milk powder
3 tablespoons vegetable oil
1 teaspoon salt
5 to 5-1/2 cups all-purpose flour
1 tablespoon butter, melted

In a large mixing bowl, dissolve yeast in 1/2 cup warm water. Stir in 1 teaspoon sugar; let stand for 5 minutes. Add the squash, milk powder, oil, salt, 2 cups flour and remaining water and sugar; beat until smooth. Add enough remaining flour to form a soft dough. Cover and let rest for 10 minutes.

Turn dough onto a floured surface; knead until smooth and elastic, about 6-8 minutes. Place in a greased bowl, turning once to grease top. Cover and let rise in a warm place until doubled, about 1 hour.

Punch dough down; turn onto a floured surface. Roll to 1-in. thickness. Cut with a 2-1/2-in. biscuit cutter. Place in a greased 13-in. x 9-in. x 2-in. baking pan. Cover and let rise until doubled, about 30 minutes. Bake at 375° for 20-25 minutes or until golden brown. Cool on a wire rack. Brush with butter. **Yield:** 15 rolls.

Winter Beet Salad

(Pictured at right and on page 54)

To save a little time, our Test Kitchen home economists recommend using packaged salad greens in this original recipe. The simple dressing is easy to assemble.

2 medium fresh beets
1 package (5 ounces) mixed
  salad greens
2 medium navel oranges,
  peeled, quartered and sliced
1 small fennel bulb, halved and
  thinly sliced
1/4 cup chopped hazelnuts,
  toasted

DRESSING:

3 tablespoons olive oil
2 tablespoons orange juice
1 tablespoon balsamic vinegar
2 teaspoons grated orange peel
1/4 teaspoon onion powder

Cut slits in beets; place on a baking sheet. Bake at 425° for 1 hour or until tender. When cool enough to handle, peel and slice beets. Divide the greens among salad plates; top with beets, oranges, fennel and hazelnuts.

In a jar with a tight-fitting lid, combine the dressing ingredients; shake well. Drizzle over salads. **Yield:** 4 servings.

THE BASICS OF BEETS

LOOK for beets with smooth, unblemished skin. The greens, if attached, should be brightly colored and not wilted.

Before storing, remove the greens. Place the beets in a plastic bag and refrigerate for up to 3 weeks.

Just before using, gently wash beets. To retain nutrients and color, don't peel until after cooking.

Stains from beets are almost impossible to remove, so protect work surfaces and consider wearing rubber or plastic gloves when handling.

Cauliflower Casserole

When making this casserole for company, I sometimes replace ordinary ham with prosciutto, an Italian-style ham found in larger grocery stores.
—*Carolyn Martin, Brewster, New York*

4 ounces fully cooked ham, chopped
4 garlic cloves, minced
6 tablespoons butter
1 large head cauliflower, broken into florets and thinly sliced
2 tablespoons all-purpose flour
1-1/2 cups half-and-half cream
1/2 cup shredded Swiss cheese
1/3 cup minced fresh parsley

In a large skillet, saute the ham and garlic in butter for 2 minutes. Add the cauliflower; cook and stir for 2 minutes. Combine the flour and cream until smooth; gradually stir into skillet. Bring to a boil; cook and stir for 1-2 minutes or until thickened.

Transfer to a greased 8-in. square baking dish. Sprinkle with cheese and parsley. Bake, uncovered, at 350° for 35-40 minutes or until heated through. **Yield:** 6-8 servings.

BUYING AND STORING CAULIFLOWER

WHEN purchasing fresh cauliflower, look for a head with compact florets that are free from yellow or brown spots. The leaves should be crisp and green, not withered or discolored.

Tightly wrap an unwashed head of cauliflower and refrigerate for up to 5 days. Before using, wash and remove the leaves at the base and trim the stem.

Chunky Cranberry Applesauce

(Pictured on page 55)

I love to cook and even have a food column in two area newspapers. This crimson-colored relish is a "must" during the holidays.
—*Gael Mustapha, Green Valley, Arizona*

6 cups chopped peeled apples
2 cups fresh *or* frozen cranberries
1 cup water
1/2 cup raisins
1/3 cup packed brown sugar
2 tablespoons red-hot candies
1 teaspoon ground cinnamon
1/8 teaspoon ground nutmeg

In a large saucepan, combine the apples, cranberries and water. Cook over medium heat until the berries pop, about 15 minutes. Reduce heat; simmer, uncovered, for 15 minutes or until apples are tender.

Stir in the raisins, brown sugar, red-hots, cinnamon and nutmeg. Simmer, uncovered, for 5-10 minutes or until candies are dissolved. Serve warm or refrigerate until serving. **Yield:** 5 cups.

ABC Salad

(Pictured at right)

Apples, broccoli and dried cranberries combine in this fresh-tasting salad. I came up with the recipe after tasting something similar at a restaurant buffet.
—Joan Sharp, El Paso, Texas

1/2 cup vegetable oil
  3 tablespoons lemon juice, *divided*
  1 teaspoon sugar
1/4 teaspoon salt
  1 cup dried cranberries
  3 large red apples, cut into 1/2-inch cubes
  2 cups fresh broccoli florets
1/2 cup chopped walnuts

In a bowl, whisk the oil, 2 tablespoons lemon juice, sugar and salt. Add cranberries; let stand for 10 minutes. In a large bowl, toss the apples with remaining lemon juice. Add the broccoli, walnuts and cranberry mixture; toss to coat. Cover and refrigerate for 2 hours or until chilled. Toss before serving. **Yield:** 6-8 servings.

Pesto Potatoes

This hearty potato dish keeps us warm during our long Alaskan winters. Each summer, I make lots of homemade pesto and freeze it to enjoy throughout the year.
—Jennifer Reese, Wasilla, Alaska

  1 cup firmly packed fresh basil leaves
1/2 cup firmly packed fresh parsley
1/2 cup grated Parmesan *or* Romano cheese
1/4 cup chopped walnuts
  1 garlic clove
1-1/4 teaspoons salt
1/2 teaspoon pepper
1/2 cup olive oil, *divided*
  4 large potatoes, peeled and cubed

  5 plum tomatoes, cut into 1/4-inch slices
  2 cups (8 ounces) shredded mozzarella cheese

In a food processor or blender, combine the first seven ingredients. Cover and process until smooth. While processing, gradually add 1/4 cup oil in a steady stream.

In a large roasting pan, combine potatoes and tomatoes; drizzle with remaining oil. Top with basil mixture; toss to coat. Bake, uncovered, at 400° for 40-45 minutes or until potatoes are tender. Sprinkle with mozzarella cheese. Bake 5 minutes longer or until cheese is melted. **Yield:** 8 servings.

Red Cabbage with Cranberries

Sweet-and-sour cabbage complements mild meats like pork and ham.
You can serve this relish warm or cold.
—Lucille Kunze, Melbourne, Florida

1 tablespoon olive oil
1/2 cup packed brown sugar, *divided*
8 garlic cloves, minced
3 cups fresh *or* frozen cranberries, *divided*
1/2 cup red wine vinegar
1 medium head red cabbage, shredded (10 cups)
1 cup dry red wine *or* apple juice
1/2 teaspoon salt
1/8 to 1/4 teaspoon cayenne pepper

In a Dutch oven or kettle, heat oil and 1/4 cup brown sugar over medium heat. Add garlic; saute for 2 minutes. Stir in 2 cups cranberries and vinegar. Cover and cook over medium heat for 3-4 minutes or until the berries have popped.

Add cabbage and wine or apple juice. Cover and cook over medium heat for 15 minutes or until the cabbage is tender, stirring occasionally. Stir in the salt, cayenne and remaining cranberries and brown sugar. Remove from the heat. Cover and let stand for 5 minutes or until berries are tender. **Yield:** 8 servings.

Layered Gelatin Salad

It's nice to offer a cool gelatin salad as an alternate to hot side dishes.
Make it ahead and relax a little on the day of your party.
—Lorraine Caland, Thunder Bay, Ontario

1 package (3 ounces) lemon gelatin
2-1/2 cups boiling water, *divided*
2 cans (8 ounces *each*) crushed pineapple
1 package (8 ounces) cream cheese, softened
1/4 cup mayonnaise
1/4 cup whipped topping
1 envelope unflavored gelatin
3/4 cup cold water, *divided*
1 package (3 ounces) lime gelatin

In a bowl, dissolve lemon gelatin in 1-1/2 cups boiling water. Drain pineapple, reserving 2/3 cup juice; set juice aside. Stir pineapple into gelatin. Pour into a 2-qt. glass bowl. Cover and refrigerate until firm.

In a small mixing bowl, combine cream cheese, mayonnaise and whipped topping; set aside. Sprinkle unflavored gelatin over 1/4 cup cold water; let stand for 1 minute. In a small saucepan, bring the reserved pineapple juice to a boil; stir in dissolved unflavored gelatin. Add to the cream cheese mixture; mix well. Carefully spread over the chilled lemon layer. Refrigerate until firm.

In a bowl, dissolve lime gelatin in remaining boiling water. Stir in remaining cold water. Chill until partially set. Beat with a portable mixer until foamy. Pour over cream cheese layer. Refrigerate until firm, about 3 hours or overnight. **Yield:** 8-10 servings.

Stuffed Artichokes

(Pictured at right)

Christmas Eve at our house isn't the same until I set out a platter of these succulent stuffed artichokes.
—Mary Ann Marino
West Pittsburgh, Pennsylvania

4 medium artichokes
8 teaspoons lemon juice
1 medium lemon, sliced
4 whole peppercorns
1 bay leaf
1 teaspoon salt, *divided*
4 cups cubed Italian bread
  (1/2-inch cubes)
1/2 cup minced fresh parsley
2 tablespoons grated Parmesan
  cheese
2 tablespoons plus 4 teaspoons
  olive oil, *divided*
2 teaspoons grated lemon peel
2 garlic cloves, minced
1/4 teaspoon pepper

Using a sharp knife, level the bottom of each artichoke and cut 3/4 in. from the top. Using kitchen scissors, snip off the tips of the outer leaves; brush cut edges with lemon juice.

Stand artichokes in a Dutch oven; add 2 in. of water. Add the lemon slices, peppercorns, bay leaf and 1/2 teaspoon salt; bring to a boil. Reduce heat; cover and simmer for 25-30 minutes or until tender and leaves near the center pull out easily. Invert artichokes to drain. Carefully scrape out the fuzzy center portion of artichokes with a spoon and discard.

In a large bowl, combine the bread cubes, parsley, Parmesan cheese, 2 tablespoons oil, lemon peel, garlic, pepper and remaining salt. Gently spread artichoke leaves apart; fill with stuffing. Place in a greased 13-in. x 9-in. x 2-in. baking dish; drizzle with the remaining oil. Bake, uncovered, at 350° for 20-25 minutes or until heated through and stuffing is lightly browned. **Yield:** 4 servings.

THE ART OF EATING WHOLE ARTICHOKES

FULLY enjoying whole artichokes is a messy, finger-licking-good experience! Here are some hints for eating this unusual vegetable.

Starting on the outside of the artichoke, remove petals, one at a time. Pull each petal through your teeth to remove the soft, pulpy portion. Discard petals.

The fuzzy center portion (which you're instructed to remove in the Stuffed Artichokes recipe above) is the "choke" and shouldn't be eaten. The meaty bottom, or heart, of the artichoke is completely edible.

Holiday Rice Salad

*It's nice to prepare a cold salad like this when entertaining because it can
be made ahead and doesn't take up valuable oven space.*
—Debra Walter, Huntington Woods, Michigan

7 cups cooked wild rice, cooled
1 cup chopped pecans, toasted
1 cup thinly sliced green onions
1/2 cup dried cranberries
1/2 cup dried cherries *or*
  additional dried cranberries
1/2 cup golden raisins
1/4 cup slivered almonds, toasted
1/2 cup minced fresh parsley
1 tablespoon chopped fresh
  mint *or* 1 teaspoon dried mint
  flakes

DRESSING:
1/2 cup orange juice
1/3 cup cider vinegar
1/4 cup olive oil
1 tablespoon lime juice
2 teaspoons sugar
1 teaspoon salt
1/8 teaspoon pepper

In a large bowl, combine the first nine ingredients. In a jar with a tight-fitting lid, combine the dressing ingredients; shake well. Pour over rice mixture and toss to coat. Cover and refrigerate for 2 hours or until serving. **Yield:** 12-14 servings.

Oyster Casserole

*The holidays are the perfect time to indulge in a rich and buttery dish like this.
You can assemble and refrigerate it the night before, then top with
the remaining crumbs and seasonings just before baking.*
—Mrs. Earl Wade, Roxboro, North Carolina

1-1/2 cups crushed butter-flavored
  crackers (about 38 crackers)
1/2 cup butter, melted
1/4 teaspoon salt
1/4 teaspoon ground nutmeg
1/4 teaspoon pepper
1 pint shucked fresh oysters,
  drained
1/3 cup condensed cream of
  mushroom soup, undiluted
2 tablespoons milk

In a small bowl, toss the cracker crumbs and butter. In another bowl, combine the salt, nutmeg and pepper. In a greased 11-in. x 7-in. x 2-in. baking dish, layer half of the crumbs, half of the oysters and 1/4 teaspoon of seasoning mixture.

Combine soup and milk; pour over the top. Layer with remaining oysters and another 1/4 teaspoon of seasoning mixture. Top with remaining crumbs and seasonings. Bake, uncovered, at 400° for 20-25 minutes or until hot and bubbly. **Yield:** 9 servings.

Curried Sweet Potato Chowder

(Pictured at right)

The flavor of curry is subtle in this creamy, comforting chowder. For fun, I sometimes sprinkle individual servings with pumpkin or sunflower kernels.
—*Kara De la vega*
Suisun City, California

3 cups cubed peeled sweet
   potatoes
2/3 cup finely chopped green
   onions
4 teaspoons butter
2 tablespoons all-purpose flour
1 teaspoon curry powder
1 teaspoon salt
1/4 teaspoon pepper
3 cups milk
2 cups frozen peas, thawed
1 cup half-and-half cream

Place 2 in. of water in a large saucepan; add sweet potatoes. Bring to a boil. Reduce heat; cover and simmer for 7-9 minutes or until tender. Drain and set aside.

In a skillet, saute onions in butter until tender. In another large saucepan, combine the flour, curry powder, salt and pepper. Gradually stir in milk until smooth. Add the sweet potatoes and onions. Bring to a boil; cook and stir for 2 minutes or until thickened. Stir in peas and cream; heat through (do not boil). **Yield:** 6 servings.

Creamy Onion Bake

The idea of onions starring in a side dish never dawned on me until my mother-in-law shared
this recipe and asked me to make it for a holiday dinner. It's been a staple ever since.
— Boni Aulwurm, Naples, Florida

6 medium onions, halved and
   thinly sliced
5 tablespoons butter, *divided*
3 tablespoons all-purpose flour
1 teaspoon salt
1/8 teaspoon pepper
1-1/2 cups half-and-half cream
2 celery ribs, diced
1/4 cup pecan halves
Grated Parmesan cheese and
   paprika

In a large skillet, saute onions in 3 tablespoons butter until tender. Remove with a slotted spoon and set aside. In the same skillet, melt remaining butter; stir in flour, salt and pepper until smooth. Gradually stir in cream. Bring to a boil; cook and stir for 2 minutes or until thickened and bubbly.

Place celery in a small saucepan and cover with water. Cover and cook over medium heat until tender; drain. In a greased 2-qt. baking dish, combine the onions, celery and pecans. Stir in the cream mixture. Sprinkle with Parmesan cheese and paprika. Cover and bake at 350° for 30-35 minutes or until bubbly and heated through. **Yield:** 6-8 servings.

Triple-Layer Vegetable Terrine

My family enjoys eating vegetables when they're pureed and
made into a tasty terrine. Although it takes a little time to prepare,
this unique cold dish can conveniently be made a day in advance.
— Sandra Barry, Ramsey, New Jersey

CARROT LAYER:
1-1/2 cups sliced carrots
2 tablespoons butter
1 egg
1 egg yolk
2 tablespoons heavy whipping
   cream
1/2 teaspoon sugar
1/2 teaspoon ground nutmeg
1/8 teaspoon ground allspice
BROCCOLI LAYER:
2 cups fresh broccoli florets
1 egg

2 tablespoons butter, softened
2 tablespoons heavy whipping cream
1/2 teaspoon ground nutmeg
1/4 teaspoon salt
POTATO LAYER:
1-1/2 cups diced peeled potatoes
1 cup chopped onion
1/4 cup butter, cubed
1 egg
1 egg yolk
1 teaspoon curry powder
1/4 teaspoon salt
White pepper to taste

Lightly grease an 8-in. x 4-in. x 2-in. loaf pan. Line with parchment paper and grease the paper; set aside. In a skillet, saute the carrots in butter until tender; cool slightly. Transfer to a food processor or blender; cover and process until pureed. Add the egg, egg yolk, cream, sugar, nutmeg and all-spice. Cover and process until well combined; set aside.

For broccoli layer, place 1 in. of water in a small saucepan; add broccoli. Bring to a boil. Reduce heat; cover and simmer for 7-9 minutes or until tender. Drain; cool slightly. Transfer to a food processor or blender; cover and process until pureed. Add the egg, butter, cream, nutmeg and salt. Cover and process until well combined; set aside.

For potato layer, in a skillet, saute potatoes and onion in butter until tender; cool slightly. Transfer to a food processor or blender; cover and process until pureed. Add the remaining ingredients. Cover and process until well combined.

Spread carrot mixture evenly in the prepared pan. Top with broccoli and potato layers. Place pan in a larger baking pan. Fill larger pan with boiling water to a depth of 1 in. Bake, uncovered, at 350° for 50-60 minutes or until a knife inserted near the center comes out clean. Let stand for 10 minutes before inverting onto a serving platter; remove parchment paper. With a sharp knife, cut into slices. **Yield:** 8-10 servings.

Confetti Long Grain And Wild Rice

(Pictured at right)

Summer squash, zucchini and sweet red pepper peek out from the tender grains of rice in this colorful side dish.
—Mary Jo Hopkins, Hobart, Indiana

2 **packages (6 ounces *each*) long grain and wild rice**
2 **teaspoons olive oil**
1 **small yellow summer squash, finely diced**
1 **small zucchini, finely diced**
1 **small sweet red pepper, finely diced**
1 **medium carrot, diced**
2 **green onions, thinly sliced**
1/4 **to 1/2 teaspoon salt**

Cook rice according to package directions. Meanwhile, in a skillet, heat oil. Add the yellow squash, zucchini, red pepper, carrot, onions and salt; saute for 5 minutes or until vegetables are tender. Transfer rice to a serving bowl; add vegetable mixture and toss gently. **Yield:** 8 servings.

Chestnut Sausage Stuffing

I discovered this recipe in a four-generation family cookbook. I'm glad I gave it a try.
It has become "the" stuffing at our holiday table.
—Judi Oudekerk, Buffalo, Minnesota

1 pound bulk pork sausage
2 cups finely chopped fresh mushrooms
1-1/2 cups finely chopped onions
2 celery ribs, chopped
1/3 cup butter
1/4 cup minced fresh parsley
2 teaspoons dried thyme
1/4 teaspoon pepper
1 cup chicken broth
4 cups day-old bread cubes
1 package (8-3/4 ounces) whole chestnuts*, coarsely chopped (about 2 cups)

In a large skillet, cook the sausage over medium heat until no longer pink; drain and set aside. In the same skillet, saute the mushrooms, onions and celery in butter until tender. Stir in the sausage, parsley, thyme and pepper. Add broth; heat through. Remove from the heat. Add bread cubes and chestnuts; toss to coat.

Transfer to a greased shallow 2-1/2-qt. baking dish. Cover and bake at 350° for 30 minutes. Uncover; bake 10-15 minutes longer or until heated through. Let stand for 5 minutes before serving. **Yield:** 8-10 servings.

*Editor's Note: These are sweet chestnuts, not water chestnuts.

Green Bean Supreme

The combination of sour cream and dill makes this a delicious variation of traditional
green bean casserole. I've had the recipe for more than 25 years.
—La Verne Hulden, Darien, Illinois

1 small onion, chopped
1 tablespoon dill weed
1 tablespoon minced fresh parsley
2 tablespoons butter
2 tablespoons all-purpose flour
1 cup (8 ounces) sour cream
1 package (16 ounces) frozen French-cut green beans
1/2 cup shredded cheddar cheese
1 cup crushed potato chips

In a large skillet, saute onion, dill and parsley in butter until onion is tender. Stir in flour and sour cream. Bring to a boil; cook and stir for 2 minutes or until thickened.

Cook the beans according to package directions; drain. Stir beans and cheese into the sour cream mixture. Transfer to a greased 1-qt. baking dish; sprinkle with potato chips. Bake, uncovered, at 350° for 30-35 minutes or until bubbly. **Yield:** 4-6 servings.

Swiss Potato Bake

(Pictured at right)

If you're tired of the same old mashed potatoes, reach for this recipe featuring Swiss cheese and lots of crunchy almonds.
—*Evelyn Plyler, Santa Maria, California*

- 5 large uncooked baking potatoes, peeled and shredded
- 1 cup (4 ounces) shredded Swiss cheese
- 3/4 cup chopped green onions
- 2 garlic cloves, minced
- 3 eggs, lightly beaten
- 2 cups (16 ounces) sour cream
- 1/4 cup butter, melted
- 1 teaspoon salt
- 1/2 teaspoon white pepper
- 1/2 cup sliced almonds

In a large bowl, combine the potatoes, Swiss cheese, onions and garlic. In another bowl, combine the eggs, sour cream, butter, salt and pepper until smooth. Pour over potato mixture; toss to coat.

Transfer to a greased 11-in. x 7-in. x 2-in. baking dish. Sprinkle with almonds. Bake, uncovered, at 350° for 55-65 minutes or until potatoes are tender and top is golden brown. **Yield:** 10 servings.

Creamy Spinach Casserole

My husband claims not to like spinach but can't stop eating it prepared this way!
Serve it alongside ham and watch it disappear.
—*Patricia Fake, Mystic, Connecticut*

- 2 eggs, beaten
- 2 packages (10 ounces *each*) frozen chopped spinach, thawed and squeezed dry
- 1 can (10-3/4 ounces) condensed cream of mushroom soup, undiluted
- 1 medium onion, chopped
- 1 cup (4 ounces) shredded cheddar cheese
- 2/3 cup mayonnaise
- 1/2 cup dry bread crumbs
- 2 tablespoons butter, melted

In a large bowl, combine the eggs, spinach, soup, onion, cheese and mayonnaise. Spoon into a greased 8-in. square baking dish. Toss the bread crumbs and butter; sprinkle over spinach mixture. Bake, uncovered, at 350° for 35-40 minutes or until heated through and topping is golden brown. **Yield:** 5-6 servings.

Make Christmas Cookies A Canvas for Creativity

FROM shopping and wrapping to cooking and entertaining, you just might discover you've painted yourself into a corner when it comes to finding time for baking Christmas cookies.

Consider this stroke of genius. Instead of baking several varieties of mouth-watering morsels, make just one kind of cutout cookie. Then add a little finesse with frosting!

In the photo at right, we made one batch of tried-and-true Vanilla Butter Rollouts, which yields 7 dozen.

Then we transformed the rich, buttery morsels into edible works of art with various decorating techniques discussed in this chapter.

So you can create mini masterpieces to share with family and friends!

COOKIE DECORATING TECHNIQUES

DRESS UP cookies with Confectioners' Sugar Glaze (page 74), Royal Icing (page 76), Buttercream Frosting (page 78) and these easy decorating techniques.

1. Glazing and Decorating. Spread Confectioners' Sugar Glaze over cookies; let dry. Pipe designs onto cookies using a contrasting color of Royal Icing.

2. Flocking. Prepare Buttercream Frosting. Combine 1 cup frosting and 1-1/2 teaspoons water; stir until smooth. Place in a pastry bag or resealable plastic bag; cut a small hole in corner of bag. Pipe desired designs onto cookies. Immediately sprinkle with colored sugar. Gently shake off excess sugar. Let dry.

3. Stenciling. Spread Buttercream Frosting over cookies. Place stencil over cookies; sprinkle colored sugar over cutout area. Carefully lift off stencil.

4. Marbling. Spread Confectioners' Sugar Glaze over cookies; let dry. For each desired color, stir 1/2 teaspoon water into 1/4 cup glaze until smooth; tint with food coloring. Tightly crumble a 12-inch square piece of waxed paper into a ball; lightly dip into colored glaze. Press onto cookies; repeat until desired pattern is achieved. Let dry completely.

5. Drizzling. Place cookies on waxed paper or a wire rack over waxed paper. Prepare Chocolate Confectioners' Sugar Glaze (page 74); stir in 1-1/2 teaspoons water until smooth. Using a spoon, drizzle evenly over cookies. Let dry completely.

6. Dipping. Prepare Chocolate Confectioners' Sugar Glaze (page 74); stir in 1 teaspoon water until smooth. Dip cookies halfway into glaze, allowing excess to drip off. Place on a wire rack over waxed paper. Let dry completely.

Vanilla Butter Rollouts

(Pictured at right and on pages 68 and 69)

Even cooks who normally shy away from rolled cookies can make these with confidence. The dough is so easy to work with after a mere 30 minutes of chilling. They can be decorated in a variety of ways.
—Colleen Sickman, Charles City, Iowa

1-1/2 cups butter, softened
1-1/2 cups sugar
   2 eggs
   1 tablespoon vanilla extract
   4 cups all-purpose flour
   1 teaspoon baking soda
   1 teaspoon cream of tartar
   1 teaspoon salt

In a large mixing bowl, cream butter and sugar. Add eggs, one at a time, beating well after each addition. Beat in vanilla. Combine the flour, baking soda, cream of tartar and salt; gradually add to the creamed mixture. Cover and refrigerate for 30 minutes or until easy to handle.

On a lightly floured surface, roll out dough to 1/4-in. thickness. Cut with floured 2-1/2-in. cookie cutters. Place 2 in. apart on ungreased baking sheets. Bake at 350° for 8-10 minutes or until edges are lightly browned. Cool for 1 minute before removing to wire racks to cool completely. Decorate as desired. **Yield:** about 7 dozen.

SUCCESSFUL CUTOUT COOKIES

FOR tender cutout cookies that bake perfectly every time, follow these tips:

- For easier handling, refrigerate the dough before rolling out.
- Lightly flour the rolling pin and work surface. Too much flour added to the dough can cause cookies to be tough.
- Work with one portion of dough at a time. Keep the remaining dough in the refrigerator to prevent it from getting too warm.
- Roll out from the center to the edge. Keep a ruler handy so you can check the thickness. If there are cutouts of varying thickness on the baking sheet, some will brown too quickly, while others will be underbaked.
- Dip the cookie cutter in flour so it doesn't stick to the dough.
- Avoid having too many scraps by placing the cookie cutters close together on the rolled-out dough. Save any scraps and reroll them only once.
- Transfer cutouts to and from the baking sheet with a large metal spatula.

Lemon Cream Cheese Spritz

*Our Test Kitchen home economists liven up ordinary spritz cookies with
lemon extract and peel. Cream cheese makes every bite tasty and tender.*

1 cup shortening
1 package (3 ounces) cream
  cheese, softened
1 cup sugar
1 egg yolk
1 teaspoon lemon extract
1 teaspoon grated lemon peel
2-1/2 cups all-purpose flour
1/4 teaspoon salt

In a large mixing bowl, beat shortening and cream cheese until blended. Add sugar; beat until creamy. Beat in egg yolk, lemon extract and peel. Combine the flour and salt; gradually add to the creamed mixture.

Using a cookie press fitted with the disk of your choice, press dough 1 in. apart onto ungreased baking sheets. Bake at 350° for 9-12 minutes or until set (do not brown). Remove to wire racks to cool. Decorate as desired. **Yield:** about 9 dozen.

Chocolate Cherry Cookies

*A juicy maraschino cherry peeks out from under a creamy frosting in this
chocolate cookie. I've been making them for years and they've never failed to satisfy.*
—Carol Hemker, Phenix City, Alabama

1/2 cup butter, softened
1 cup sugar
1 egg
2 teaspoons maraschino cherry
  juice
1-1/2 teaspoons vanilla extract
1-1/2 cups all-purpose flour
1/2 cup baking cocoa
1/4 teaspoon salt
1/4 teaspoon baking powder
1/4 teaspoon baking soda
24 maraschino cherries, drained
  and halved
FROSTING:
1 cup (6 ounces) semisweet
  chocolate chips
1/2 cup sweetened condensed
  milk
1 teaspoon maraschino cherry
  juice

In a large mixing bowl, cream butter and sugar. Beat in the egg, cherry juice and vanilla. Combine the flour, cocoa, salt, baking powder and baking soda; gradually add to the creamed mixture.

Roll into 1-in. balls. Place 2 in. apart on ungreased baking sheets. Using the end of a wooden spoon handle, make an indentation in the center of each. Place a cherry half in each indentation.

In a small saucepan over low heat, melt chocolate chips with milk, stirring constantly. Remove from the heat; stir in cherry juice until blended. Spoon about 1 teaspoon over each cherry (frosting will spread over cookies during baking). Bake at 350° for 9-11 minutes or until set. Remove to wire racks to cool. **Yield:** 4 dozen.

Chocolate-Dipped Cookies

(Pictured at right)

This tender, flavorful cookie from our Test Kitchen is made even better by being dipped in chocolate. The contrasting drizzle is a fancy finishing touch.

1/2 cup butter, softened
3/4 cup sugar
   1 egg
   1 teaspoon vanilla extract
   1 cup all-purpose flour
1/3 cup baking cocoa
1/2 teaspoon baking soda
1/4 teaspoon salt
1/2 cup chopped almonds
1/2 cup miniature semisweet
     chocolate chips
  12 ounces white candy coating
     disks, melted
  12 ounces dark chocolate candy
     coating disks, melted
   2 ounces milk chocolate candy
     coating disks, melted

In a large mixing bowl, cream butter and sugar. Beat in egg and vanilla. Combine the flour, cocoa, baking soda and salt; gradually add to the creamed mixture. Stir in almonds and chocolate chips. Cover and refrigerate for 2 hours. Divide dough in half. Shape into two 8-in. rolls; wrap each in plastic wrap. Refrigerate for 3 hours or until firm.

Unwrap and cut into 1/4-in. slices. Place 2 in. apart on greased baking sheets. Bake at 350° for 8-10 minutes or until set. Remove to wire racks to cool.

Dip half of the cookies in white coating; place on waxed paper. Dip remaining cookies in dark chocolate coating; place on waxed paper. Place milk chocolate coating in a resealable plastic bag; cut a small hole in one corner of the bag. Pipe designs on cookies. Let stand for 30 minutes or until set. **Yield:** 4-1/2 dozen.

EASY CHOCOLATE-COVERED COOKIES

IF you don't have time to make Chocolate-Dipped Cookies (above) from scratch, simply purchase cream-filled chocolate sandwich cookies and dip into melted candy coating. Then drizzle with a contrasting chocolate.

It's an easy yet elegant way to enhance the offerings on your cookie tray!

Confectioners' Sugar Glaze

This versatile glaze is shared by our Test Kitchen. You can make the basic recipe and tint it with food coloring if desired. For chocolate lovers, skip the food coloring and stir in some baking cocoa.

2 cups confectioners' sugar
2 tablespoons plus 1 teaspoon water
1/2 teaspoon clear vanilla extract
Food coloring, optional

In a bowl, combine the confectioners' sugar, water and vanilla; stir until combined and smooth (mixture will be thick). Tint with food coloring if desired. With a butter knife or small metal spatula, lightly spread glaze on cooled cookies. Let dry for 1 hour. **Yield:** 3/4 cup.

Chocolate Confectioners' Sugar Glaze: Prepare Confectioners' Sugar Glaze. Stir in 4 teaspoons baking cocoa until smooth.

Apricot Shortbread Squares

These fruity bars taste and look so good, people will have a hard time believing how quick they can be prepared. They're bound to become a favorite with your family.
— Terry Grossmann, Libertyville, Illinois

1 cup butter, softened
1 cup sugar
2 eggs, *separated*
2 teaspoons vanilla extract
3-1/2 cups all-purpose flour
1 teaspoon baking powder
1/4 teaspoon baking soda
1/4 teaspoon salt
2 jars (12 ounces *each*) apricot preserves
1 cup finely chopped walnuts

In a large mixing bowl, cream butter and sugar. Add egg yolks and vanilla; mix well. Combine the flour, baking powder, baking soda and salt; add to the creamed mixture and mix well (mixture will be crumbly). Press into a greased 15-in. x 10-in. x 1-in. baking pan. Carefully spread with apricot preserves.

In a small mixing bowl, beat egg whites until stiff peaks form. Carefully spread over preserves (egg white layer will be thin). Sprinkle with walnuts. Bake at 350° for 25-30 minutes or until golden brown and edges are bubbly. Cool on a wire rack. Cut into squares. Refrigerate leftovers. **Yield:** 4 dozen.

Rugalach

(Pictured at right)

The crisp texture of these crescent-shaped cookies makes them a terrific treat to serve alongside a steaming mug of hot chocolate or coffee.
—Becky Phillips
Chippewa Falls, Wisconsin

  1 cup butter, softened
  1 package (8 ounces) cream
    cheese, softened
  2 cups all-purpose flour
1/2 teaspoon salt
FILLING:
  1 cup sugar
  2 tablespoons ground cinnamon
1/2 cup butter, melted, *divided*
1/2 cup finely chopped pecans

In a mixing bowl, cream butter and cream cheese. Combine flour and salt; gradually add to the creamed mixture. Divide dough into fourths. Wrap each portion in plastic wrap; refrigerate for 1 hour or until easy to handle.

Roll out each portion between two sheets of waxed paper into a 12-in. circle. Remove top sheet of waxed paper. Combine sugar and cinnamon. Brush each circle with 1 tablespoon melted butter. Sprinkle each with 3 tablespoons cinnamon-sugar and 2 tablespoons pecans. Cut each into 12 wedges.

Roll up wedges from the wide end; place pointed side down 2 in. apart on ungreased baking sheets. Curve ends to form a crescent shape. Bake at 350° for 24-26 minutes or until golden brown. Remove to wire racks. Brush warm cookies with remaining butter; sprinkle with remaining cinnamon-sugar. **Yield:** 4 dozen.

WHAT IS RUGALACH?

RUGALACH (ruhg-uh-lukh) is a traditional Jewish cookie normally prepared for Hanukkah. The dough for these bite-size, crescent-shaped cookies is prepared with cream cheese, which results in a dense texture and rich flavor. Rugalach can be made with a variety of fillings, including fruit, raisins, nuts, jam and poppy seeds.

Royal Icing

Our home economists share the recipe for this classic decorating icing that sets up and dries quickly. It's nice to use when cookies will be stacked on a plate.

2 cups confectioners' sugar
2 tablespoons plus 2 teaspoons water
4-1/2 teaspoons meringue powder
1/4 teaspoon cream of tartar
Food coloring, optional

In a small mixing bowl, combine the confectioners' sugar, water, meringue powder and cream of tartar; beat on low speed just until combined. Beat on high for 4-5 minutes or until stiff peaks form. Tint with food coloring if desired. Keep unused icing covered at all times with a damp cloth. If necessary, beat again on high speed to restore texture.

To decorate, place icing in a pastry bag. For border decorations and dots, use #3 round pastry tip. For small detailed decorations, use #1 or #2 round pastry tip. **Yield:** about 1 cup.

Editor's Note: Use of a coupler ring will allow you to easily change pastry tips for different designs. Meringue powder can be ordered by mail from Wilton Industries, Inc. Call 1-800/794-5866 or visit their Web site, *www.wilton.com*.

Pistachio Cranberry Cookies

I came up with this recipe one year when looking for a cookie that had a little red and green in it. The combination of cranberries and pistachios is delicious.
—Arlene Kroll, Vero Beach, Florida

1/2 cup butter, softened
1/2 cup vegetable oil
1/2 cup sugar
1/2 cup packed brown sugar
1 egg
1 teaspoon vanilla extract
1-3/4 cups all-purpose flour
1/2 teaspoon salt
1/2 teaspoon baking powder
1/2 teaspoon baking soda
1 cup crisp rice cereal
1/2 cup old-fashioned oats
1/2 cup dried cranberries
1/2 cup chopped pistachios

In a large mixing bowl, cream the butter, oil and sugars. Beat in egg and vanilla. Combine the flour, salt, baking powder and baking soda; gradually add to the creamed mixture. Stir in the cereal, oats, cranberries and pistachios.

Drop by tablespoonfuls 2 in. apart onto ungreased baking sheets. Bake at 350° for 10-12 minutes or until lightly browned. Remove to wire racks to cool. **Yield:** 5 dozen.

PURCHASING PISTACHIOS

WHEN buying unshelled pistachios, look for ones with the shell partially open so it's easier to retrieve the nut. Also, a closed shell indicates an immature nut.

Fudge-Filled Toffee Cookies

(Pictured at right)

I combined three recipes to come up with these crisp cookies topped with a sweet chocolate center. They're a nice addition to a holiday cookie tray.
—Karen Barto, Churchville, Virginia

1/2 cup butter, softened
1/2 cup sugar
1/2 cup confectioners' sugar
1/2 cup vegetable oil
1 egg
1/2 teaspoon almond extract
1/4 teaspoon coconut extract
1-3/4 cups all-purpose flour
1/2 cup whole wheat flour
1/2 teaspoon salt
1/2 teaspoon baking soda
1/2 teaspoon cream of tartar
3/4 cup English toffee bits *or* almond brickle chips
2/3 cup chopped pecans
2/3 cup flaked coconut
Additional sugar
FILLING:
1-1/2 cups semisweet chocolate chips, melted
3/4 cup sweetened condensed milk
1-1/2 teaspoons vanilla extract
1-1/4 cups pecan halves

In a large mixing bowl, cream butter and sugars. Beat in the oil, egg and extracts. Combine the flours, salt, baking soda and cream of tartar; gradually add to the creamed mixture. Stir in the toffee bits, pecans and coconut. Cover and refrigerate for 1 hour or until easy to handle.

Shape dough into 1-in. balls; roll in sugar. Place 2 in. apart on ungreased baking sheets. Using the end of a wooden spoon handle, make an indentation in the center of each.

In a bowl, combine the melted chocolate, milk and vanilla until smooth. Spoon 1 teaspoon into the center of each cookie. Top with a pecan half. Bake at 350° for 12-14 minutes or until lightly browned. Remove to wire racks to cool. **Yield:** 5-1/2 dozen.

Buttercream Frosting

*Our home economists suggest keeping the recipe for this creamy frosting handy
because it deliciously tops cakes as well as cookies.*

1 cup butter, softened
8 cups confectioners' sugar
6 tablespoons milk
2 teaspoons vanilla extract
Food coloring, optional

In a large mixing bowl, beat butter, confectioners' sugar, milk and vanilla (frosting will be thick). Add food coloring if desired. **Yield:** 5 cups.

Maple Macadamia Nut Cookies

*My son, Jason, and I had fun coming up with this cookie recipe. Every bite is packed with
maple flavor, vanilla chips, milk chocolate chips and chopped macadamia nuts.*
—Vanda Pozzanghera, Rochester, New York

1-1/4 cups butter, softened
1-1/2 cups confectioners' sugar
1 egg
2 tablespoons maple flavoring
1 teaspoon vanilla extract
2 cups all-purpose flour
1 teaspoon baking soda
1 teaspoon cream of tartar
2 cups quick-cooking oats
3/4 cup vanilla *or* white chips
3/4 cup milk chocolate chips
3/4 cup chopped macadamia nuts
MAPLE ICING:
1-1/2 cups confectioners' sugar
1/4 cup heavy whipping cream
3 teaspoons maple flavoring
1 teaspoon vanilla extract
1/8 teaspoon salt

In a large mixing bowl, cream butter and confectioners' sugar. Beat in the egg, maple flavoring and vanilla. Combine the flour, baking soda and cream of tartar; gradually add to the creamed mixture. Stir in the oats, chips and nuts.

Drop by heaping tablespoonfuls 2 in. apart onto greased baking sheets. Bake at 350° for 10-12 minutes or until lightly browned. Remove to wire racks to cool. In a bowl, combine icing ingredients until smooth; drizzle over cookies. Store in the refrigerator. **Yield:** about 4-1/2 dozen.

LEARN ABOUT MACADAMIA NUTS

THE MACADAMIA nut tree originated in Queensland, Australia and was brought to Hawaii in 1882. Today, virtually all of the world's macadamias are grown on the Big Island. It takes about 7 years for a macadamia to bear fruit, making the nut an in-demand delicacy.

It takes 300 pounds of pressure per square inch to crack the shell of the macadamia, making it one of the hardest of all nuts to crack open. Because of that, macadamia nuts are mostly sold shelled.

Holiday Pinwheels

(Pictured at right)

The first time I made these pretty cookies, my husband ate the whole batch in just a few days! The fun green swirls are also great for St. Patrick's Day.
— Tejay Kuechenmeister
Brookings, South Dakota

1 cup butter, softened
1-1/4 cups sugar
2 eggs
1/4 cup light corn syrup
1 tablespoon vanilla extract
3 cups all-purpose flour
3/4 teaspoon baking powder
1/2 teaspoon baking soda
1/2 teaspoon salt
1/2 teaspoon peppermint extract
Green food coloring

In a large mixing bowl, cream butter and sugar. Add eggs, one at a time, beating well after each addition. Beat in corn syrup and vanilla. Combine the flour, baking powder, baking soda and salt; gradually add to creamed mixture. Divide dough in half. To one portion, add peppermint extract and food coloring. Wrap each portion in plastic wrap; refrigerate for 2 hours or until firm.

On a baking sheet, roll out each portion between two sheets of waxed paper into a 14-in. x 9-in. rectangle. Refrigerate for 30 minutes. Remove waxed paper. Place plain rectangle over green rectangle. Roll up tightly jelly-roll style, starting with a long side; wrap in plastic wrap. Refrigerate for 2 hours or until firm.

Unwrap and cut into 1/4-in. slices. Place 2 in. apart on greased baking sheets. Bake at 350° for 8-10 minutes or until set. Cool for 2 minutes before removing to wire racks. **Yield:** 4-1/2 dozen.

Snowy Apricot Bars

A dusting of confectioners' sugar adds to the appeal of these soft and chewy apricot bars.
A packaged baking mix makes them a snap to prepare.
—Jean Mathis, Hayesville, North Carolina

1 package (7 ounces) dried
  apricots
1 cup water
2-1/2 cups plus 2/3 cup biscuit/
  baking mix, *divided*
1/2 cup sugar
1/2 cup cold butter
2 cups packed brown sugar
4 eggs
1 cup chopped walnuts
1 teaspoon vanilla extract
Confectioners' sugar

In a saucepan, bring the apricots and water to a boil. Reduce heat; simmer, uncovered, for 10 minutes. Drain and cool. Chop apricots and set aside.

In a bowl, combine 2-1/2 cups biscuit mix and sugar. Cut in butter until crumbly. Pat into an ungreased 15-in. x 10-in. x 1-in. baking pan. Bake at 350° for 10-12 minutes or until edges are lightly browned. Cool on a wire rack.

In a large mixing bowl, beat brown sugar and eggs until blended. Stir in the apricots, walnuts, vanilla and remaining biscuit mix; spread over crust. Bake for 20-25 minutes or until golden brown. Cool on a wire rack. Cut into bars. Dust with confectioners' sugar. Store in the refrigerator. **Yield:** 5 dozen.

Dutch Almond Cookies

This recipe comes from ladies of Dutch descent at my sister's church.
The pleasant almond flavor pairs well with a cup of coffee.
—Linda DeJong, Lynden, Washington

1 cup butter, softened
2 cups sugar
2 eggs
1 teaspoon almond extract
3-1/2 cups all-purpose flour
1 teaspoon baking powder
1 teaspoon baking soda
1/2 teaspoon salt
6 tablespoons almond paste
1 egg white, lightly beaten
3 dozen whole almonds

In a large mixing bowl, cream butter and sugar. Beat in eggs and extract. Combine the flour, baking powder, baking soda and salt; gradually add to the creamed mixture and mix well. Cover and refrigerate for 1 hour or until easy to handle.

On a lightly floured surface, roll out dough to 1/4-in. thickness; cut with a floured 2-in. round cookie cutter. Place half of the circles 2 in. apart on ungreased baking sheets. Crumble 1/2 teaspoon almond paste over each; top with remaining circles. Pinch edges to seal.

Cut a small slit in top of each cookie. Brush with egg white. Press an almond in each slit. Bake at 350° for 10-12 minutes or until lightly browned. Remove to wire racks to cool. **Yield:** 3 dozen.

Fig-Filled Cookies

(Pictured at right)

Family and friends know I have a fondness for Christmas cookies. Each year after Thanksgiving, they begin asking when the cookies will be ready!
—Linda Kappelt, Linesville, Pennsylvania

1/2 cup butter, softened
1/4 cup sugar
1/4 cup packed brown sugar
1 egg
1 teaspoon vanilla extract
1-3/4 cups all-purpose flour
1/2 teaspoon baking soda
1/4 teaspoon salt
FILLING:
2/3 cup finely chopped raisins
1/2 cup finely chopped dates
1/2 cup finely chopped dried figs
1/2 cup orange juice
1/3 cup finely chopped dried
    cherries *or* cranberries
2 teaspoons sugar
1 teaspoon grated lemon peel
1/4 teaspoon ground cinnamon
1/2 cup finely chopped pecans
GLAZE:
3/4 cup confectioners' sugar
2 to 3 teaspoons lemon juice

In a large mixing bowl, cream butter and sugars. Beat in egg and vanilla. Combine the flour, baking soda and salt; stir into the creamed mixture. Divide dough in half; cover and refrigerate for at least 3 hours.

In a saucepan, combine the first eight filling ingredients. Bring to a boil. Reduce heat; simmer, uncovered, for 4-6 minutes or until the fruit is tender and liquid is absorbed, stirring occasionally. Remove from the heat; stir in pecans. Cool to room temperature.

Roll out each portion of dough between two pieces of waxed paper into a 10-in. x 8-in. rectangle. Cut each into two 10-in. x 4-in. rectangles. Spread 1/2 cup filling down the center of each rectangle. Starting at a long side, fold dough over filling; fold other side over top. Pinch to seal seams and edges. Place seam side down on parchment paper-lined baking sheets.

Bake at 375° for 10-15 minutes or until lightly browned. Cut each rectangle diagonally into 1-in. strips. Remove to wire racks to cool. Combine glaze ingredients; drizzle over cookies. **Yield:** about 2-1/2 dozen.

Ginger Diamonds

These soft delicious ginger cookies were a favorite of my son, who passed away years ago.
I think of him each time I make them and know your family will enjoy them, too.
—Fran Williamson, Washington, Indiana

1 cup shortening
1-1/2 cups sugar
1/2 cup molasses
2 eggs
3-1/2 cups all-purpose flour
1 teaspoon baking soda
1 teaspoon ground cinnamon
1 teaspoon ground cloves
1/2 teaspoon salt
1/2 teaspoon ground ginger
Additional sugar

In a large mixing bowl, cream shortening and sugar. Beat in molasses. Add eggs, one at a time, beating well after each addition. Combine the flour, baking soda, cinnamon, cloves, salt and ginger; gradually add to the creamed mixture. Cover and refrigerate for 30 minutes or until easy to handle.

Divide dough in half. On a lightly floured surface, roll out each portion to 1/4-in. thickness. With a sharp knife, make cuts 1-1/2 in. apart in one direction, then make diagonal cuts 1-1/2 in. apart in the opposite direction. Generously sprinkle with additional sugar.

Place 1 in. apart on ungreased baking sheets. Bake at 350° for 10-11 minutes or until edges are golden brown. Remove to wire racks to cool. **Yield:** 7 dozen.

Butter Ball Chiffons

The combination of lemon pudding and toffee candy bars sets these crisp cookies apart
from all others. Keep the ingredients on hand for when you need a treat in a hurry.
—Myla Harvey, Stanton, Michigan

1 cup butter, softened
1/4 cup confectioners' sugar
1 package (3.4 ounces) instant lemon pudding mix
2 teaspoons water
1 teaspoon vanilla extract
2 cups all-purpose flour
1 cup chopped pecans *or* walnuts
2 Heath candy bars (1.4 ounces *each*), chopped
Additional confectioners' sugar

In a mixing bowl, cream butter and confectioners' sugar. Beat in the pudding mix, water and vanilla. Gradually add flour. Stir in nuts and chopped candy bars.

Roll into 1-in. balls. Place 2 in. apart on ungreased baking sheets. Bake at 325° for 12-15 minutes or until lightly browned. Cool for 3 minutes before removing to wire racks. Sprinkle with additional confectioners' sugar. **Yield:** 5 dozen.

Editor's Note: This recipe does not use eggs.

Frosted Maple Pyramids

(Pictured at right)

The cute shape of these cookies makes them a splendid sight on a Christmas cookie tray. You could use star-shaped cookie cutters in place of the round ones.
—Wanda Goodell, Kent, Washington

1/2 cup shortening
1/3 cup packed brown sugar
  1 egg
  1 teaspoon vanilla extract
1/4 teaspoon maple flavoring
1-1/4 cups all-purpose flour
1/4 teaspoon salt
1/4 teaspoon baking powder
FROSTING:
  1/4 cup butter, softened
  3/4 cup confectioners' sugar
  1 teaspoon vanilla extract
Red candied cherries, halved

In a mixing bowl, cream shortening and brown sugar. Beat in the egg, vanilla and maple flavoring. Combine the flour, salt and baking powder; gradually add to the creamed mixture. Cover and refrigerate for 2 hours or until easy to handle.

On a lightly floured surface, roll out dough to 1/8-in. thickness. With floured 2-in. round cookie cutters, cut out 18 circles. Repeat with 1-1/2-in.

and 1-in. round cookie cutters. Place 1 in. apart on greased baking sheets. Bake at 375° for 7-9 minutes or until lightly browned. Remove to wire racks to cool.

In a small mixing bowl, cream butter and confectioners' sugar. Beat in vanilla. To assemble cookies, place a 2-in. cookie on waxed paper. Spread with 1 teaspoon frosting. Top with a 1-1/2-in. cookie; frost. Top with a 1-in. cookie; frost. Garnish with candied cherries. **Yield:** about 1-1/2 dozen.

'TIS THE Season

A Jolly Spread of Just Desserts!

ENTERTAINING around the holidays doesn't mean you have to spend all day in the kitchen preparing a multi-course meal.

Your relatives and friends will be sweet on the idea of getting together on a weeknight for a few hours of great conversation and a dazzling assortment of dressed-up desserts!

Like Cheese-Filled Shortbread Tartlets, Harlequin Cake and Chocolate-Macadamia Freezer Pie (all shown at right), many of the irresistible recipes in this chapter have handy make-ahead components.

So the only last-minute fussing you'll have is putting on a pot of coffee!

Happy Holidays

SWEETS FOR SANTA
(Clockwise from top left)

Cheese-Filled Shortbread Tartlets (p. 88)

Harlequin Cake (p. 86)

Chocolate-Macadamia Freezer Pie (p. 87)

Harlequin Cake

(Pictured on page 85)

This chocolate cake looks as impressive as it tastes.
— Pat Fredericks, Oak Creek, Wisconsin

1/2 cup butter, cubed
1/4 cup water
  3 tablespoons baking cocoa
  1 cup all-purpose flour
  1 cup sugar
1/2 teaspoon baking soda
1/4 teaspoon salt
  1 egg
1/4 cup buttermilk
  1 teaspoon vanilla extract
TOPPING:
  1 cup heavy whipping cream
  3 tablespoons sugar
  1 can (12 ounces) raspberry *or*
    strawberry filling
  1 can (12 ounces) apricot filling
1/4 cup sliced almonds, toasted
  4 plain milk chocolate candy
    bars (1.55 ounces *each*)

In a small saucepan, bring butter, water and cocoa to a boil, stirring constantly. Remove from the heat; set aside. In a small mixing bowl, combine the flour, sugar, baking soda and salt. Add the egg, buttermilk and vanilla; mix well. Beat in cocoa mixture. Pour into a greased and floured 9-in. round baking pan. Bake at 350° for 35-40 minutes or until a toothpick inserted near the center comes out clean. Cool for 10 minutes before removing from pan to a wire rack to cool completely.

In a small mixing bowl, beat cream and sugar until soft peaks form. Place cake on a serving platter. Set aside a fourth of the whipped cream. Frost top and sides of cake with remaining whipped cream. Spoon the reserved whipped cream into a pastry bag with a star tip; pipe a diamond-pattern lattice design on cake top. Pipe a border around top edge of cake.

Spoon raspberry filling into every other diamond in lattice. Spoon apricot filling into remaining diamonds. Sprinkle with almonds. Divide each chocolate bar into 12 rectangles, following scored lines. Arrange chocolate pieces around side of cake with smooth sides out and edges overlapping; press into whipped cream. Refrigerate until serving. **Yield:** 13 servings.

Eggnog Sauce

Use this dessert sauce to dress up bread pudding, pound cake, ice cream or fresh fruit.
— Helen Hunden, Orem, Utah

  3 tablespoons all-purpose flour
  2 tablespoons sugar
1/2 teaspoon salt
  2 cups eggnog*

In a double boiler, combine the flour, sugar and salt. Gradually stir in eggnog until smooth. Cook and stir over medium heat for 6-8 minutes or until thickened. Remove from the heat; cool. Cover and refrigerate until serving. **Yield:** 2 cups.

  *Editor's Note: This recipe was tested with commercially prepared eggnog.

Chocolate-Macadamia Freezer Pie

(Pictured at right and on page 84)

The rich filling for this make-ahead pie resembles chocolate mousse. Macadamia nuts in both the filling and crust are a nice touch.
—Martha Lercher, Cabot, Arkansas

1-1/4 cups crushed chocolate wafers
  2 cups finely chopped macadamia nuts, *divided*
1/3 cup butter, melted
  1 package (8 ounces) cream cheese, softened
  1 cup sugar, *divided*
  1 cup (6 ounces) semisweet chocolate chips, melted and cooled
  1 teaspoon vanilla extract
1-1/2 cups heavy whipping cream

In a small bowl, combine the wafer crumbs, 1/2 cup nuts and butter. Press onto the bottom and up the sides of a greased 9-in. pie plate. Bake at 350° for 8 minutes. Cool completely on a wire rack.

In a mixing bowl, beat cream cheese and 1/2 cup sugar until smooth. Add chocolate and vanilla; mix well. Stir in the remaining nuts. In another mixing bowl, beat cream until soft peaks form. Gradually add the remaining sugar, beating until stiff peaks form. Fold into the chocolate mixture. Spoon into crust. Cover and freeze for several hours or overnight. Remove from the freezer 30 minutes before serving. **Yield:** 6-8 servings.

WRITING IN CHOCOLATE

PRESENT wedges of Chocolate-Macadamia Freezer Pie (above) with a seasonal sentiment handwritten on the rim of the serving platter.

Melt about 2 tablespoons semisweet chocolate chips in a microwave-safe bowl. Transfer to a pastry bag fitted with a small round tip. Lightly touch the tip to the surface of the platter, squeezing the melted chocolate out as you write. Release pressure and gently touch the platter to stop.

The chocolate writing can be done early in the day; set aside until chocolate becomes firm. Top with your choice of dessert and any additional garnishes just before serving.

Cheese-Filled Shortbread Tartlets

(Pictured on page 84)

*Bite-size treats are a nice addition to a dessert buffet. You can store cooled, baked tart shells in
an airtight container at room temperature overnight or in the freezer for a few weeks.*
—*Cathy Walerius, Mound, Minnesota*

1 package (8 ounces) cream
  cheese, softened
1 cup sweetened condensed
  milk
1/3 cup lemon juice
1 teaspoon vanilla extract
1 cup butter, softened
1-1/2 cups all-purpose flour
1/2 cup confectioners' sugar
1 tablespoon cornstarch
Fresh raspberries and mint leaves

In a small mixing bowl, beat cream cheese until smooth. Gradually beat in milk, lemon juice and vanilla. Cover and refrigerate for 8 hours or overnight.

In another mixing bowl, beat the butter, flour, confectioners' sugar and cornstarch until smooth. Roll into 1-in. balls. Place in greased miniature muffin cups; press onto the bottom and up the sides. Prick with a fork. Bake at 325° for 20-25 minutes or until golden brown. Immediately run a knife around each tart to loosen completely. Cool in pans on wire racks.

Spoon 1 tablespoon cheese filling into each tart shell. Cover and refrigerate until set. Just before serving, garnish with raspberries and mint. **Yield:** 3 dozen.

Cranberry Mousse

*After indulging in a rich holiday meal, a refreshing treat like this is a welcome sight.
My holiday dinners aren't complete without this cool, colorful dessert.*
—*Mitzi Sentiff, Alexandria, Virginia*

3/4 cup sugar
3 tablespoons cornstarch
1-1/2 cups cranberry-raspberry
  juice
1/2 cup cranberry-orange sauce*
1 cup heavy whipping cream,
  whipped

In a small saucepan, combine the sugar, cornstarch and juice until smooth. Bring to a boil over medium heat; cook and stir for 1 minute or until thickened. Remove from the heat. Stir in cranberry-orange sauce. Pour into a bowl; cover and refrigerate for 2 hours or until chilled.

Stir cranberry mixture; fold in whipped cream. Spoon into dessert dishes. Refrigerate for 30 minutes or until set. **Yield:** 4-6 servings.

***Editor's Note:** This recipe was tested with Indian Trail cranberry-orange sauce. Look for it in the freezer section of your grocery store.

Almond-Cream Puff Ring

(Pictured at right)

Although individual cream puffs are an awesome dessert, they require a lot of preparation time...and time is one thing I often don't have enough of! That's why I rely on this recipe.
—Carolyn Johannsen, Melvin, Illinois

1 cup water
1/2 cup butter
1/4 teaspoon salt
1 cup all-purpose flour
4 eggs
FILLING:
1-1/4 cups cold milk
1 package (3.4 ounces) instant vanilla pudding mix
1/2 teaspoon almond extract
1 cup heavy whipping cream, whipped
GLAZE:
1/2 cup semisweet chocolate chips
1 tablespoon butter
1-1/2 teaspoons light corn syrup
1-1/2 teaspoons milk

Cover a baking sheet with foil; grease the foil. Trace a 12-in. circle onto foil; set aside. In a large saucepan, bring the water, butter and salt to a boil. Add flour all at once and stir until a smooth ball forms. Remove from the heat; let stand for 5 minutes. Add eggs, one at a time, beating well after each addition. Continue beating until mixture is smooth and shiny.

Drop batter by rounded tablespoonfuls along the inside of the circle (mounds should be slightly touching). Bake at 400° for 40-45 minutes or until golden brown. Lift foil and transfer to a wire rack. Immediately cut a slit in the side of each puff to allow steam to escape; cool. Carefully cut ring in half horizontally and set top aside; remove soft dough from inside with a fork. Transfer to a serving plate.

In a bowl, whisk the milk, pudding mix and extract for 2 minutes. Chill for 5 minutes or until thickened. Fold in whipped cream. Spread over bottom of ring; replace top. In a microwave, melt chocolate chips and butter; stir until smooth. Stir in corn syrup and milk. Drizzle over ring. Refrigerate until serving. **Yield:** 10-12 servings.

Apricot Strudel Sticks

When I share this recipe, folks often do a double take when they see ice cream in the pastry!
The recipe makes 6 dozen, so you have plenty to both keep and share.
—Caroline Anderson, Toledo, Ohio

4 cups all-purpose flour
1/4 teaspoon salt
2 cups cold butter
2 cups French vanilla ice cream,
    softened
Confectioners' sugar
1 can (12 ounces) apricot filling
1/2 cup golden raisins
1/2 cup chopped pecans
Cinnamon-sugar

In a large bowl, combine the flour and salt; cut in butter until crumbly. Add ice cream, tossing with a fork until a ball forms. Refrigerate overnight.

Shape dough into six balls. Lightly sprinkle work surface with confectioners' sugar; roll out each ball into a 13-in. x 8-in. rectangle. Spread apricot filling evenly over dough to within 1/2 in. of edges. Top with raisins and pecans; sprinkle with cinnamon-sugar. Roll up jelly-roll style into a tight roll, starting with a long side; pinch seam to seal.

Carefully place on three greased baking sheets. Bake at 350° for 25-30 minutes or until lightly browned. Remove to wire racks to cool completely. Cut each roll into 12 slices; sprinkle cut sides with confectioners' sugar. **Yield:** 6 dozen.

Chocolate Caramel Tart

Look no further when you want a dessert that's gooey and good!
Each piece is like a big candy bar on a plate.
—Margaret Peterson, Forest City, Iowa

2 cups crushed chocolate wafers
    (about 35 wafers)
1/3 cup butter, melted
30 caramels*
1/2 cup caramel ice cream
    topping
1/2 cup heavy whipping cream,
    divided
2 cups chopped pecans
3/4 cup semisweet chocolate chips

In a bowl, combine the wafer crumbs and butter; press onto the bottom of a greased 9-in. springform pan. Place pan on a baking sheet. Bake at 350° for 10 minutes. Cool on a wire rack.

In a heavy saucepan, cook and stir the caramels and caramel topping over low heat until smooth. Remove from the heat; stir in 1/4 cup cream and pecans. Spread over crust. Cover and refrigerate for 1 hour. In a saucepan, melt chocolate chips with remaining cream. Drizzle over tart. Cover and refrigerate for 1 hour or until serving. **Yield:** 12 servings.

*Editor's Note: This recipe was tested with Hershey caramels.

Ricotta Nut Torte

(Pictured at right)

This pretty layered Italian cake is called cassata. It takes some time to prepare this eye-catching dessert but it conveniently chills overnight.
—*Karen Albert, Prineville, Oregon*

2 cartons (15 ounces *each*)
   ricotta cheese
1-1/2 cups sugar
  1 teaspoon vanilla extract
  1 cup chopped pecans
  1 milk chocolate candy bar
   (7 ounces), grated

BATTER:
 2/3 cup shortening
1-2/3 cups sugar
  3 eggs
1-1/2 teaspoons vanilla extract
2-1/2 cups all-purpose flour
2-1/2 teaspoons baking powder
  1 teaspoon salt
1-1/4 cups milk

FROSTING:
  2 cups heavy whipping cream
 1/4 cup confectioners' sugar
 1/2 teaspoon vanilla extract
Whole hazelnuts and chocolate
  curls, optional

For filling, in a small mixing bowl, beat ricotta cheese and sugar until smooth; beat in vanilla. Fold in pecans and chocolate. Cover and refrigerate.

In a large mixing bowl, cream shortening and sugar until light and fluffy. Add eggs, one at a time, beating well after each addition. Beat in vanilla. Combine the flour, baking powder and salt; add to the creamed mixture alternately with milk. Pour into three waxed paper-lined 9-in. round baking pans. Bake at 350° for 25-30 minutes or until a toothpick inserted near the center comes out clean. Cool for 10 minutes before removing from pans to wire racks to cool completely.

Split each cake in half. Place one bottom layer on a serving plate; spread with 1 cup filling. Repeat layers four times. Top with remaining cake. Cover and refrigerate overnight.

In a mixing bowl, beat cream until thickened. Add confectioners' sugar and vanilla; beat until stiff peaks form. Spread over top and sides of cake. Garnish with hazelnuts and chocolate curls if desired. Refrigerate leftovers. **Yield:** 12 servings.

Pumpkin Chiffon Pie

*This delicious pie is so light and fluffy that folks will have room for a slice
no matter how full they are! Guests are always delighted with the delicate flavor.*
—*Linda Gartner, Feasterville, Pennsylvania*

- 1 envelope unflavored gelatin
- 1/2 cup cold water
- 3/4 cup milk
- 1 cup packed brown sugar
- 1 cup canned pumpkin
- 1/2 teaspoon ground ginger
- 1/2 teaspoon ground cinnamon
- 1/4 teaspoon salt
- 1-1/2 cups whipped topping
- 1 graham cracker crust (9 inches)

In a small bowl, sprinkle gelatin over cold water; let stand for 1 minute. In a saucepan, heat milk over medium heat until bubbles form around sides of saucepan. Add gelatin mixture; stir until dissolved. Stir in brown sugar until dissolved. Remove from the heat. Add the pumpkin, ginger, cinnamon and salt; mix well. Refrigerate until thickened, about 1-1/2 hours.

Fold whipped topping into pumpkin mixture. Pour into crust. Refrigerate for at least 4 hours or until firm. Refrigerate leftovers. **Yield:** 6-8 servings.

Winter Celebrations Cake

*I came up with this dessert by adapting my recipe for July Fourth Celebrations Cake, which calls
for fresh fruit. It's a delicious way to dress up angel food cake for any season.*
—*Collette Mooney, Sayward, British Columbia*

- 1 package (16 ounces) angel food cake mix
- 2 packages (12 ounces *each*) frozen unsweetened mixed berries, thawed
- 1 package (10 ounces) frozen unsweetened sliced strawberries, thawed
- 2 packages (3 ounces *each*) raspberry gelatin
- 1 pint vanilla ice cream
- 2 cups heavy whipping cream
- 1/2 cup applesauce

Prepare and bake cake according to package directions for a 10-in. tube pan. Drain the berries, reserving juice in a 2-cup measuring cup; add enough water to the juice to measure 1-1/4 cups. Set berries aside.

Pour juice mixture into a microwave-safe bowl; cover and microwave on high for 3-4 minutes or until mixture comes to a boil. Stir in gelatin until dissolved. Stir in the ice cream until melted. Fold in the berries. Refrigerate for 30 minutes or until set but not firm.

For frosting, beat cream in a mixing bowl until thickened. Add applesauce; beat until stiff peaks form. Set aside. Cut a 1-in. slice off the top of cake; set aside. Using a sharp knife, cut a tunnel out of the cake, leaving a 1-in. wall on all sides; carefully remove cake from inside and save for another use. Fill tunnel with berry mixture; replace cake top. Spread frosting over top and sides of cake. Store in the refrigerator. **Yield:** 12-16 servings.

Chocolate Hazelnut Gateau

(Pictured at right)

Gateau (pronounced ga-tow) is the French word for any rich and fancy cake. I think you'll agree this dense chocolate dessert has just the right amount of sweetness.
—Michelle Krzmarzick
Redondo Beach, California

2/3 **cup butter, softened**
3/4 **cup sugar**
3 **eggs,** *separated*
1 **cup (6 ounces) semisweet chocolate chips, melted and cooled**
1 **teaspoon vanilla extract**
3/4 **cup all-purpose flour**
1/2 **teaspoon salt**
1/4 **cup milk**
2/3 **cup ground hazelnuts, toasted**
GLAZE:
3 **tablespoons butter**
2 **tablespoons light corn syrup**
1 **tablespoon water**
1 **cup (6 ounces) semisweet chocolate chips**
Toasted slivered almonds and fresh mint leaves

In a large mixing bowl, cream butter and sugar until light and fluffy. Beat in egg yolks, melted chocolate and vanilla. Combine the flour and salt; gradually add to creamed mixture alternately with milk. Stir in the hazelnuts.

In a small mixing bowl, beat egg whites until stiff peaks form; carefully fold into batter. Spread into a greased 9-in. springform pan. Place pan on a baking sheet. Bake at 350° for 30-35 minutes or until a toothpick inserted near the center comes out clean. Cool on a wire rack for 10 minutes. Carefully run a knife around edge of pan to loosen; remove sides of pan. Cool completely.

In a saucepan, bring the butter, corn syrup and water to a boil, stirring constantly. Remove from the heat. Add the chocolate chips; stir until smooth. Cool to room temperature. Spread over top and sides of gateau. Garnish with almonds and mint. **Yield:** 12 servings.

Nutty Butterscotch Bites

*With butterscotch pudding mix, peanuts, caramels, chocolate and more,
these treats have something for everyone. They take some time to prepare,
but I don't mind because the recipe makes a big batch.*
—*Karen Van Beek, Holland, Minnesota*

1 cup butter, softened
3/4 cup packed brown sugar
1/4 cup sugar
2 eggs
1 teaspoon vanilla extract
2-1/4 cups all-purpose flour
1 package (3.4 ounces) instant
   butterscotch pudding mix
1 teaspoon baking soda
1-1/3 cups butterscotch chips
FILLING:
1/4 cup butter, cubed
1 cup sugar
1/4 cup evaporated milk
1 jar (7 ounces) marshmallow
   creme
1/4 cup peanut butter
1 teaspoon vanilla extract
1-1/2 cups salted peanuts
CARAMEL LAYER:
1 package (14 ounces) caramels
1/4 cup heavy whipping cream
TOPPING:
1 cup semisweet chocolate chips
1 cup butterscotch chips
1 teaspoon shortening
1/4 cup peanut butter

In a large mixing bowl, cream butter and sugars. Add eggs, one at a time, beating well after each addition. Beat in vanilla. Combine the flour, pudding mix and baking soda; gradually add to creamed mixture. Stir in butterscotch chips. Spread into a greased 15-in. x 10-in. x 1-in. baking pan. Bake at 350° for 20-25 minutes or until a toothpick inserted near the center comes out clean. Cool on a wire rack.

For filling, melt butter in a heavy saucepan over medium heat. Add sugar and milk; bring to a gentle boil. Reduce heat to medium-low; boil and stir for 5 minutes. Remove from the heat. Stir in the marshmallow creme, peanut butter and vanilla until blended and smooth. Stir in peanuts. Spread over crust. Refrigerate until set.

In a saucepan, cook and stir the caramels and cream over low heat until melted and smooth; cook and stir 4 minutes longer. Spread over filling. Refrigerate until set.

Melt the chocolate chips, butterscotch chips and shortening. Stir in peanut butter. Spread over caramel layer. Refrigerate for 4 hours or overnight. Remove from the refrigerator 20 minutes before cutting. Cut into 1-in. squares. **Yield:** about 12 dozen.

Editor's Note: Reduced-fat or generic brands of peanut butter are not recommended for this recipe. This recipe was tested with Hershey caramels.

Raspberry Vanilla Trifle

(Pictured at right)

When I was growing up, my English mother made this as the centerpiece at our traditional Christmas Day tea. Presented in a cut glass bowl, it's absolutely stunning.
—Joyce Toth, Wichita Falls, Texas

2 cups milk
1 package (3 ounces) cook-and-serve vanilla pudding mix
1 loaf (10-3/4 ounces) frozen pound cake, thawed
1/4 cup seedless raspberry jam
1/4 cup orange juice
10 soft macaroon cookies
2 cups fresh *or* frozen unsweetened raspberries, thawed and drained
1 cup heavy whipping cream
2 tablespoons confectioners' sugar
1/4 cup sliced almonds, toasted

In a small saucepan, combine milk and pudding mix. Cook and stir over medium heat until mixture comes to a full boil. Cool. Cut cake into 1-in. slices; spread with jam. Cut into 1-in. cubes. Place cubes jam side up in a 3-qt. trifle or glass bowl. Drizzle with orange juice.

Place macaroons in a food processor or blender; cover and process until coarse crumbs form. Set aside 1/4 cup crumbs for garnish; sprinkle remaining crumbs over cake cubes. Top with berries and pudding. Cover and refrigerate overnight.

Just before serving, in a small mixing bowl, beat cream until thickened. Beat in confectioners' sugar until stiff peaks form. Spread over trifle. Sprinkle with almonds and reserved macaroon crumbs. **Yield:** 10-12 servings.

BUYING AND STORING RASPBERRIES

PURCHASE raspberries that are brightly colored without the hulls attached.

When you get home, discard any raspberries that are soft, shriveled or moldy. Quickly rinse remaining berries in water, then place in a single layer in a paper towel-lined bowl. They'll stay fresh in the refrigerator for up to 3 days.

One-half pint equals about 1 cup.

Cranberry Peach Tart

Dinner guests will be impressed with the interesting pairing of fruit in this lovely tart.
I think you'll agree it tastes almost too good to share!
— Dorothy Smith, El Dorado, Arkansas

Pastry for single-crust pie
  (9 inches)
    3 cups frozen sliced peaches,
      thawed
    1 cup fresh *or* frozen
      cranberries, thawed
  1/2 cup sugar
  1/4 cup all-purpose flour
  1/2 teaspoon ground nutmeg
  1/4 teaspoon salt
TOPPING:
  1/3 cup all-purpose flour
  1/4 cup packed brown sugar
  1/4 teaspoon ground cinnamon
    3 tablespoons cold butter
  1/4 cup slivered almonds, toasted

Press pastry into an ungreased 9-in. fluted tart pan with removable bottom or press onto the bottom and 1 in. up the sides of an ungreased 9-in. springform pan. Line unpricked pastry shell with a double thickness of heavy-duty foil. Bake at 425° for 5 minutes. Remove foil; bake 5 minutes longer or until lightly browned. Cool on a wire rack.

In a bowl, gently toss the peaches, cranberries, sugar, flour, nutmeg and salt. Pour into crust. For topping, combine the flour, brown sugar and cinnamon in a bowl; cut in butter until mixture resembles coarse crumbs. Stir in almonds. Sprinkle over filling. Bake at 375° for 40-45 minutes or until bubbly, covering loosely with foil during the last 20 minutes of baking. **Yield:** 6-8 servings.

Poppy Seed Citrus Cheesecake

When I have time to spend in the kitchen, I like making desserts that are sure to please.
This cheesecake fills the bill. The citrus glaze is a perfect topping.
— Diane Babcock, Richmond, British Columbia

  3/4 cup graham cracker crumbs
    (about 12 squares)
  3/4 cup ground almonds
    1 tablespoon sugar
  1/4 cup butter, melted
FILLING:
    2 packages (8 ounces *each*)
      cream cheese, softened
    1 cup sugar
  3/4 cup heavy whipping cream
  1/4 cup orange juice
    3 tablespoons all-purpose flour

    2 tablespoons poppy seeds
    1 teaspoon grated orange peel
    4 eggs, beaten
GLAZE:
    2 eggs
  3/4 cup sugar
  1/4 cup lemon juice
    2 tablespoons orange juice
    2 tablespoons butter
    1 teaspoon grated orange peel
    1 teaspoon grated lemon peel

In a bowl, combine cracker crumbs, almonds and sugar; stir in butter. Press onto the bottom and 1 in. up the sides of a greased 9-in. springform pan. Place pan on a baking sheet. Bake at 350° for 8 minutes. Cool on a wire rack.

In a mixing bowl, beat cream cheese and sugar until smooth. Add cream, orange juice, flour, poppy seeds and orange peel; mix until well blended. Add eggs; beat on low speed just until combined. Pour over crust. Return pan to baking sheet.

Bake at 350° for 45-50 minutes or until center is almost set. Cool on a wire rack for 10 minutes. Carefully run a knife around edge of pan to loosen. Cool 1 hour longer.

In a small saucepan, whisk eggs until foamy. Whisk in remaining glaze ingredients; cook and stir over low heat until mixture reaches 160° and is smooth and thickened. Refrigerate cheesecake and glaze overnight. Remove sides of pan. Serve glaze over cheesecake. **Yield:** 12-14 servings.

Fruit-and-Cheese Bars

(Pictured at right)

One pan of these sweet, rich bars goes a long way. Colorful candied fruit makes it especially festive.
— *Tina Hagen, Emo, Ontario*

1/2 cup butter, softened
1/2 cup packed brown sugar
  1 cup all-purpose flour
  1 package (8 ounces) cream cheese, softened
1/4 cup sugar
  1 egg
  1 tablespoon lemon juice
1/2 cup chopped mixed candied fruit

In a small mixing bowl, cream butter and brown sugar. Add flour; beat until crumbly. Set aside 1/2 cup for topping. Press remaining crumb mixture into a greased 8-in. square baking dish. Bake at 350° for 10-12 minutes or until lightly browned.

Meanwhile, in a mixing bowl, beat cream cheese and sugar until smooth. Beat in the egg and lemon juice. Stir in candied fruit. Spread over crust; sprinkle with reserved crumb mixture. Bake 18-20 minutes longer or until firm. Cool on a wire rack. Store in the refrigerator. **Yield:** about 2-1/2 dozen.

Pistachio-Chocolate Chiffon Roll

This cake roll keeps well in the freezer; just thaw and glaze before serving.
I sometimes add crushed peppermint candies to the filling.
—Rosemary Sukowatey, South Byron, Wisconsin

3/4 cup cake flour
3/4 cup sugar, *divided*
  1 teaspoon baking powder
1/4 teaspoon salt
  3 egg yolks
1/4 cup vegetable oil
  2 ounces German sweet
    chocolate, melted and cooled
1/3 cup water
  4 egg whites
1/4 teaspoon cream of tartar

FILLING:
1-1/4 cups heavy whipping cream
  2 tablespoons confectioners'
    sugar
  1 teaspoon vanilla extract
1/2 teaspoon almond extract
  2 drops green food coloring
  1 drop yellow food coloring
1/3 cup chopped pistachios

GLAZE:
  1 package (4 ounces) German
    sweet chocolate, melted and
    cooled
  1 tablespoon butter, softened
  1 cup confectioners' sugar
1/8 teaspoon salt
  2 tablespoons plus 2 teaspoons
    milk

Line a greased 15-in. x 10-in. x 1-in. baking pan with waxed paper and grease the paper; set aside. In a mixing bowl, combine the flour, 10 tablespoons sugar, baking powder and salt. Combine the egg yolks, oil and chocolate; add to the flour mixture and beat until well combined. Add water; beat until smooth.

In another mixing bowl, beat egg whites and cream of tartar on medium speed until soft peaks form. Gradually add remaining sugar, beating on high until stiff peaks form. Fold into the chocolate mixture. Pour into prepared pan. Bake at 350° for 20 minutes or until a toothpick inserted near the center comes out clean.

Cool for 5 minutes. Invert cake onto a towel dusted with confectioners' sugar. Roll up cake in the towel, starting with a short side. Cool completely on a wire rack.

For filling, in a mixing bowl, beat the cream, sugar and extracts until soft peaks form. Add food coloring; mix well. Unroll cake; spread filling to within 1/2 in. of edges. Sprinkle with pistachios. Roll up again. In a small mixing bowl, combine the glaze ingredients; beat until smooth. Spread over cake. Cover and refrigerate for 1 hour before serving. **Yield:** 8-10 servings.

THE POWER OF PISTACHIOS

PISTACHIOS date back to the Holy Land in the Middle East and were a rare delicacy prized by royalty. One legend says that if you stood under a pistachio tree on moonlit nights and heard the shells cracking open, good fortune would come your way.

In the late 1800s, American traders began importing pistachios primarily for U.S. citizens of Middle Eastern origin.

Pretty Cake Pedestals

(Pictured at right)

THE PRESENTATION of foods on a buffet can have as much impact as the impressive desserts themselves!

One way to add a stunning sight to your table is by decorating an ordinary cake pedestal.

We started with a white raised cake plate that has a lacy apron, then transformed it by adding easy embellishments.

Pretty Paper. Beautiful scrapbook paper (like the pink striped paper shown on page 84 and the green striped one shown above right) can be found at any arts and crafts store. Buy enough paper to go around the pedestal. Cut the paper's bottom edge with a decorative-edge scissors. Adhere the paper to the pedestal's apron with double-stick tape.

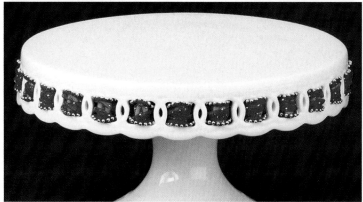

Wrap It with Ribbon. Weave wire-edge ribbon in and out of the holes on the pedestal's apron. You can either tucks in the ends or tie the ends together into a bow.

Fragrant Fresh Greens. Add festive color—and a subtle fragrance—to your table by tucking delicate-looking juniper branches into the holes of the pedestal's apron. You can assemble this pretty pedestal ahead of time and store it in the refrigerator.

Have a Ball! For a whimsical look, tie cording onto miniature ornaments and place in the apron's holes. Attach with tape under the pedestal. You can also hang the baubles from the apron with ornament hooks.

Holiday Gifts from The Kitchen

NOT SURE what to give neighbors, friends, relatives, teachers and other important people in your life this Christmas season?

You don't have to spend hours—or lots of money—at the mall to come up with thoughtful gifts that are sure to please.

Just turn the page, head to the kitchen and whip up some yummy Yuletide treats! After all, nothing shows you care more than a gift made with love by your own hands.

Popcorn Nut Treat, Eggnog Mini Loaves and Orange-Cinnamon Chocolate Chip Cookies (all recipes shown at right) are just a sample of the snacks, breads, sweets and relishes found in this chapter.

We also provide some innovative packaging ideas so you can present these goodies in a special way.

Christmas blessings to you and yours

Madelin

HOMEMADE FROM THE HEART
(Clockwise from top right)

Popcorn Nut Treat (p. 102)

Eggnog Mini Loaves (p. 103)

**Orange-Cinnamon
Chocolate Chip Cookies** (p. 102)

Popcorn Nut Treat

(Pictured on page 101)

You need only five ingredients to make this special snack mix featuring popcorn, cereal and nuts. The pairing of salty nuts and sweet honey is delicious.
—Kay Young, Flushing, Michigan

2 quarts popped popcorn
3 cups Wheat *or* Rice Chex
1 can (11-1/2 ounces) salted mixed nuts
1/2 cup butter, cubed
1/2 cup honey

In a large bowl, combine the popcorn, cereal and nuts. In a microwave-safe bowl, heat butter and honey until butter is melted; stir until smooth. Pour over popcorn mixture and toss to coat.

Transfer to two ungreased 15-in. x 10-in. x 1-in. baking pans. Bake at 350° for 15-20 minutes or until popcorn is golden brown, stirring every 5 minutes. Cool, stirring occasionally. **Yield:** about 2-1/2 quarts.

Orange-Cinnamon Chocolate Chip Cookies

(Pictured on page 100)

I developed this recipe after years of searching for a chocolate chip cookie that would stand out from all others. Orange and cinnamon are tasty additions.
—Daniel Kaepp, Coldwater, Michigan

1 cup butter, softened
3/4 cup sugar
3/4 cup packed brown sugar
2 eggs
1 tablespoon grated orange peel
1 teaspoon vanilla extract
3-1/2 cups all-purpose flour
1-1/2 teaspoons baking soda
1-1/4 teaspoons ground cinnamon
3/4 teaspoon salt
2 cups (12 ounces) semisweet chocolate chips
1 cup chopped walnuts

In a large mixing bowl, cream butter and sugars. Beat in the eggs, orange peel and vanilla. Combine the flour, baking soda, cinnamon and salt; gradually add to the creamed mixture. Stir in the chips and walnuts. Cover and chill for 2 hours or until easy to handle.

On a lightly floured surface, roll out dough to 1/2-in. thickness. Cut with a 3-in. round cookie cutter. Place 1 in. apart on greased baking sheets. Bake at 375° for 12-14 minutes or until lightly browned. Remove to wire racks to cool. **Yield:** about 3 dozen.

Eggnog Mini Loaves

(Pictured at right and on page 100)

The seasonal flavors of eggnog, rum extract and nutmeg shine through in these moist, golden loaves. Tender slices go great with a cup of coffee.
—Beverly Elmore, Spokane, Washington

2-1/4 cups all-purpose flour
    2 teaspoons baking powder
1/2 teaspoon salt
1/2 teaspoon ground cinnamon
1/2 teaspoon ground nutmeg
    2 eggs
    1 cup sugar
    1 cup eggnog*
1/2 cup butter, melted
    2 teaspoons vanilla extract
    2 teaspoons rum extract

In a large bowl, combine the flour, baking powder, salt, cinnamon and nutmeg. In another bowl, beat the eggs, sugar, eggnog, butter and extracts; stir into dry ingredients just until moistened.

Pour into three greased 5-3/4-in. x 3-in. x 2-in. loaf pans. Bake at 350° for 30-35 minutes or until a toothpick inserted near the center comes out clean. Cool for 10 minutes before removing from pans to wire racks. **Yield:** 3 loaves.

*Editor's Note: This recipe was tested with commercially prepared eggnog.

Family Traditions

My passion for making gifts of food at the holidays is shared by my daughter. (Homemade fudge is one of our specialties!) It all began when she was a teen and I enlisted her to knead 22 batches of dough for my mom's caramel cinnamon rolls, which I presented to friends and co-workers. I'm proud I instilled in her a love of giving from the heart...and hands.
    —*Mary Ann Kosmas*
    Minneapolis, Minnesota

Versatile Seasoning Mix

One year, I gave salt shakers filled with this mix to Sunday school instructors.
When one teacher asked for a refill, I knew this recipe was a winner!
—*Karla Weaver, Greenville, Ohio*

1/3 cup garlic powder
1/4 cup celery salt
1/4 cup Italian seasoning
1/4 cup lemon-pepper seasoning
1/4 cup dried rosemary, crushed
1/4 cup paprika
3 tablespoons garlic salt
4 teaspoons pepper

In a bowl, combine all of the ingredients. Store in shaker-topped containers. Sprinkle on soups, stews, salads or baked potatoes or use as a meat rub. **Yield:** 1-1/3 cups.

Gingered Cranberry Chutney

I've been making this versatile chutney for more than two decades.
It pairs well with poultry and pork. We also enjoy it on toasted
English muffins or spread over a block of cream cheese for a quick appetizer.
—*Janie Layman, Bethel Park, Pennsylvania*

5-1/4 cups water, *divided*
1/2 medium lime
5 whole cloves
1 cup packed dark brown sugar
3/4 cup apricot preserves
1/2 cup cider vinegar
1 tablespoon minced fresh gingerroot
3/4 teaspoon curry powder
1/4 teaspoon ground cinnamon
1 medium pear, peeled and diced
1 medium tart apple, peeled and diced
3 cups fresh *or* frozen cranberries, thawed
1/2 cup golden raisins
1/2 cup chopped walnuts

In a large saucepan, bring 4 cups water to a boil. Add lime; cover and boil for 2 minutes. Drain and immediately place lime in ice water. Discard lime seeds; finely chop lime with peel and set aside. Place cloves on a double thickness of cheesecloth; bring up corners of cloth and tie with string to form a bag.

In a saucepan, combine the brown sugar, preserves, vinegar, ginger, curry, cinnamon and remaining water. Add spice bag. Bring to a boil over medium heat, stirring constantly. Add the pear, apple and reserved lime; return to a boil. Reduce heat; simmer, uncovered, for 10 minutes.

Add cranberries and raisins. Simmer, uncovered, for 20-25 minutes until the berries pop and mixture is thickened. Discard spice bag. Stir in walnuts. Cool. Cover and refrigerate until serving. **Yield:** 5 cups.

Million-Dollar Chocolate Fudge

(Pictured at right)

As the name suggests, this candy tastes like a million bucks! The recipe came from a local cooking show, which aired in the 1950s.
—Helen Webb, Mason, Michigan

1-1/2 teaspoons plus 1/4 cup butter, *divided*
2-1/4 cups sugar
  3/4 cup plus 2 tablespoons evaporated milk
  1/2 teaspoon salt
    1 cup marshmallow creme
    2 packages (4 ounces *each*) German sweet chocolate, chopped
    3 milk chocolate candy bars with almonds (1.45 ounces *each*), chopped
    1 cup (6 ounces) semisweet chocolate chips
    2 cups chopped blanched almonds
1-1/2 teaspoons vanilla extract

Line a 13-in. x 9-in. x 2-in. pan with foil and grease the foil with 1-1/2 teaspoons butter; set aside. In a heavy saucepan, combine the sugar, milk, salt and remaining butter. Cook and stir over medium heat until sugar is dissolved. Bring to a rapid boil, stirring constantly for 5 minutes. Remove from the heat.

Stir in the marshmallow creme, chocolate, candy bars and chips until chocolate is melted and mixture is blended. Fold in almonds and vanilla. Immediately spread into prepared pan. Cool. Using foil, lift fudge out of pan. Discard foil; cut fudge into squares. Store in a cool dry place. **Yield:** about 3 pounds.

Peanut Butter Chocolate Meltaways

People are amazed how easy it is to make these impressive-looking chocolate peanut butter cup candies. The recipe makes a big batch for you to share.
—*Darcie Vezzi, McDonald, Pennsylvania*

1 package (10 to 12 ounces) vanilla *or* white chips
1 cup (6 ounces) semisweet chocolate chips
1 cup creamy peanut butter
2 tablespoons butter-flavored shortening

In a microwave-safe bowl, combine all of the ingredients. Cover and microwave on high for 1-1/2 minutes; stir. Microwave, uncovered, on high 30 seconds longer; stir until smooth. Pour into miniature muffin liners. Place on a baking sheet; refrigerate until set. Store in the refrigerator. **Yield:** about 4 dozen.

Editor's Note: This recipe was tested in a 1,100-watt microwave. Reduced-fat or generic brands of peanut butter are not recommended for this recipe.

Cranberry Brownies in a Jar

I rarely attend a holiday open house without this brownie mix in tow. It makes a great hostess gift. To make a gift basket, include a 9-inch square baking pan, wooden spoon and oven mitts.
—*Margery Richmond, Fort Collins, Colorado*

1/3 cup baking cocoa
1 cup plus 2 tablespoons all-purpose flour
2/3 cup packed brown sugar
2/3 cup sugar
1/2 cup dried cranberries
1/2 cup vanilla *or* white chips
1/2 cup semisweet chocolate chips
ADDITIONAL INGREDIENTS:
3 eggs
1/2 cup vegetable oil
1 teaspoon vanilla extract

In a glass quart jar, layer the first seven ingredients in the order given. Cover and store in a cool dry place for up to 6 months. **Yield:** 1 batch (about 4 cups total).

To Prepare Brownies: In a large bowl, whisk the eggs, oil and vanilla. Add brownie mix and stir with a wooden spoon. Spread into a greased 9-in. square baking pan. Bake at 350° for 30-35 minutes or until a toothpick inserted near the center comes out clean. Cool on a wire rack. **Yield:** 1-1/2 dozen.

Strawberry Coffee Cake

(Pictured at right)

I came across this winning recipe when helping my mom organize her extensive recipe collection.
—Caroline Roggenbuck
Pullman, Washington

1 tablespoon cornstarch
1 package (10 ounces) frozen sweetened sliced strawberries, thawed
1/4 teaspoon ground cinnamon
1/4 teaspoon almond extract
2-1/3 cups all-purpose flour
3/4 cup sugar
3/4 cup cold butter
1/2 teaspoon baking powder
1/2 teaspoon baking soda
1/8 teaspoon salt
3/4 cup buttermilk
1 egg, lightly beaten

In a large saucepan, combine cornstarch and strawberries until blended. Bring to a boil over medium heat, stirring constantly. Cook and stir for 2 minutes or until thickened. Remove from the heat. Stir in cinnamon and almond extract; set aside.

In a large bowl, combine flour and sugar. Cut in butter until mixture is crumbly. Set aside 1/2 cup for topping. Add baking powder, baking soda and salt to the remaining flour mixture. Stir in buttermilk and egg until moistened.

Spread 1-1/2 cups of batter into a greased 8-in. square baking dish. Carefully spread with the strawberry mixture. Drop remaining batter by tablespoonfuls over strawberry mixture. Sprinkle with reserved crumb mixture. Bake at 350° for 35-40 minutes or until golden brown. Cool on a wire rack. **Yield:** 9 servings.

Santa's Snack Mix

At Christmas, I love to make gifts in a jar, from jellies and jams to cookie and snack mixes.
—Lori Daniels, Beverly, West Virginia

2 cups Honey Nut Cheerios
2 cups chow mein noodles
1 cup honey roasted peanuts
1/2 cup raisins
1/2 cup holiday milk chocolate M&M's

1/2 cup peanut butter chips
1/2 cup vanilla *or* white chips

In two wide-mouth quart jars, layer all of the ingredients. Cover jars. Decorate with fabric and ribbon. To serve, pour into a bowl and stir to combine. **Yield:** 7 cups.

CREATIVE GIFT CONTAINERS

AFTER you've taken the time to prepare an assortment of homemade foods for friends and family, why not take the extra step and package them in a unique way?

Some of the creative containers featured in this chapter's photos are merely clever conversation pieces. Others are actually part of the gift itself and will be enjoyed long after the goodies are gobbled up.

- **A Colander of Cookies.** Instead of relying on an ordinary wicker basket or Christmas tin to hold Orange-Cinnamon Chocolate Chip Cookies (page 102), we fashioned a container out of a colander! You may want to line the colander with a napkin to catch any crumbs. (See the photo on page 100 for this innovative idea.)

- **It's in the Can.** Surprise someone with a paint can brimming with homemade snack mix! (See photo on page 101.)

  Purchase a new can and lid (available in gallon or quart sizes) at a hardware store. Wash and dry. Line the inside of the can with plastic wrap. Add some crumbled tissue paper if desired. Fill the can with Popcorn Nut Treat (page 102). Set the lid on top and gently tap with a hammer to close.

  Wrap the outside of the can with festive wrapping or scrapbook paper. Or simply set a decorative wreath on top of an undecorated silver can.

  Another idea is to write or type a holiday greeting on a piece of paper and slip it into a small magnetic photo frame. Place the frame on the lid. And don't forget to include a clean paint-can opener so the recipient can easily unlatch the munchies inside!

- **The Great Frame Up.** Inexpensive picture frames (measuring 5 in. x 7 in.) serve as unique "trays" that can be put to good use long after Eggnog Mini Loaves (page 103)

have been enjoyed.

  Cut a decorative piece of paper to size and place it inside the frame under the glass. Clean the glass and set a cellophane-wrapped loaf of bread on top. Hold the frame and bread together with a wide ribbon. (Can't picture it? Turn to pages 100 and 103.)

- **Clever Candy Dish.** Looking for a way to butter up people this holiday season? Start by making a batch of Million-Dollar Chocolate Fudge. Then cut a large piece of fudge to fit the dimensions of a new, clean butter dish. (We found the inexpensive dish featured on page 105 in the housewares section of a large hardware store.) In keeping with the theme, include a butter knife for sweet slicing!

- **Dress Up a Disposable Pan.** If you want to give Strawberry Coffee Cake away as a gift, but fret about not getting your good baking pan back, bake it in a disposable aluminum foil pan, then dress it up! Look for a pan that comes with a clear plastic cover. When the coffee cake is cool, cover and wrap with sheer fabric. Attach a bow and a copy of the recipe. (Turn to page 107 for the photo.)

- **Special Snack Caddy.** On the opposite page, we transformed an ordinary condiment caddy into a unique snack basket. Look in department and variety stores for two glasses and a condiment caddy that can hold the glasses and two soda bottles.

  Fill one glass with Zesty Pretzel Nuggets and the other with Spicy Nuts. (To prevent spilling when transporting, cover the filled glasses with plastic wrap.) Place the glasses and soda bottles in the caddy. Attach an ornament, gift tag or bow...and you're ready to go!

Spicy Nuts

(Pictured at right)

*Cayenne pepper gives nuts a bit of a kick.
My son-in-law can't get enough of these.*
—Laurene Nickel
Niagara-on-the-Lake, Ontario

1 tablespoon vegetable oil
2 cups cashews *or* whole
   unblanched almonds
1/2 to 1 teaspoon cayenne pepper
1/2 teaspoon ground coriander
1/4 teaspoon salt
Dash *each* ground cinnamon
   and cloves

In a heavy skillet, heat oil over medium heat; add nuts. Cook and stir for 3-5 minutes or until lightly browned; drain. Add the seasonings; stir to coat. Cool completely. To serve warm, place in a baking pan. Heat at 300° for 5 minutes. **Yield:** 2 cups.

Zesty Pretzel Nuggets

(Pictured above)

*Ordinary pretzels just don't compare to these easily seasoned nuggets.
I've been making them for guests during the holidays for years and they never fail to please.*
—Joyce Daubert, Pine Grove, Pennsylvania

4 packages (10 ounces *each*)
   pretzel nuggets
1 cup vegetable oil
1 envelope ranch salad dressing
   mix
1 tablespoon steak seasoning*
2 to 3 teaspoons cayenne
   pepper
1 teaspoon dill weed

Place pretzels in a large bowl. In a small bowl, combine the oil, dressing mix, steak seasoning, cayenne and dill. Pour over pretzels; toss to coat evenly. Transfer to two ungreased 15-in. x 10-in. x 1-in. baking pans. Bake at 250° for 50-60 minutes, stirring every 15 minutes. Cool. Store in an airtight container. **Yield:** 4 quarts.

   *Editor's Note: This recipe was tested with McCormick's Grill Mates Montreal Steak Seasoning.

GIVING *Thanks*

For a twist on the traditional at Thanksgiving,
turn the page for a mouth-watering meal of
succulent goose and all the trimmings. You'll also
uncover a cornucopia of entrees, side dishes, breads
and desserts featuring some of the season's finest
flavors...pumpkin, sweet potatoes, apples,
cranberries, squash and more. Your family and friends
are certain to fall for these newfound favorites
and offer up thanks to the host!

GIVING *Thanks*

An Elegant Thanksgiving Dinner

GATHER with your family this Thanksgiving for a distinguished dinner that pleases the eye as well as the stomach!

For an attractive entree that guests will be wild about, roast a succulent Mandarin Goose. Then set this golden bird on a bed of beautiful Roasted Autumn Vegetables.

Crimson-colored cranberries—a favorite fall fruit—shine in both Cranberry Tossed Salad and Cran-Apple Pie. (All recipes shown at right.)

Complement this lovely autumn dinner with two other splendid sides—Gingered Long Grain and Wild Rice, and Cornmeal Pan Rolls.

A MEMORABLE MEAL
(Clockwise from top left)

Cranberry Tossed Salad (p. 115)

Mandarin Goose with Roasted Autumn Vegetables (p. 116)

Cran-Apple Pie (p. 117)

THANKSGIVING DINNER AGENDA

A Few Weeks Before:
- Order a 12- to 14-pound domestic goose from your butcher.
- Prepare two grocery lists—one for nonperishable items to purchase now and one for perishable items to purchase a few days before Thanksgiving.
- Bake Cornmeal Pan Rolls; cool. Freeze in heavy-duty resealable plastic bags.

A Few Days Before:
- Buy the goose and any remaining grocery items, including fruit for the Sugared Fruit Centerpiece (see page 118).
- Toast bread cubes for Gingered Long Grain and Wild Rice. Cool and store in an airtight container at room temperature.

The Day Before:
- Set the table.
- For Cranberry Tossed Salad, make the dressing; cover and chill. Wash and dry salad greens; refrigerate in a resealable plastic bag. Wash and chop broccoli and cauliflower; place in a resealable plastic bag and chill.
- Bake Cran-Apple Pie. Store loosely covered at room temperature.
- Later in the day, make the Sugared Fruit Centerpiece.

Thanksgiving Day:
- In the morning, peel sweet potatoes for Roasted Autumn Vegetables and cut into wedges. Cover with cold water and refrigerate.
- Thaw Cornmeal Pan Rolls at room temperature.
- Assemble Gingered Long Grain and Wild Rice; cover and chill. Remove from the refrigerator 30 minutes before baking as directed.
- Bake the Mandarin Goose.
- Assemble Roasted Autumn Vegetables; bake as directed.
- Remove salad dressing from the refrigerator 30 minutes before dinner; combine all salad ingredients. Just before serving, shake dressing and drizzle over the salad; toss.
- Let the cooked goose stand for 10 to 15 minutes before carving. Meanwhile, make the gravy.
- Set out the Cornmeal Pan Rolls.
- Serve Cran-Apple Pie for dessert.

Gingered Long Grain and Wild Rice

Although I just recently added this recipe to my collection, it's already a favorite.
—*Paula Magnus, Republic, Washington*

2 slices bread, cut into 1/2-inch cubes
2 packages (6 ounces *each*) long grain and wild rice mix
4 celery ribs, chopped
1 medium onion, chopped
1 tablespoon minced fresh gingerroot
6 tablespoons butter
1/4 cup chicken broth
1 can (8 ounces) water chestnuts, drained, chopped

Place bread cubes on a baking sheet. Bake at 250° for 35 minutes or until toasted. Meanwhile, prepare rice according to package directions. In a skillet, saute the celery, onion and ginger in butter until tender. Add to the rice.

Stir in broth, water chestnuts and bread cubes. Transfer to a greased shallow 3-qt. baking dish. Bake, uncovered, at 350° for 30-35 minutes or until heated through. **Yield:** 10-12 servings.

Cranberry Tossed Salad

(Pictured at right and on page 112)

Dinner guests rave about this salad's poppy seed dressing.
—*Marilyn Bue, Princeton, Minnesota*

10 cups torn mixed salad greens
1 cup chopped broccoli
1 cup chopped cauliflower
1 cup (4 ounces) crumbled blue cheese
1 cup dried cranberries
DRESSING:
1/3 cup sugar
1/3 cup vegetable oil
2 tablespoons chopped onion
2 tablespoons cider vinegar
1 tablespoon jellied cranberry sauce
1/2 teaspoon salt
1/2 teaspoon Dijon mustard
1/4 teaspoon poppy seeds

In a large salad bowl, combine the first five ingredients. In a blender, combine the sugar, oil, onion, vinegar, cranberry sauce, salt and mustard; cover and process until blended. Add poppy seeds; cover and pulse for 5-10 seconds. Drizzle over salad; toss to coat. Serve immediately. **Yield:** 12 servings.

Mandarin Goose

(Pictured on page 113)

*With mountains to the east, west and south of us and Canada to the north,
we have ample opportunity to hunt. This succulent goose is one of our favorite dishes.*
—*Paula Magnus, Republic, Washington*

1 domestic goose (12 to 14 pounds)
Salt
1 tablespoon all-purpose flour
1 tablespoon ground mustard
1/2 cup port wine *or* 1/4 cup grape juice plus 1/4 cup chicken broth
1/4 cup orange juice
1 medium onion, quartered
1/4 cup plum *or* red raspberry jam
2 tablespoons cornstarch
2 tablespoons cold water
1 can (11 ounces) mandarin oranges, drained

Sprinkle inside of goose with salt. Prick skin well; place breast side up on a rack in a large shallow roasting pan. In a small bowl, combine the flour and mustard; stir in wine and orange juice until smooth. Pour over goose. Add onion to pan. Bake, uncovered, at 350° for 3 to 3-1/2 hours or until a meat thermometer reads 180° (cover with foil during the last hour to prevent overbrowning).

Discard onion. Cover goose and let stand 10-15 minutes before carving. Pour pan drippings into a 2-cup measuring cup; skim off fat. Add enough water to measure 2 cups. In a saucepan, combine juices and jam. Combine cornstarch and water until smooth; add to juices. Bring to a boil; cook and stir for 2 minutes or until thickened. Stir in oranges. Serve with goose. **Yield:** 8-10 servings.

Roasted Autumn Vegetables

(Pictured on page 113)

*This colorful vegetable dish with mild garlic flavor was developed in our Test Kitchen.
It conveniently bakes at the same temperature as the Mandarin Goose.*

1 medium whole garlic bulb, peeled
1/2 cup butter, melted
1 tablespoon minced fresh thyme *or* 1 teaspoon dried thyme
1/2 teaspoon salt
1/4 teaspoon pepper
4 medium sweet potatoes, peeled and cut into wedges
1 pound fresh brussels sprouts, halved

2 medium onions, cut into 1/2-inch wedges

Separate garlic bulb into cloves. Mince two cloves; place in a small bowl. Add the butter, thyme, salt and pepper. In a large bowl, combine the sweet potatoes, brussels sprouts, onions and remaining garlic cloves. Drizzle with butter mixture; toss to coat.

Transfer to a greased 13-in. x 9-in. x 2-in. baking dish. Cover and bake at 350° for 30 minutes. Uncover; bake 40-45 minutes longer or until vegetables are tender. Stir before serving. **Yield:** 10 servings.

Cran-Apple Pie

(Pictured at right and on page 112)

Our home economists capture the flavor of fall in this pretty lattice fruit pie.

5 cups sliced peeled Golden
    Delicious apples
3/4 cup plus 2 tablespoons apple
    juice, *divided*
3/4 cup sugar
3/4 teaspoon ground cinnamon
1/4 teaspoon salt
1/4 teaspoon ground nutmeg
  2 tablespoons plus 2 teaspoons
    cornstarch
  2 cups cranberries
PASTRY:
2-3/4 cups all-purpose flour
  3/4 teaspoon salt
  3/4 cup plus 2 tablespoons
    shortening
  8 to 9 tablespoons cold water
  1 egg, lightly beaten
Additional sugar

In a saucepan, combine apples, 3/4 cup apple juice, sugar, cinnamon, salt and nutmeg; bring to a boil over medium heat, stirring occasionally. Combine cornstarch and remaining juice until smooth; add to saucepan. Return to a boil, stirring constantly. Cook and stir for 1 minute or until thickened. Remove from heat; cool to room temperature. Stir in cranberries.

In a bowl, combine the flour and salt; cut in shortening until crumbly. Gradually add cold water, tossing with a fork until dough forms a ball. Divide dough in half. Roll out one portion to fit a 9-in. pie plate. Transfer to pie plate. Trim pastry to 1 in. beyond edge of plate.

Pour fruit filling into crust. Divide the remaining dough in half. Roll out one portion; cut into six 1/2-in.-wide strips. Place three strips over filling in each direction, forming a lattice crust; trim edges of strips.

For decorative cutouts, roll out remaining dough and cut out with a 1-1/2-in. leaf-shaped cookie cutter. With a sharp knife, lightly score cutouts to resemble veins on leaves. Lightly brush lattice and edge of crust with egg. Overlap cutouts on the lattice and along edge of pie. Brush cutouts with egg; sprinkle lightly with sugar.

Cover edges loosely with foil coated with nonstick cooking spray. Bake at 400° for 20 minutes. Remove foil; bake 15-20 minutes longer or until crust is golden brown and filling is bubbly. Cool on a wire rack. **Yield:** 6-8 servings.

A LOVELY LEAF-TOPPED LATTICE PIE

1. Lightly brush lattice with beaten egg; overlap leaf cutouts on top.

2. Brush pie edge with beaten egg. Place leaf cutouts lengthwise along edge, overlapping slightly. Lightly press cutouts onto lattice and pie edge to secure.

Sugared Fruit Centerpiece

(Pictured at right and on page 113)

For an elegant table topper, create this centerpiece showcasing simple-to-make sugared fruit. It's not only eye-catching but edible as well!

15 to 20 pieces assorted fruit
3 envelopes unflavored gelatin
3/4 cup cold water
2 cups superfine sugar
Edible *or* silk leaves, optional

Scrub fruit in soapy water; rinse and dry completely. In a microwave-safe bowl, sprinkle gelatin over cold water; let stand for 1 minute. Microwave on high for 1-2 minutes, stirring every 20 seconds, until gelatin is completely dissolved. Whisk until slightly frothy.

Lightly brush mixture over all sides of fruit. Place on a wire rack over waxed paper. Sprinkle with sugar. Let stand at room temperature for up to 24 hours. Arrange as desired, adding leaves if desired.

Editor's Note: Fruit should not be refrigerated because the sugar will dissolve. This recipe was tested in a 1,100-watt microwave.

MAKING SUGARED FRUIT

1. Working with one piece of fruit at a time, lightly brush gelatin mixture over entire surface with a pastry brush. Place on a wire rack over waxed paper.

2. With a spoon, sprinkle superfine sugar over all sides of the fruit until the desired look is achieved. Repeat with remaining fruit. Let dry completely before handling.

SECRETS FOR SUCCESSFUL SUGARED FRUIT

A STUNNING Sugared Fruit Centerpiece is guaranteed if you review these helpful hints before beginning.

- You can sugar whole pieces of fruit as well as cut pieces. For cut pieces, it's best to use citrus—not fruits that turn brown when exposed to air, like apples and pears. Because cut fruit will be a bit juicy, the sugar may not adhere as well. Dab the cut side with paper towel and let air dry a few hours before brushing with the gelatin mixture and sprinkling with sugar.
- Sugared grape clusters become very stiff when dry. So if you would like them to have a little bend when arranging your centerpiece, drape the grapes over an inverted bowl until dry.
- If desired, you can sprinkle the fruits with additional sugar before completely dry to achieve a more dramatic effect.
- Sugar-coated fruit can be kept at room temperature for up to 24 hours; do not refrigerate.
- When arranging the centerpiece, handle fruit as little as possible so that the heat from your hands doesn't dissolve the sugar.

Cornmeal Pan Rolls

After I moved away from home, I realized I had better learn to cook if I wanted to enjoy wonderful meals like Mom used to make! Now my mom has me make these rolls every holiday. They're terrific topped with butter or jam.
—Sawyer Tremble, Bird Creek, Arkansas

1-2/3 cups milk
2/3 cup cornmeal
2/3 cup sugar
1/2 cup butter, cubed
1 teaspoon salt
2 tablespoons active dry yeast
1/4 cup warm water (110° to 115°)
2 eggs
1 cup whole wheat flour
3 cups all-purpose flour

In a saucepan, bring milk to a simmer. Gradually whisk in cornmeal; simmer for 3-4 minutes or until thickened. Stir in the sugar, butter and salt. Remove from the heat; cool to 110°-115°.

In a mixing bowl, dissolve yeast in warm water. Add cornmeal mixture, eggs and whole wheat flour; beat until smooth. Stir in enough all-purpose flour to form a soft dough (dough will be sticky). Do not knead. Place in a greased bowl, turning once to grease top. Cover and let rise in a warm place until doubled, about 1-1/4 hours.

Punch dough down. Turn onto a lightly floured surface; divide into 15 pieces. Shape each piece into a roll. Place in a greased 13-in. x 9-in. x 2-in. baking pan. Cover and let rise until doubled, about 30 minutes. Bake at 375° for 20-25 minutes or until golden brown. **Yield:** 15 rolls.

A Bountiful Autumn Harvest

FALL is a fantastic time to head back to the kitchen for a host of full-flavored foods.

Not only does autumn's cool weather trigger hearty appetites, but gardens and farmers markets are bursting with a bounty of palate-pleasing produce.

Celebrate this special season and dig into any (or all!) of the entrees, breads, side dishes and desserts on the following pages.

To show your family they're the apple of your eye, serve an inviting entree like Baked Pork Chops with Apple Slices.

Dinner guests will cheer for root vegetables when presented in Glazed Vegetable Medley.

Pumpkin-shaped Sweet Potato Biscuits are a festive addition to any fall meal. (All recipes shown at right.)

FALL'S FINEST
(Clockwise from top left)

Sweet Potato Biscuits (p. 123)

Baked Pork Chops with Apple Slices (p. 124)

Glazed Vegetable Medley (p. 122)

Glazed Vegetable Medley

(Pictured on page 120)

Our home economists came up with this recipe to showcase late summer and early fall produce. The slightly sweet glaze coats every delicious piece.

2 medium parsnips, peeled and
   cut into 1/2-inch pieces
3 medium carrots, cut into
   1/4-inch pieces
1 small onion, halved and sliced
1 garlic clove, minced
1 tablespoon olive oil
1 medium zucchini, halved and
   cut into 1/4-inch slices
1 medium sweet red pepper,
   thinly sliced and halved
1 tablespoon butter
1 tablespoon brown sugar
1/2 teaspoon cornstarch
3 tablespoons water
1/2 teaspoon seasoned salt
1/4 teaspoon lemon-pepper
   seasoning
1/4 teaspoon dill weed

Place parsnips in a large saucepan; cover with water. Bring to a boil. Reduce heat; simmer, uncovered, for 5 minutes. Add the carrots. Cook 7-9 minutes longer or until vegetables are crisp-tender; drain and keep warm.

In a large skillet, saute onion and garlic in oil for 1 minute. Add the zucchini and red pepper; cook and stir for 5 minutes or until crisp-tender. Remove from the skillet and keep warm. In the same skillet, melt butter; stir in the brown sugar and cornstarch until smooth. Gradually stir in the water, seasoned salt, lemon-pepper and dill. Bring to a boil; cook and stir for 1-2 minutes or until slightly thickened. Add the vegetables; stir to coat. **Yield:** 6 servings.

PARSNIPS POINTERS

PARSNIPS are a root vegetable that is similar to carrots. Look for small to medium parsnips that are firm and have smooth skin. Don't buy parsnips that are shriveled, limp, cracked or spotted.

Store parsnips in a plastic bag for up to 2 weeks. Peel and trim ends just before using.

One pound is equivalent to about 4 medium parsnips or 2 cups peeled and chopped.

Sweet Potato Biscuits

(Pictured at right and on page 120)

A pumpkin cookie cutter can be used for sweet treats and for savory biscuits as well. These biscuits are a fun addition to any meal in fall.
—Flo Burnett, Gage, Oklahoma

1-1/2 cups all-purpose flour
   2 teaspoons baking powder
1/2 teaspoon salt
1/4 teaspoon ground cinnamon
1/8 teaspoon ground nutmeg
1/3 cup cold butter
   1 cup cold mashed sweet potato
     (prepared without milk *or*
     butter)
1/3 cup milk
   1 egg, lightly beaten
1/2 teaspoon sugar

In a bowl, combine the first five ingredients. Cut in butter until crumbly. Combine sweet potato and milk; stir into crumb mixture just until moistened. Turn onto a floured surface; knead 10-15 times. Roll out to 1/2-in. thickness; cut with a floured 2-1/2-in. pumpkin-shaped cookie cutter or biscuit cutter.

Place 2 in. apart on a greased baking sheet. Brush with egg; sprinkle with sugar. Bake at 425° for 10-12 minutes or until golden brown. Serve warm. **Yield:** 1 dozen.

Family Traditions

I don't let autumn come and go without a trip to a local apple orchard with my two nieces and sister-in-law. We take a hay ride into the orchard, pick until our baskets are overflowing, then stop to select pumpkins from the field before heading home. We look forward to this outing every year!
—Susie Stoner, Milwaukee, Wisconsin

Baked Pork Chops With Apple Slices

(Pictured on page 121)

*A friend who raises pork shared this recipe with me. The lightly breaded chops with simple
glazed apples on the side make a mouth-watering meal.*
—*Mrs. Burlin Jones, Beloit, Wisconsin*

3 tablespoons all-purpose flour
1-1/2 teaspoons salt
1/2 teaspoon pepper
6 bone-in pork loin chops (1-1/2
    inches thick)
1/4 cup water
1 jar (12 ounces) currant jelly
3 to 4 unpeeled green tart
    apples, thinly sliced

In a shallow bowl, combine the flour, salt and pepper. Coat
pork chops. Place in a greased 15-in. x 10-in. x 1-in. baking pan. Add water to pan. Bake, uncovered, at 350° for 1
hour or until a meat thermometer reads 160°.

In a large skillet, melt the jelly. Add apples. Cook over low
heat for 5-7 minutes or until apples are tender, turning occasionally. Serve with pork chops. **Yield:** 6 servings.

Veggie Chicken Stir-Fry

*To highlight autumn vegetables, our Test Kitchen home economists came up with
this seasonal stir-fry. Apple juice is a nice addition to the teriyaki sauce.*

1-1/2 pounds boneless skinless
    chicken breasts, cut into
    strips
1 garlic clove, minced
1 tablespoon minced fresh
    gingerroot
3 tablespoons vegetable oil
2 medium carrots, julienned
2 medium parsnips, peeled,
    halved and thinly sliced
1 can (14-1/2 ounces) chicken
    broth
3/4 cup apple juice *or* cider
3 tablespoons teriyaki sauce
2 cups fresh broccoli florets
3/4 cup frozen pearl onions

1/4 cup cornstarch
1/2 cup cold water
Hot cooked rice

In a large skillet or wok, stir-fry the chicken, garlic and
ginger in oil until chicken is no longer pink. Remove chick-
en and keep warm. Drain excess oil from skillet; add the carrots, parsnips, broth, apple juice and teriyaki sauce. Bring
to a boil. Reduce heat to medium; cover and cook for 5
minutes. Add broccoli and onions. Cover and cook for 3-4
minutes or until vegetables are almost crisp-tender.

Return chicken to skillet. Combine the cornstarch and
water until smooth; stir into chicken mixture. Bring to a boil;
cook and stir for 2 minutes or until thickened. Serve over
rice. **Yield:** 6 servings.

Creamy Carrot Soup

(Pictured at right)

I first sampled this colorful carrot soup at a local Victorian tea room and wouldn't leave until I had the recipe in hand. The chef was kind enough to share it with me so I could enjoy it anytime at home.
—Carole Martin, Coffeeville, Mississippi

3/4 cup chopped onion
  3 tablespoons butter, *divided*
  3 cups chopped carrots
  3 cups chicken broth
  2 tablespoons uncooked long
    grain rice
1/2 cup heavy whipping cream
  1 to 2 tablespoons tomato paste
1/2 teaspoon salt
1/4 teaspoon white pepper

In a large saucepan, saute the onion in 2 tablespoons butter. Add the carrots, broth and rice. Bring to a boil. Reduce heat; cover and simmer for 25 minutes or until carrots and rice are tender. Cool slightly. Transfer to a blender or food processor; cover and process until smooth. Return to pan. Add the cream, tomato paste, salt, pepper and remaining butter; heat through. **Yield:** 4-5 servings.

CLEVER CARROT SOUP GARNISH

ENHANCE individual servings of Creamy Carrot Soup (above) with a cute carrot garnish. Here's how:
   Spoon some sour cream into a resealable plastic bag; cut a small hole in one corner. Gently squeeze the bag and pipe a carrot shape over each bowl of soup. For the carrot tops, add sprigs of carrot greens or parsley.

Rustic Mashed Turnips

My husband is a big fan of turnips, so I created this recipe just for him.
It has more texture than typical mashed potatoes.
—Jennifer Musgrove, Wheatland, Iowa

1 medium turnip, peeled and chopped
3 medium carrots, peeled and chopped
1 medium potato, peeled and diced
1/4 cup butter, cubed
1/4 cup sour cream
1 tablespoon sugar
1/2 teaspoon salt
Dash pepper

Place the turnip, carrots and potato in a large saucepan; cover with water. Bring to a boil. Reduce heat; cover and cook for 15-20 minutes or until vegetables are tender. Drain and place in a bowl. Add the butter, sour cream, sugar, salt and pepper; mash. **Yield:** 4 servings.

Cheese Soup in Squash Bowls

This unique recipe combines two dishes in one—cheese soup and baked squash.
It's so hearty you could almost serve it as a meatless meal!
—Paula Marchesi, Lenhartsville, Pennsylvania

4 small acorn squash (about 12 ounces *each*), halved and seeded
1 tablespoon butter, melted
2 medium tart apples, peeled and chopped
2/3 cup chopped carrot
1/2 cup chopped onion
2 tablespoons vegetable oil
3 cups chicken broth
1 tablespoon brown sugar
2 teaspoons Dijon mustard
1/4 teaspoon ground allspice
1/8 teaspoon ground ginger
1/8 teaspoon white pepper
1 cup cubed process cheese (Velveeta)

1/4 cup heavy whipping cream
Sour cream and minced chives

Place squash cut side up in two 13-in. x 9-in. x 2-in. baking dishes. Brush insides of squash with butter. Add 1/2 in. of hot water to each dish. Cover and bake at 400° for 35-40 minutes or until squash is tender.

Meanwhile, in a large saucepan, cook the apples, carrot and onion in oil until tender. Add broth; bring to a boil. Reduce heat; cover and simmer for 20 minutes. Stir in the brown sugar, mustard, allspice, ginger and pepper. Cool slightly. Process in small batches in a blender until smooth. Return to the pan. Add cheese and cream; cook and stir until smooth and blended. Place squash halves on serving plates; fill with soup. Garnish with sour cream and chives. **Yield:** 8 servings.

Sweet Potato Stuffed Apples

(Pictured at right)

I inherited this recipe for baked dessert apples from my grandmother and make it every chance I get, especially in fall.
— Howie Wiener, Spring Hill, Florida

5 medium tart apples
1 can (15 ounces) cut sweet
   potatoes, drained and mashed
3 tablespoons brown sugar
3 tablespoons maple syrup
1 tablespoon butter, melted
1/2 teaspoon ground cinnamon
1/4 teaspoon salt
2 tablespoons slivered almonds,
   divided

Core apples and scoop out pulp, forming a 2-in. cavity; discard seeds. Chop pulp; place in a bowl. Add the sweet potatoes, brown sugar, syrup, butter, cinnamon, salt and 1 tablespoon almonds. Spoon into apples; sprinkle with remaining almonds. Place in an ungreased 11-in. x 7-in. x 2-in. baking dish. Bake, uncovered, at 350° for 30-35 minutes or until apples are tender. **Yield:** 5 servings.

New England Sweet Potatoes

The sweet potato lovers in my family think this side dish is tops!
— Michelle Armistead, Keyport, New Jersey

4 large sweet potatoes (about
   3-1/2 pounds)
1/4 cup maple syrup
2 teaspoons minced fresh
   gingerroot
1/2 teaspoon salt
1/4 teaspoon cayenne pepper
1/4 cup dried cranberries
1/3 cup chopped pecans, toasted

Place sweet potatoes on a foil-lined baking sheet. Bake at 375° for 1 hour or until tender. Cool. Cut potatoes in half. Scoop out the pulp into a mixing bowl; discard potato skins. Mash potatoes. Add the syrup, ginger, salt and cayenne; mix well. Fold in cranberries. Set aside 1-2 tablespoons pecans for topping. Stir remaining pecans into potato mixture.

Transfer to a greased 1-1/2-qt. baking dish. Sprinkle with reserved pecans. Bake, uncovered, at 375° for 15-20 minutes or until heated through. **Yield:** 8 servings.

Maple Zucchini Cake

The preparation of this special pan cake is so simple.
I've been making this recipe for my family for years.
—Margaret Jeram, Greenwich, New York

3 eggs
2 cups all-purpose flour
2 cups shredded zucchini
1 cup sugar
1 cup vegetable oil
1 cup maple syrup
3 teaspoons ground cinnamon
2 teaspoons vanilla extract
2 teaspoons baking soda
1 teaspoon baking powder
1 teaspoon salt

1-1/2 cups chopped walnuts
1 cup raisins
Cream cheese frosting

In a large mixing bowl, combine the first 11 ingredients; beat on medium speed for 1-2 minutes or until well blended. Fold in walnuts and raisins. Transfer to a greased 13-in. x 9-in. x 2-in. baking pan. Bake at 350° for 45-50 minutes or until a toothpick inserted near the center comes out clean. Cool completely on a wire rack. Frost with cream cheese frosting. **Yield:** 16-20 servings.

Grandma's Squash Pie

Like my Grandma Bessie did, I grow my own squash, cook it, then freeze it in
two-cup portions to use in this recipe. It rivals any pumpkin pie!
—Cathi Holt, Lebanon, Kansas

2 cups mashed cooked winter squash
1/3 cup packed brown sugar
1 teaspoon ground cinnamon
1 teaspoon pumpkin pie spice
1/2 teaspoon ground nutmeg
2 eggs, *separated*
1 can (14 ounces) sweetened condensed milk
1 unbaked pastry shell (9 inches)

In a bowl, combine the first five ingredients. Whisk in egg yolks and milk. In a small mixing bowl, beat egg whites until stiff peaks form; gently fold into squash mixture. Pour into pastry shell. Bake at 425° for 15 minutes. Reduce heat to 350°; bake 30-35 minutes longer or until a knife inserted near the center comes out clean. Cool on a wire rack for 1 hour. Store in the refrigerator. **Yield:** 6-8 servings.

Cranberry Nut Dessert

(Pictured at right)

My family manages a cranberry marsh so we've seen our share of recipes featuring that tart and tasty berry. We're especially fond of this easy-to-make, no-crust pie.
—Leigh Nordback
Stone Lake, Wisconsin

1-1/4 cups fresh *or* frozen
     cranberries
1/4 cup packed brown sugar
1/4 cup chopped walnuts
  1 egg
1/2 cup sugar
1/2 cup all-purpose flour
1/3 cup butter, melted

Place cranberries in a greased 9-in. pie plate; sprinkle with brown sugar and nuts. In a small mixing bowl, beat egg; gradually add sugar. Beat in the flour and butter; mix well. Pour over berries. Bake at 325° for 40-45 minutes or until golden brown. Serve warm. **Yield:** 6-8 servings.

Apple 'n' Beef Bean Bake

Slightly sweet apples blend beautifully with savory ground beef and baked beans. You can easily double the recipe for a potluck.
—Nancy Beckman, Helena, Montana

  1 pound ground beef
  2 medium onions, chopped
  2 cans (16 ounces *each*) baked
     beans, undrained
  3 medium tart apples, diced
2/3 cup ketchup
1/4 cup packed brown sugar
  1 tablespoon prepared mustard
  1 teaspoon rubbed sage
1/4 teaspoon pepper

In a large skillet, cook beef and onions over medium heat until meat is no longer pink; drain. Stir in the remaining ingredients. Transfer to a greased 3-qt. baking dish. Bake, uncovered, at 350° for 40-45 minutes or until apples are tender. **Yield:** 6-8 servings.

Cranberry Dressing

*I've fine-tuned this recipe over the years. Now it's the only dressing
my family lets me make at Thanksgiving.*
—*Rin Hansen, Adams, Tennessee*

1 package (12 ounces) fresh *or*
  frozen cranberries, thawed
1 cup chopped peeled tart apple
1-1/4 cups sugar
1-1/4 cups water
2 celery ribs, finely chopped
1 large onion, finely chopped
1 garlic clove, minced
1/2 teaspoon rubbed sage
1/8 teaspoon pepper
1/4 cup butter
1 package (8 ounces) seasoned stuffing croutons

In a large saucepan, combine the cranberries, apple, sugar and water. Bring to a boil. Reduce heat; simmer, uncovered, for 10 minutes or until tender. Remove from the heat; set aside.

In a large skillet, saute the celery, onion, garlic, sage and pepper in butter until tender. Remove from the heat; stir in cranberry mixture and croutons. Transfer to a greased 2-qt. baking dish. Bake, uncovered, at 350° for 25-30 minutes or until heated through. **Yield:** 8 servings.

Golden Corn Muffins

*When I was little, my grandmother made corn bread in a cast-iron skillet in a
wood-burning oven. This recipe is the closest I've come to being as good as hers.*
—*Mary Rea, Orangeville, Ontario*

1 cup all-purpose flour
1 cup yellow cornmeal
1/4 cup packed brown sugar
2 teaspoons baking powder
1 teaspoon salt
1/2 teaspoon baking soda
1 egg, beaten
3/4 cup cubed butternut squash,
  cooked and mashed
3/4 cup buttermilk
2 tablespoons vegetable oil
1/2 cup frozen corn, thawed

In a large bowl, combine the flour, cornmeal, brown sugar, baking powder, salt and baking soda. Combine the egg, squash, buttermilk and oil; stir into the dry ingredients just until blended. Fold in corn. Fill greased or paper-lined muffin cups two-thirds full. Bake at 400° for 12-15 minutes or until a toothpick comes out clean. Cool for 5 minutes before removing from pan to a wire rack. **Yield:** 1 dozen.

BUYING AND STORING WINTER SQUASH

THE MOST COMMON varieties of winter squash are butternut, acorn, hubbard, spaghetti and turban.

Look for squash which feel heavy for their size and have hard, deep-colored rinds that are free of blemishes. Unwashed winter squash can be stored in a dry, cool, well-ventilated place for up to 1 month.

Chunky Apple Pumpkin Bread

(Pictured at right)

This moist quick bread combines both apples and pumpkin, making it a must in autumn. Every slice is chock-full of nuts and spices.
—*Lyletta Searle, Morgan, Utah*

1-1/2 cups sugar
   1 cup canned pumpkin
  1/2 cup water
  1/3 cup vegetable oil
   2 eggs
1-2/3 cups all-purpose flour
   1 teaspoon baking soda
  3/4 teaspoon salt
  1/2 teaspoon ground cinnamon
  1/2 teaspoon ground nutmeg
  1/4 teaspoon baking powder
  1/4 teaspoon ground cloves
   1 cup chopped peeled tart apples
  3/4 chopped walnuts

In a large mixing bowl, combine the sugar, pumpkin, water, oil and eggs; mix well. Combine the flour, baking soda, salt, cinnamon, nutmeg, baking powder and cloves; add to the pumpkin mixture. Beat on low speed just until moistened. Fold in apples and walnuts.

Pour into a greased 9-in. x 5-in. x 3-in. loaf pan. Bake at 325° for 1-1/2 to 1-3/4 hours or until a toothpick inserted near the center comes out clean. Cool for 10 minutes before removing from pan to a wire rack. **Yield:** 1 loaf.

Sweet Treats Fit for Fall

WHEN the sun starts sinking in the sky and the breeze becomes a bit more brisk, give your family a warm welcome home by dishing out a homemade dessert at dinner.

Packed with seasonal produce like pumpkin, cranberries and nuts, the delectable desserts featured in this chapter are fitting finales for all of your fall menus, including Thanksgiving dinner.

In addition to serving ever-popular pumpkin pie, consider making crowd-pleasing Marbled Pumpkin Cheesecake.

Fruity treats like Individual Cranberry Trifles and Berry Nut Tarts will also become favorites with your family. (All recipes shown at right.)

SEASONAL TREATS
(Clockwise from top left)

Marbled Pumpkin
Cheesecake (p. 134)

Individual Cranberry
Trifles (p. 135)

Berry Nut Tarts (p. 136)

Marbled Pumpkin Cheesecake

(Pictured on page 132)

A gingersnap crust pairs well with the pumpkin and cream cheese filling.
—Judy Shatzer, Upper Strasburg, Pennsylvania

1 cup finely crushed
   gingersnaps (about 20 cookies)
3 tablespoons butter, melted
FILLING:
4 packages (8 ounces *each*)
   cream cheese, softened
1 cup sugar
3 tablespoons cornstarch,
   divided
1 cup (8 ounces) sour cream
1-1/2 teaspoons vanilla extract
1/4 teaspoon salt
3 eggs
1 teaspoon lemon juice
3/4 cup canned pumpkin
3 tablespoons dark brown sugar
1 tablespoon molasses
2 teaspoons ground cinnamon
3/4 teaspoon ground ginger
1/2 teaspoon ground nutmeg
1/8 teaspoon ground cloves

In a small bowl, combine cookie crumbs and butter. Press onto the bottom of a greased 9-in. springform pan. Place pan on a baking sheet. Bake at 325° for 10-15 minutes or until set. Cool on a wire rack.

In a large mixing bowl, beat the cream cheese, sugar and 2 tablespoons cornstarch until smooth. Beat in the sour cream, vanilla and salt. Add eggs; beat on low speed just until combined. Remove 3-1/2 cups filling to a bowl; stir in lemon juice and set aside. Add the pumpkin, brown sugar, molasses, spices and remaining cornstarch to the remaining filling; set aside 1/2 cup. Pour half of the remaining pumpkin filling over crust; top with half of the plain filling. Repeat layers. Dot with spoonfuls of the reserved pumpkin filling. Cut through filling with a knife to swirl.

Place pan on a double thickness of heavy-duty foil (about 16 in. square); securely wrap foil around pan. Place pan in a large baking pan. Add 1 in. of hot water to larger pan. Bake at 325° for 70-75 minutes or until center is almost set. Remove springform pan from water bath. Cool on a wire rack for 10 minutes. Carefully run a knife around edge of pan to loosen; cool 1 hour longer. Remove foil. Refrigerate overnight. Remove sides of pan. Refrigerate leftovers. **Yield:** 12-14 servings.

MAKING CHEESECAKES IN ADVANCE

COOL AND CREAMY cheesecakes are a rich, filling dessert that feed a crowd. So, usually no other dessert is needed. Best of all, cheesecakes can be made in advance, meaning there's one less thing to do on the day you're entertaining.

Cheesecakes can be covered and refrigerated for up to 3 days. For even more convenience, bake a cheesecake weeks in advance and freeze it! Here's how:

Place a whole cheesecake or individual slices on a baking sheet; freeze until firm. Wrap in plastic wrap and place in a heavy-duty resealable plastic bag. Freeze for up to 2 months. Defrost whole cheesecakes in the refrigerator overnight. Individual pieces can be defrosted in the refrigerator or at room temperature for 30 minutes before serving.

Individual Cranberry Trifles

(Pictured at right and on page 133)

If you don't have enough individual parfaits, you can make this dessert from our Test Kitchen in a trifle bowl. Either way, it's sure to bring you rave reviews.

1 package (16 ounces) angel
    food cake mix
2 packages (8 ounces *each*)
    cream cheese, softened
2 cups confectioners' sugar
1 cup (8 ounces) sour cream
1 teaspoon vanilla extract
1 carton (12 ounces) frozen
    whipped topping, thawed
2 cans (16 ounces *each*)
    whole-berry cranberry sauce
2 tablespoons sugar
2 to 3 teaspoons grated orange
    peel
Fresh cranberries and mint,
    optional

Prepare, bake and cool angel food cake according to package directions. Cut into 1-in. cubes; set aside. In a large mixing bowl, combine cream cheese, confectioners' sugar, sour cream and vanilla; beat until smooth. Fold in whipped topping. In a bowl, combine the cranberry sauce, sugar and orange peel.

In individual parfait glasses or a 3-qt. trifle bowl, layer half of the cake cubes, cranberry mixture and whipped topping mixture. Repeat layers. Refrigerate until serving. Garnish with cranberries and mint if desired. **Yield:** 14-16 servings.

Berry Nut Tarts

(Pictured on page 132)

Cranberries are a delicious addition to this spin on individual pecan pies.
Folks have a hard time eating only one.
—*Lena Ehlert, Vancouver, British Columbia*

1/2 cup butter, softened
1 package (3 ounces) cream
  cheese, softened
1 cup all-purpose flour
FILLING:
1-1/2 cups packed brown sugar
2 tablespoons butter, melted
2 eggs, lightly beaten
2 teaspoons vanilla extract
2/3 cup finely chopped
  cranberries
1/3 cup chopped pecans

In a small mixing bowl, beat the butter and cream cheese; add flour and mix well. Cover and refrigerate for 1 hour or until easy to handle.

Cut dough into 12 portions. Press onto the bottom and all the way up the sides of greased muffin cups. In a bowl, combine the brown sugar, butter, eggs and vanilla. Stir in the cranberries and pecans. Spoon into prepared crusts.

Bake at 350° for 25-30 minutes or until edges are golden brown. Cool for 5 minutes before removing from pan to a wire rack to cool completely. Store in the refrigerator. **Yield:** about 1 dozen.

Bread Pudding with Lemon Sauce

This bread pudding is a little lighter than most and is enhanced by a lovely lemon sauce.
I've also served the sauce over slices of angel food cake.
—*Margaret Anderson, Salmon, Idaho*

2 cups milk
4 eggs
1/2 cup sugar
5 slices white bread, cut into
  1-inch cubes
1/3 cup semisweet chocolate chips
1/8 teaspoon ground cinnamon
LEMON SAUCE:
1 cup sugar
1/2 cup butter, melted
1/4 cup water
2 tablespoons lemon juice
1 egg yolk
1 teaspoon grated lemon peel

In a large bowl, combine the milk, eggs and sugar. Stir in bread cubes; let stand for 5 minutes, stirring occasionally. Pour into a greased 1-1/2-qt. baking dish. Sprinkle with chocolate chips and cinnamon. Bake at 350° for 55-60 minutes or until a knife inserted near the center comes out clean.

For sauce, combine the sugar, butter, water and lemon juice in a saucepan. Whisk in egg yolk. Bring to a boil over medium heat, stirring constantly. Cook and stir for 1 minute. Remove from the heat; stir in lemon peel. Serve over pudding. **Yield:** 8 servings.

Maple Pecan Cookies

(Pictured at right)

When I bake cookies for the annual youth ski trip, I try at least one new recipe. When I received recipe requests for these frosted goodies, I knew I had a winner.
—Nancy Johnson, Laverne, Oklahoma

   1 cup shortening
1/2 cup butter, softened
   2 cups packed brown sugar
   2 eggs
   1 teaspoon vanilla extract
   1 teaspoon maple flavoring
   3 cups all-purpose flour
   2 teaspoons baking soda
   1 package (10 to 12 ounces)
     vanilla *or* white chips
1/2 cup chopped pecans
FROSTING:
1/4 cup butter, softened
   4 cups confectioners' sugar
   1 teaspoon maple flavoring
   3 to 5 tablespoons milk
1-1/2 cups pecan halves

In a large mixing bowl, cream the shortening, butter and brown sugar. Add eggs, one at a time, beating well after each addition. Beat in vanilla and maple flavoring. Combine flour and baking soda; gradually add to the creamed mixture. Stir in vanilla chips and pecans.

Drop by tablespoonfuls 2 in. apart onto ungreased baking sheets. Bake at 350° for 9-11 minutes or until golden brown. Cool for 2 minutes before removing to wire racks.

In a mixing bowl, cream the butter, confectioners' sugar, maple flavoring and enough milk to achieve spreading consistency. Frost each cookie with 1 teaspoon frosting; top with a pecan half. **Yield:** 7 dozen.

Hickory Nut Cake

As a girl, I'd help my dad and grandpa gather hickory nuts for Grandma's classic cake.
We could hardly wait for dinner to be over so we could indulge in a generous slice.
—*Gloria Fee, McArthur, Ohio*

1/2 cup butter, softened
1-1/2 cups sugar
1 teaspoon vanilla extract
2 cups cake flour
2 teaspoons baking powder
1/2 teaspoon salt
3/4 cup milk
1 cup finely chopped hickory nuts *or* walnuts, toasted
4 egg whites
BUTTER FROSTING:
3/4 cup butter, softened
5 cups confectioners' sugar
1/2 teaspoon vanilla extract
1/8 teaspoon salt
4 to 5 tablespoons half-and-half cream

In a large mixing bowl, cream the butter, sugar and vanilla. Combine the flour, baking powder and salt; add to creamed mixture alternately with milk. Stir in nuts. In a small mixing bowl, beat egg whites on high speed until soft peaks form; fold into batter. Pour into two greased and floured 9-in. round baking pans. Bake at 350° for 25-30 minutes or until a toothpick inserted near the center comes out clean. Cool for 10 minutes before removing from pans to wire racks to cool completely.

For frosting, in a large mixing bowl, beat butter and sugar on low speed for 1 minute. Beat in the vanilla, salt and enough cream until a fluffy consistency is achieved. Spread between layers and over top and sides of cake. **Yield:** 12-16 servings.

Spiced Butterscotch Fudge

This butterscotch fudge is a nice change from the more typical chocolate varieties.
When I have a craving for a little sweet, this fits the bill.
—*Cathy Steinkuhler, Burr, Nebraska*

1 tablespoon plus 3/4 cup butter, *divided*
3 cups sugar
1 can (5 ounces) evaporated milk
1/2 cup canned pumpkin
1/2 teaspoon ground cinnamon
1/2 teaspoon ground nutmeg
1 package (11 ounces) butterscotch chips
1 jar (7 ounces) marshmallow creme
1 cup chopped pecans, optional
1 teaspoon vanilla extract

Line a 13-in. x 9-in. x 2-in. pan with foil and grease the foil with 1 tablespoon butter; set aside. In a large saucepan, combine the sugar, milk, pumpkin, cinnamon, nutmeg and remaining butter. Bring to a boil over medium heat, stirring constantly. Reduce heat; cook until a candy thermometer reaches 238° (soft-ball stage), stirring occasionally.

Remove from the heat. Stir in chips until melted. Stir in marshmallow creme, pecans if desired and vanilla. Spread into prepared pan. Cool to room temperature; cover and refrigerate. Using foil, lift fudge out of pan. Discard foil; cut fudge into 1-in. squares. **Yield:** about 3-1/4 pounds.

Editor's Note: We recommend that you test your candy thermometer before each use by bringing water to a boil; the thermometer should read 212°. Adjust your recipe temperature up or down based on your test.

Mincemeat Pumpkin Pie

(Pictured at right)

Instead of serving separate pumpkin and mincemeat pies one Thanksgiving, I served this one pie that combines those wonderful flavors. It was a hit!
—*Joann Frazier Hensley*
McGaheysville, Virginia

  2 cups prepared mincemeat
  1 unbaked pastry shell
    (9 inches)
  1 egg
  1 cup canned pumpkin
1/3 cup sugar
1/2 teaspoon ground cinnamon
1/4 teaspoon ground ginger
1/4 teaspoon ground nutmeg
1/8 teaspoon salt
1/8 teaspoon ground cloves
3/4 cup evaporated milk

Spread mincemeat over the bottom of pastry shell. In a large mixing bowl, beat the egg, pumpkin, sugar, cinnamon, ginger, nutmeg, salt and cloves just until smooth. Gradually stir in milk. Pour over mincemeat. Bake at 400° for 55-60 minutes or until a knife inserted near the center comes out clean. Cool on a wire rack. Store in the refrigerator. **Yield:** 6-8 servings.

Ginger Pear Pie

This recipe comes from my grandmother, who had lots of pear trees on her land.
A gingersnap crust complements the pleasant taste of pears.
—Mildred Sherrer, Bay City, Texas

1 unbaked pastry shell
  (9 inches)
1/2 cup gingersnap crumbs (about
  9 cookies)
1/4 cup sugar
1/4 cup packed brown sugar
1 tablespoon all-purpose flour
1/2 teaspoon salt
1/2 teaspoon ground cinnamon
1/4 cup cold butter
5 cups thinly sliced peeled
  pears (about 5 medium)

Line unpricked pastry shell with a double thickness of heavy-duty foil. Bake at 450° for 8 minutes. Remove foil; bake 5 minutes longer. Cool on a wire rack.

In a bowl, combine gingersnap crumbs, sugars, flour, salt and cinnamon. Cut in butter until crumbly. Place half of the pear slices in crust. Top with half of the crumb mixture. Repeat layers. Cover edges loosely with foil. Bake at 350° for 55-60 minutes or until golden. Cool on a wire rack. Store in the refrigerator. **Yield:** 6-8 servings.

Pear Pointers

PURCHASE pears that are firm, fragrant and free of blemishes or soft spots.

To ripen pears, place them in a paper bag at room temperature for several days. When the pears give in slightly to pressure, store in the refrigerator. Pears used for cooking should be a little more firm.

Before cooking pears, use a vegetable peeler or paring knife to remove the skin, which turns dark and tough when exposed to heat.

One pound of pears equals about 3 medium or 3 cups sliced.

To prevent pear slices from discoloring, toss with a little lemon juice.

Peanut Butter Maple Ice Cream Pie

Homemade pie can't get any easier than this! The recipe makes two pies,
so you can enjoy one now and keep the other in the freezer for drop-in guests.
—Linda Markauskas, Walkerton, Ontario

2 quarts vanilla ice cream,
  softened
1 cup maple syrup
3/4 cup peanut butter
2 graham cracker crusts (9
  inches)

1/2 cup finely chopped peanuts

In a large mixing bowl, combine the ice cream, syrup and peanut butter until smooth. Transfer half into each crust. Cover and freeze for 2-3 hours. Just before serving, sprinkle with peanuts. **Yield:** 2 pies (6-8 servings each).

Raisin Pumpkin Bars

(Pictured at right)

Chocolate-covered raisins are a fun surprise inside these moist pumpkin bars. The traditional cream cheese frosting never fails to please.
—*Margaret Wilson, Hemet, California*

2 cups sugar
3/4 cup vegetable oil
4 eggs
2 cups canned pumpkin
2 cups all-purpose flour
2 teaspoons baking powder
1 teaspoon baking soda
1 teaspoon ground cinnamon
1 teaspoon ground nutmeg
1/2 teaspoon ground ginger
1/4 teaspoon ground cloves
1 cup chopped walnuts
1 cup chocolate-covered raisins
   for baking
FROSTING:
1/3 cup butter, softened
1 package (3 ounces) cream
   cheese, softened
2 cups confectioners' sugar
1 tablespoon milk
1 teaspoon orange extract
Decorator sprinkles, optional

In a large mixing bowl, beat sugar and oil. Add eggs, one at a time, beating well after each addition. Add pumpkin; mix well. Combine the flour, baking powder, baking soda and spices; gradually add to the pumpkin mixture. Stir in walnuts and chocolate-covered raisins. Pour into a greased 15-in. x 10-in. x 1-in. baking pan. Bake at 350° for 25-30 minutes or until a toothpick inserted near the center comes out clean. Cool on a wire rack.

For frosting, in a mixing bowl, cream the butter, cream cheese and confectioners' sugar. Add milk and orange extract; beat until smooth. Frost bars. Decorate with sprinkles if desired. Cut into bars. Store in the refrigerator. **Yield:** 4 dozen.

EASTER
Gatherings

When spring has sprung and the Easter bunny has
made an appearance at your home, it's time to usher
in a fresh, new season! Whether you celebrate this
holiday with a late-morning brunch or a formal
sit-down dinner, you'll discover a sunny selection of
main courses, side dishes, desserts and more in this
chapter. Or why not start a new tradition in your family
by baking up a selection of specialty Easter breads?

Hop to It with Easter Brunch!

LITTLE girls donning beautiful bonnets...pretty baskets brimming with pastel-colored candies...decorated eggs dotting the lush green lawn.

When you catch a glimpse of time-honored traditions such as these, there's no doubt that Easter has arrived.

Get the celebration of spring under way by hosting a memorable late-morning brunch.

Topped with flavorful ruby-red tomatoes, Spinach Brunch Pie will elicit compliments for the cook. And folks will flip over Banana Hotcakes when served alongside Baked Canadian-Style Bacon. (All recipes shown at right.)

EARLY-DAY DINING
(Clockwise from top right)

Banana Hot Cakes (p.147)

Baked Canadian-Style Bacon (p.148)

Spinach Brunch Pie (p.148)

Ham Onion Tart

Even folks who don't care for onions can't resist this delicious quiche.
Pair it with fresh fruit for a flavorful breakfast.
—Anthony Lemoine, Alexandria, Louisiana

3 large onions
3 tablespoons butter, cubed
1/2 pound ground fully cooked ham
1/2 cup chopped fresh mushrooms
1 tablespoon all-purpose flour
3 egg yolks
1/2 cup heavy whipping cream
1/8 teaspoon salt
1/8 teaspoon pepper
1 pastry shell (9 inches), baked
1/2 cup shredded Swiss cheese

Cut one slice off one onion; set aside for topping. Chop remaining onions. In a large skillet, melt butter. Saute ham and chopped onions until onions are tender. Add mushrooms; saute for 2 minutes. Stir in flour until blended; cook 1 minute longer. Remove from the heat.

In a small bowl, beat the egg yolks, cream, salt and pepper. Stir into ham mixture. Pour into pastry shell. Sprinkle with cheese. Separate reserved onion slice into rings; place in center of tart. Bake at 375° for 25-30 minutes or until top begins to brown and a knife inserted near the center comes out clean. **Yield:** 6-8 servings.

Potatoes Olé

I came up with this potato and egg recipe one summer when relatives came to visit.
It was a well received by everyone! To save time, you can use frozen hash browns.
—Lori Pierce, Cottage Grove, Minnesota

3/4 cup chopped onion
3/4 cup *each* chopped green, sweet red and yellow pepper
2 tablespoons butter
2 pounds red potatoes, cooked, peeled and cubed (1/4-inch cubes)
1 can (4 ounces) chopped green chilies, drained
5 eggs, beaten
1 cup evaporated milk
1 cup (4 ounces) shredded

Monterey Jack cheese
3/4 teaspoon salt
1/4 teaspoon pepper
Salsa and sour cream, optional

In a large skillet, saute onion and peppers in butter until tender. Add potatoes and chilies; toss to combine. Transfer to a greased 2-qt. baking dish. In a large bowl, combine the eggs, milk, cheese, salt and pepper; pour over the potato mixture. Bake, uncovered, at 400° for 35-40 minutes or until set and top is golden brown. Serve with salsa and sour cream if desired. **Yield:** 8 servings.

Banana Hotcakes

(Pictured at right and on page 145)

*My daughter came across this recipe and
had me add it to my recipe collection.
Topped with a homemade honey butter,
these flapjacks are fabulous!*
—Harriet Stichter, Milford, Indiana

HONEY PECAN BUTTER:
 1/2 cup butter, softened
 1/4 cup honey
 1/3 cup chopped pecans, toasted
HOTCAKES:
 1 cup all-purpose flour
 2 tablespoons sugar
 2 teaspoons baking powder
 1/2 teaspoon salt
 1/8 teaspoon ground cinnamon
 1 egg
 1 cup milk
 1 cup mashed ripe bananas
   (about 2 medium)
 3 tablespoons vegetable oil
 2 teaspoons lemon juice
Maple syrup, optional

In a small mixing bowl, beat butter and
honey until smooth. Stir in pecans; set
aside. In a large bowl, combine the
flour, sugar, baking powder, salt and
cinnamon. In a small bowl, whisk the
egg, milk, bananas, oil and lemon juice;
stir into dry ingredients just until
moistened.

 Pour batter by 1/4 cupfuls onto a
greased hot griddle. Turn when bubbles form on top; cook until second
side is golden brown. Serve with honey pecan butter and syrup if desired.
Yield: 6 servings.

BANANA BASICS

LOOK for plump bananas that are evenly yellow-
colored. Green bananas are under-ripe, while a fleck-
ing of brown flecks indicates ripeness.

 If bananas are too green, place in a paper bag until
ripe. Adding an apple to the bag will speed the process.

 Store ripe bananas at room temperature. To prevent bruises, a banana hook or hanger is a great inexpensive investment. For longer storage, you can
place ripe bananas in a tightly sealed plastic bag
and refrigerate. The peel will become brown but the
flesh will remain unchanged.

 One pound of bananas equals about 3 medium or
1-1/3 cups mashed.

Spinach Brunch Pie

(Pictured at right and on page 144)

You won't believe how easy it is the assemble this egg dish. With tomatoes,
eggs and spinach, every bite is colorful and flavorful.
—*Gertie Kwant, Stanwood, Washington*

1 **package (10 ounces) frozen chopped spinach, drained and squeezed dry**
1 **teaspoon white vinegar**
1/2 **teaspoon ground nutmeg**
3 **eggs**
1 **cup (8 ounces) small-curd cottage cheese**
1 **cup (8 ounces) sour cream**
1/2 **cup biscuit/baking mix**
1/4 **cup butter, melted**
3 **small tomatoes, thinly sliced**
2 **tablespoons shredded Parmesan cheese**

In a small bowl, combine the spinach, vinegar and nutmeg. Spread into a greased 9-in. pie plate. In a blender, combine the eggs, cottage cheese, sour cream, biscuit mix and butter; cover and process until smooth. Pour over spinach mixture.

Bake, uncovered, at 350° for 25-30 minutes or until almost set. Arrange tomato slices over the top; sprinkle with Parmesan cheese. Bake 5-10 minutes longer or until set (pie has a soft-set). Let stand for 10 minutes before serving. **Yield:** 6 servings.

SECRET FOR SLICING TOMATOES

THE BEST WAY to cut through the skin of a tomato is with a serrated, not straight-edged, knife.

Cut a tomato vertically, from stem end to blossom end, for slices that will be less juicy and hold their shape better.

Baked Canadian-Style Bacon

(Pictured on page 144)

Brown sugar, pineapple juice and ground mustard nicely season slices of Canadian bacon.
You can easily double the recipe when entertaining a crowd.
—*Myra Innes, Auburn, Kansas*

1 **pound sliced Canadian bacon**
1/4 **cup packed brown sugar**
1/4 **cup pineapple juice**
1/4 **teaspoon ground mustard**

Place the bacon in a greased 11-in. x 7-in. x 2-in. baking dish. In a bowl, combine the brown sugar, pineapple juice and mustard. Pour over the bacon. Cover and bake at 325° for 25-30 minutes or until heated through. **Yield:** 6-8 servings.

Burgundy Salad Dressing

(Pictured at right)

A spiced wine salad dressing deliciously tops off your favorite fruits. Serve it as a side dish or light dessert.
—*Donna Warner, Tavares, Florida*

   2 cinnamon sticks (3 inches), broken
 16 whole cloves
   1 cup red Burgundy wine *or* grape juice
 2/3 cup sugar
   2 tablespoons red wine vinegar
Melon balls and halved grapes and strawberries

Place cinnamon sticks and cloves on a double thickness of cheesecloth; bring up corners of cloth and tie with kitchen string to form a bag. In a saucepan, combine the wine or grape juice, sugar and vinegar; add spice bag. Bring to a boil. Reduce heat; simmer, uncovered, for 10 minutes. Discard spice bag. Cool dressing slightly. Cover and refrigerate for 2 hours or until chilled. Serve over fruit. **Yield:** 1 cup.

Family Traditions

Grandma Gert introduced our family to Swieconka (sh-vee-en-soon-kah), the Polish tradition of blessing Easter food. On Holy Saturday, Grandma, Mom and I would head to church, our picnic baskets brimming with hard-cooked eggs, rye bread, Polish sausage, ham, lamb-shaped butter...a sampling of the food to be served on Easter Day. A wonderful aroma filled the church and whetted our appetites for the next morning! —*Barb Gumieny Wauwatosa, Wisconsin*

Wine 'n' Cheese Strata

When hosting a shower or brunch, I double this recipe's ingredients and use
two 13 x 9 dishes. You don't need many other foods to complete the meal.
— Tiffany Mitchell, Susanville, California

1 pound day-old Italian bread, cubed
3 tablespoons butter, melted
1-1/3 cups shredded Swiss cheese
1 cup shredded Monterey Jack cheese
2 ounces salami, coarsely chopped
8 eggs
1-1/2 cups milk
1/4 cup dry white wine *or* water
2 green onions, chopped
1-1/2 teaspoons spicy brown mustard
1/4 teaspoon pepper

Dash crushed red pepper flakes
3/4 cup sour cream
1/2 cup shredded Parmesan cheese

Place bread cubes in a greased 13-in. x 9-in. x 2-in. baking dish; drizzle with butter. Sprinkle with cheeses and salami. In a bowl, beat the eggs, milk, wine or water, onions, mustard, pepper and pepper flakes. Pour evenly over top. Cover and refrigerate overnight.

Remove from the refrigerator 30 minutes before baking. Cover and bake at 325° for 1 hour. Uncover; spread sour cream evenly over the top. Sprinkle with Parmesan cheese. Bake 10 minutes longer or until cheese is melted. **Yield:** 10-12 servings.

Creamed Eggs on English Muffins

I came across this magazine when I first got married more than 20 years ago.
It's still my husband's favorite for breakfast or brunch.
—Barbara Peterson, Indianapolis, Indiana

1/4 cup chopped onion
1 tablespoon butter
1/4 cup coarsely chopped fresh mushrooms
3/4 cup milk
1 package (8 ounces) cream cheese, cubed
1/2 cup grated Parmesan cheese
2 tablespoons minced fresh parsley
1 teaspoon Dijon mustard

Salt and pepper to taste
6 hard-cooked eggs, coarsely chopped
4 English muffins, split and toasted

In a saucepan, saute onion in butter until almost tender. Add mushrooms; saute until mushrooms and onion are tender. Stir in milk and cream cheese; cook and stir until cheese is melted and blended. Stir in the Parmesan cheese, parsley, mustard, salt and pepper. Add eggs; heat through. Serve over English muffins. **Yield:** 4 servings.

Fruit-Filled Puff Pancake

(Pictured at right)

My husband and I often make a meal of this fruity puff pancake. The combination of cinnamon, blueberries and bananas is wonderful.
—LeAnne Senger, Oregon City, Oregon

   1 tablespoon butter
1/3 cup all-purpose flour
   3 tablespoons sugar, *divided*
1/4 teaspoon salt
   3 eggs, beaten
1/2 cup milk
1-1/2 cups fresh *or* frozen
      blueberries
   1 medium ripe banana, sliced
1/4 teaspoon ground cinnamon

Place butter in a 9-in. pie plate. Bake at 400° for 4-5 minutes or until melted. Meanwhile, in a bowl, combine the flour, 1 tablespoon sugar and salt. Add eggs and milk; whisk until smooth. Pour into hot pie plate.

Bake at 400° for 10-12 minutes or until edges are puffed and golden brown. Meanwhile, combine blueberries and banana. In a small bowl, combine cinnamon and remaining sugar. Spoon fruit mixture into pancake; sprinkle with cinnamon-sugar. Cut into wedges. Serve immediately. **Yield:** 4 servings.

Artichoke Quiche

Oklahoma may be meat-and-potatoes country. But even good ol' boys have been known to eat this quiche!
—*Jone Kendrick, Idabel, Oklahoma*

1 small onion, finely chopped
1 garlic clove, minced
2 teaspoons vegetable oil
4 eggs
1/4 cup soft bread crumbs
2 tablespoons minced fresh parsley
1/4 teaspoon salt
1/8 teaspoon dried oregano
1/8 teaspoon pepper
1/8 teaspoon hot pepper sauce

2 cups (8 ounces) shredded cheddar cheese
1 can (14 ounces) water-packed artichoke hearts, drained and chopped

In a skillet, saute onion and garlic in oil until tender; set aside. In a large bowl, whisk the eggs, bread crumbs, parsley, salt, oregano, pepper and hot pepper sauce. Stir in cheese, artichokes and onion mixture. Pour into a greased 9-in. pie plate. Bake at 350° for 22-26 minutes or until a knife inserted near the center comes out clean. **Yield:** 6 servings.

Salmon Tartlets

I like to serve these bite-size snacks as the first course of an Easter or Christmas brunch. The lemon herb sauce nicely complements the salmon filling.
—*Monica Steiner, Olathe, Kansas*

1 cup butter, softened
1 package (8 ounces) cream cheese, softened
2 cups all-purpose flour
FILLING:
2 eggs
1/2 cup milk
1 tablespoon butter, melted
1 teaspoon lemon juice
1/2 cup dry bread crumbs
1-1/2 teaspoons dried parsley flakes
1/2 teaspoon rubbed sage
1/2 teaspoon salt
1/4 teaspoon pepper
1 can (14-3/4 ounces) salmon, drained, bones and skin removed and flaked
1/2 cup chopped celery
1 green onion, finely chopped

LEMON HERB SAUCE:
3/4 cup mayonnaise
1-1/2 to 2 teaspoons lemon juice
1 teaspoon prepared horseradish
1/2 teaspoon dried thyme
Salt and pepper to taste

In a small mixing bowl, beat the butter, cream cheese and flour until smooth. Press onto the bottom and up the sides of greased miniature muffin cups. In a bowl, combine the eggs, milk, butter and lemon juice. Stir in the bread crumbs, parsley, sage, salt and pepper; mix well. Add the salmon, celery and onion. Spoon into prepared crusts.

Bake at 350° for 30-35 minutes or until a knife inserted near the center comes out clean. In a bowl, combine the sauce ingredients. Serve with tartlets. **Yield:** 2 dozen.

Twice-Baked Cheese Souffles

(Pictured at right)

You'll easily impress guests with these individual cheese souffles from our home economists. Partially bake and refrigerate them early in the morning. Then simply sprinkle with cheese and finish baking when ready to eat.

3 tablespoons butter
1/4 cup all-purpose flour
2 cups plus 2 tablespoons milk
1/4 teaspoon onion powder
1/4 teaspoon salt
1/8 teaspoon ground nutmeg
1/8 teaspoon pepper
2 cups (8 ounces) shredded cheddar cheese, *divided*
3 eggs, *separated*

In a saucepan, melt butter. Stir in flour until smooth. Gradually add milk, onion powder, salt, nutmeg and pepper. Bring to a boil; cook and stir for 2 minutes or until thickened. Reduce heat; add 1 cup cheese and stir until melted. Remove from the heat; set aside.

In a small mixing bowl, beat egg yolks until thick and lemon-colored, about 3 minutes. Stir in 1/3 cup hot cheese sauce. Return all to the pan; cook and stir for 1-2 minutes. Cool completely.

In another mixing bowl, beat egg whites on high speed until stiff peaks form. Gently fold into cooled cheese mixture. Pour into ungreased 1-cup souffle dishes or custard cups. Place in a shallow baking pan. Add 1 in. of hot water to pan. Bake, uncovered, at 325° for 20 minutes. Remove custard cups to wire racks to cool. Cover and refrigerate for up to 4 hours.

Remove from the refrigerator 30 minutes before baking. Uncover; sprinkle with remaining cheese. Bake at 425° for 15-20 minutes or until puffed and golden brown. **Yield:** 4 servings.

Dessert Corn Crepes

Although I'm in my 80s, I still love to cook. I often serve these crepes as a unique dessert.
You can replace apricot jam with your favorite filling.
—Mildred Pavek, Eagle River, Wisconsin

1 cup fresh corn
3 tablespoons cornstarch
1/3 cup all-purpose flour
3/4 cup plus 1 tablespoon milk
2 eggs, beaten
2 tablespoons butter, melted
1/2 teaspoon salt
11 tablespoons apricot jam
Confectioners' sugar
LEMON CREAM:
1 cup (8 ounces) sour cream
1/4 cup confectioners' sugar
1 to 2 tablespoons grated lemon
   peel

Place corn in a blender; cover and process until smooth. In a large mixing bowl, whisk cornstarch, flour and milk until smooth. Stir in the eggs, pureed corn, butter and salt until blended. Cover and refrigerate for 1 hour.

Heat a lightly greased 8-in. nonstick skillet; pour 3 tablespoons batter into the center of skillet. Lift and tilt pan to evenly coat bottom. Cook until top appears dry; turn and cook 15-20 seconds longer. Remove to a wire rack. Repeat with remaining batter, greasing skillet as needed. When cool, stack crepes with waxed paper or paper towels in between.

Spread 1 tablespoon apricot jam over each crepe. Fold in half, then fold in half again, making triangles. Dust with confectioners' sugar. In a small bowl, combine the lemon cream ingredients. Serve with crepes. **Yield:** 11 crepes.

MAKING NATURAL EGG DYES

Onion Skin Dye. To make dye from yellow onion skins, place several skins in a large pot of water. Bring to a boil; let cool and discard skins.

Based on the number of onion skins used and the amount of time the eggs soak, you'll get warm tones that can range from gold to a rich terra cotta. (See photo at right, top.)

Brewed Coffee Dye. Simply brew a pot of strong coffee and cool.

The color can range from a light speckled tan to a more solid dark tan depending on how strong the coffee is and how long the egg soaks. (See photo at right, middle.)

Cranberry Dye. To make a dye from fresh cranberries, boil 4 cups cranberries in 2 cups cold water until the berries burst. Let cool. Drain the mixture, saving the liquid and discarding the cranberries.

To create a light blue-toned egg, soak for only a short time. (See photo at right, bottom.) We found that soaking an egg longer results in a dark gray color.

Naturally Dyed Easter Eggs

(Pictured at right and on page 145)

IN ANCIENT TIMES, eggs were an important symbol of rebirth during the spring equinox festival and were dyed in the petals and leaves of colorful flowers.

Today, you can purchase a variety of Easter egg dye kits, such as pastel, neon, marble and glitter.

But for a more natural look to Easter eggs that is reminiscent of days gone by, consider dyeing them with everyday kitchen ingredients.

For the eggs pictured here, we made three dyes—one from yellow onion skins, one from fresh cranberries and one from strong brewed coffee. (See the directions for making these natural egg dyes on the opposite page.)

Before you begin, you'll need hard-cooked eggs that are completely dry and room temperature.

For each color of dye, find a container that won't get stained or that you can discard when finished. Make sure it is big enough to completely submerge an egg or several eggs.

Place an egg in the container. Pour dye over the egg, covering completely. Refrigerate until the desired color is achieved. (The longer the egg sits in the dye, the darker the color.) Remove the egg and let dry; refrigerate.

Decorated eggs can be displayed in egg cups or simply set on the table. You can also make a nest egg centerpiece (as in the photo above) by placing the dyed eggs on an excelsior-lined grapevine wreath.

Don't eat hard-cooked eggs that have stood at room temperature for more than 2 hours. If you plan on displaying eggs, it's best to cook extra eggs for eating.

Easter Dinner Is Sure To Delight

MOST FOLKS agree that Easter just isn't the same without a home-baked ham.

Your guests will be eager for the call that dinner is ready when they smell Peach-Glazed Ham baking in the oven. Peach preserves, brown sugar and mustard fabulously flavor every bite.

(If there are seafood lovers in your clan, why not surprise them by serving impressive Baked Whole Salmon instead?)

A medley of mouth-watering meal mates includes Chilled Green Beans Italiano, Bread Machine Crescent Rolls and Pineapple Raisin Stuffing.

A happy ending to the meal is guaranteed when you serve Coconut Cake or Grandma's Baked Rice Custard.

HAM FOR THE HOLIDAY
(Clockwise from top)

Coconut Cake (p.159)

Bread Machine Crescent Rolls (p.162)

Chilled Green Beans Italiano (p.158)

Peach-Glazed Ham (p.160)

EASTER DINNER TIMETABLE

A Few Weeks Before:
- From your butcher, order an 8- to 10-pound bone-in fully cooked ham or, if making Baked Whole Salmon, a 10-pound whole salmon.
- Prepare two grocery lists—one for non-perishable items to purchase now and one for perishable items to purchase a few days before Easter.
- Bake Bread Machine Crescent Rolls; cool and freeze.

Two to Three Days Before:
- Buy remaining groceries.
- Purchase items needed for the Dramatic Hydrangea Display (page 163).

The Day Before:
- Set the table.
- Assemble the hydrangea centerpiece.
- Prepare the glaze for Peach-Glazed Ham; cover and refrigerate.

- If making Baked Whole Salmon, combine and cook the first eight ingredients as directed. Cover; chill.
- Make and refrigerate Chilled Green Beans Italiano.
- Bake Coconut Cake; store covered at room temperature.
- If serving Grandma's Baked Rice Custard, assemble, cover and chill.

Easter Day:
- In the morning, assemble Pineapple Raisin Stuffing. Cover and chill.
- Thaw Bread Machine Crescent Rolls at room temperature.
- Bake the ham or salmon as directed.
- Remove stuffing from the refrigerator 30 minutes before baking.
- Serve green bean salad and rolls.
- Remove rice custard from the refrigerator; let stand for 30 minutes. Bake as directed during dinner.
- Serve Coconut Cake.

Chilled Green Beans Italiano

(Pictured on page 157)

Chopped red onion contrasts nicely with the colorful green beans in this unique vegetable salad.
—*Mrs. Frances Avazier, Tucson, Arizona*

2 pounds fresh green beans, cut into 2-inch pieces
1/2 cup chopped red onion
4 teaspoons olive oil
1 teaspoon Italian seasoning
3/4 teaspoon salt
1/4 teaspoon pepper

Place beans in a large saucepan and cover with water; bring to a boil. Reduce heat; cover and simmer for 8-10 minutes or until crisp-tender. Rinse with cold water; drain and pat dry. Place in a bowl. Add the remaining ingredients; toss to coat. Cover and refrigerate for 2 hours or until chilled. **Yield:** 8-10 servings.

Coconut Cake

(Pictured at right and on page 157)

My grandmother and mother usually made this lovely layer cake for holidays and served it with scoops of homemade custard.
—Joyce Lee, Saltville, Virginia

1/2 cup butter, softened
1/2 cup shortening
2 cups sugar
2 eggs
5 egg yolks
3 cups cake flour
1-1/2 teaspoons baking powder
1 teaspoon baking soda
1-2/3 cups buttermilk
3 teaspoons lemon extract
FROSTING:
1-3/4 cups sugar
4 egg whites
1/2 cup water
1/2 teaspoon cream of tartar
1 teaspoon vanilla extract
1 cup flaked coconut, *divided*

In a large mixing bowl, cream butter, shortening and sugar until light and fluffy. Add eggs and yolks; mix well. Combine the flour, baking powder and baking soda; add to the creamed mixture alternately with buttermilk. Beat in extract.

Pour into three greased and floured 9-in. round baking pans. Bake at 350° for 30-35 minutes or until a toothpick inserted near the center comes out clean. Cool for 10 minutes before removing from pans to wire racks.

In a heavy saucepan, combine the sugar, egg whites, water and cream of tartar. With a portable mixer, beat on low speed for 1 minute. Continue beating on low speed over low heat until frosting reaches 160°, about 9 minutes. Pour into a large mixing bowl; add vanilla. Beat on high until frosting forms stiff peaks, about 7 minutes.

Place one cake layer on a serving plate; spread with 1/2 cup frosting and sprinkle with 1/3 cup coconut. Repeat. Spread remaining frosting over top and sides of cake; sprinkle remaining coconut over the top. **Yield:** 12 servings.

Editor's Note: A stand mixer is recommended for beating the frosting after it reaches 160°.

DRESS UP A PLAIN CAKE

TO ADD some color and a bit of elegance to Coconut Cake (above), we added a gorgeous garland garnish! Place fresh blueberries over the top and down the sides of cake. Tuck in fresh mint and lemon leaves.

Peach-Glazed Ham

(Pictured on page 156)

This recipe for our family's traditional Easter ham is my own creation.
It truly is a winner and even took first place in a local recipe contest.
—Helen McLain, Quinlan, Texas

1 bone-in fully cooked ham (8 to 10 pounds)
Whole cloves
1 can (12 ounces) lemon-lime soda
1-1/2 cups packed dark brown sugar, *divided*
1 cup water
1 jar (12 ounces) peach preserves
6 tablespoons butter, cubed
1/4 cup honey
1 teaspoon prepared mustard
1 teaspoon Liquid Smoke, optional
Dash ground cloves

1 can (8 ounces) sliced pineapple, drained
3 canned peach halves

Score the surface of the ham, making diamond shapes 1/2 in. deep; insert a clove into each diamond. Place on a rack in a well-greased foil-lined roasting pan. Pour soda over ham. Spread 1 cup brown sugar over ham. Add water to pan. Cover and bake at 325° for 1-1/2 to 2 hours.

In a saucepan, combine the preserves, butter, honey, mustard, Liquid Smoke if desired, ground cloves and remaining brown sugar. Cook and stir over low heat until butter is melted and sugar is dissolved. Uncover ham; brush with glaze.

Arrange the pineapple slices and peach halves over ham, securing with wooden toothpicks. Bake, uncovered, for 25-30 minutes or until a meat thermometer reads 140° and ham is heated through. Discard toothpicks before carving. **Yield:** 16-20 servings.

Pineapple Raisin Stuffing

A co-worker gave me this stuffing recipe years ago. I added cinnamon and
raisins for even more flavor. It accompanies ham dinners throughout the year.
—Kay Brolly, Philadelphia, Pennsylvania

1/2 cup butter, softened
1 cup sugar
1 to 2 teaspoons ground cinnamon
4 eggs
4 cans (8 ounces *each*) crushed pineapple, undrained
1 cup raisins
1 package (14 ounces) seasoned stuffing croutons

In a small mixing bowl, cream the butter, sugar and cinnamon. Add eggs, one at a time, beating well after each addition. Stir in pineapple and raisins. Place stuffing croutons in a large bowl; stir in pineapple mixture.

Transfer to a greased shallow 3-qt. baking dish. Cover and bake at 325° for 60-75 minutes or until a thermometer reads 160°. **Yield:** 12-14 servings.

Baked Whole Salmon

(Pictured at right)

We don't get much fresh seafood around here. So when I see some whole salmon in the grocery store, I snap it up and make this elegant entree.
—*Dixie Harmon, Bainville, Montana*

3/4 cup white wine *or* chicken broth
3/4 cup chopped celery leaves
  1 small onion, minced
  2 lemon slices
  8 fresh basil leaves
  2 teaspoons dried tarragon
  1 teaspoon dried rosemary, crushed
1/4 teaspoon dried thyme
  1 whole salmon (about 10 pounds)
1-1/2 teaspoons salt
WINE SAUCE:
  2 green onions, chopped
1/2 cup butter
  6 tablespoons all-purpose flour
2-1/3 cups water
2-1/3 cups white wine *or* chicken broth
  2 egg yolks, lightly beaten
1/2 cup heavy whipping cream
Salt and pepper to taste

In a saucepan over medium heat, combine the first eight ingredients. Bring to a boil. Reduce heat; simmer, uncovered, for 30 minutes.

Remove head and tail from salmon if desired. Place a double thickness of heavy-duty foil on a baking sheet (longer than the length of the fish). Grease foil. Place salmon on foil; sprinkle the cavity with salt. Pour herb sauce over fish. Fold foil over fish and seal tightly. Bake at 375° for 60-75 minutes or until fish flakes easily with a fork.

Place salmon on a serving platter and keep warm. Strain cooking juices, reserving 1/3 cup. In a large saucepan, saute green onions in butter until tender. Stir in flour until blended. Gradually stir in the water, wine or broth and reserved cooking juices. Bring to a boil; cook and stir for 2 minutes or until thickened.

Reduce heat. Stir a small amount of hot liquid into the egg yolks; return all to the pan, stirring constantly. Add the cream, salt and pepper. Cook and stir until mixture reaches 160°. Serve with the salmon. **Yield:** 12-14 servings.

Bread Machine Crescent Rolls

(Pictured on page 157)

Leftover mashed potatoes never last long around our house...
I simply turn them into these easy-to-make crescent rolls!
—Jennifer Ann Unsell, Germantown, Tennessee

1/2 cup warm milk (70° to 80°)
1/4 cup water (70° to 80°)
1 egg, lightly beaten
1 teaspoon salt
1/4 cup butter, softened
3/4 cup warm mashed potatoes (prepared with milk and butter)
1/4 cup sugar
4-1/4 cups bread flour
1-1/2 teaspoons active dry yeast
Additional butter, melted

In bread machine pan, place the first nine ingredients in order suggested by manufacturer. Select dough setting (check dough after 5 minutes of mixing; add 1 to 2 tablespoons of water or flour if needed).

When cycle is completed, turn dough onto a lightly floured surface. Divide in half; roll each portion into a 12-in. circle. Cut each circle into 12 wedges; roll up wedges from the wide end. Place pointed side down 2 in. apart on greased baking sheets. Curve ends down to form a crescent shape. Cover and let rise for 20-25 minutes or until doubled.

Bake at 400° for 10-15 minutes or until golden brown. Remove to wire racks. Brush warm rolls with melted butter. **Yield:** 2 dozen.

Editor's Note: If your bread machine has a time-delay feature, we recommend you do not use it for this recipe.

Grandma's Baked Rice Custard

While growing up in Italy in the 1900s, my mother lived a very basic life. But when Easter Sunday arrived, my grandmother would make this dessert as a special treat.
—Antonetta Matteo, Smithfield, Rhode Island

14 eggs, beaten
1-1/2 cups sugar
4 cups milk
1 carton (15 ounces) ricotta cheese
1-1/2 cups cooked rice
1 can (8 ounces) crushed pineapple, undrained
1 cup evaporated milk
3 teaspoons vanilla extract
Ground cinnamon

In a bowl, combine the eggs and sugar; mix well. Stir in the milk, ricotta cheese, rice, pineapple, evaporated milk and vanilla. Pour into a greased 13-in. x 9-in. x 2-in. baking dish and a greased 11-in. x 7-in. x 2-in. baking dish. Sprinkle with cinnamon.

Bake, uncovered, at 350° for 40-45 minutes or until a knife inserted near the center comes out clean. Serve warm or cold. Refrigerate leftovers. **Yield:** 20-22 servings.

Dramatic Hydrangea Display

(Pictured at right)

BRING a little of the outdoors inside at Easter with this beautiful hydrangea-and-candle centerpiece. Hydrangeas come in an amazing array of colors, so look for a shade that coordinates with your dishes and table linens.

Before you begin, visit your local garden center or nursery and purchase a clear plastic flowerpot saucer (the saucer we used measured 12 inches in diameter), a piece of floral foam big enough to fit inside the saucer and about seven large hydrangea blossoms in the color of your choice.

If you don't want the floral foam to be visible when the centerpiece is on display, you may want to adhere a coordinating ribbon around the plastic saucer with double-stick tape.

Soak the floral foam until completely saturated. With a serrated knife, cut the foam to fit inside the saucer. (The top should be level with the rim.) Place three candlesticks in a triangle on top of the foam.

Cut hydrangea blossoms from stems and separate into small clumps. Starting at the outside edge, push the hydrangea stems into the floral foam. Add hydrangeas to the middle of the centerpiece until the foam is completely covered. Place candles in candlesticks.

You can assemble this centerpiece in advance as long as the hydrangea stems remain in the water-soaked floral foam.

ASSEMBLING THE HYDRANGEA CENTERPIECE

SOAK floral foam in water and cut to fit inside a clear plastic flowerpot saucer. If desired, adhere a ribbon around the saucer. Set candlesticks on top of the foam.

Starting at the outside edge and working toward the center, push the hydrangea stems into the floral foam. Put candles in the candlesticks.

EASTER *Gatherings*

Seasonal Breads Rise to the Occasion

THROUGH HISTORY, people have baked rich, elaborate breads to announce the arrival of spring and to celebrate the end of sparse meals associated with religious fasting.

Why not bake up a delicious Easter morning tradition of your own and prepare one of the specialty breads featured here?

Italian Easter Bread is a sweet yeast bread dotted with colorful nesting eggs.

For fruit-filled favorites, try Strawberry Braid and Crumb-Topped Blueberry Muffins. (All recipes shown at right.)

If you're looking to complement your Easter dinner, this chapter also offers a savory selection of oven-fresh breads.

FESTIVELY FRESH
(Clockwise from top)

Crumb-Topped
Blueberry Muffins (p.168)

Strawberry Braid (p.167)

Italian Easter Bread (p.166)

Italian Easter Bread

(Pictured on page 164)

*This traditional Easter bread is topped with colored raw eggs, which cook as
the bread bakes. It makes for a pretty centerpiece.*
—June Formanek, Belle Plaine, Iowa

2-3/4 to 3-1/4 cups all-purpose flour
    1/4 cup sugar
      **1 package (1/4 ounce) active
dry yeast**
      1 teaspoon salt
    2/3 cup milk
      3 tablespoons butter, *divided*
      2 eggs
    **1/2 cup chopped mixed candied
fruit**
    **1/4 cup chopped blanched
almonds**
    1/2 teaspoon aniseed
      5 uncooked eggs, dyed
GLAZE:
      1 cup confectioners' sugar
    1/4 teaspoon vanilla extract
      1 to 2 tablespoons milk
Decorator candies, optional

In a large mixing bowl, combine 1 cup flour, sugar, yeast and salt. In a saucepan, heat milk and 2 tablespoons butter to 120°-130°. Add to dry ingredients; beat on medium speed for 2 minutes. Add eggs; mix well. Stir in enough remaining flour to form a soft dough. Turn onto a lightly floured surface; knead until smooth and elastic, about 6-8 minutes. Place in a greased bowl, turning once to grease top. Cover and let rise in a warm place until doubled, about 1 hour.

Punch dough down; turn onto a lightly floured surface. Knead in fruit, almonds and aniseed until blended. Let rest for 10 minutes. Divide dough in half. Shape each portion into a 24-in. rope. Loosely twist ropes together; place on a greased baking sheet and form into a ring. Pinch ends together. Melt remaining butter; brush over dough. Gently separate ropes and tuck dyed eggs into openings. Cover and let rise until doubled, about 40 minutes.

Bake at 350° for 30-35 minutes or until golden brown. Cool on a wire rack. For glaze, in a bowl, combine the confectioners' sugar, vanilla and enough milk to achieve desired consistency; drizzle over bread. Sprinkle with candies if desired. **Yield:** 1 loaf.

MAKING ITALIAN EASTER BREAD

WITH your hands, gently separate ropes of dough. Tuck dyed raw eggs into the openings. Cover and let rise until doubled, about 40 minutes. Bake as directed.

Strawberry Braid

(Pictured at right and on page 164)

Before moving to Oklahoma, I owned a catering business in Tennessee. This recipe was a favorite with my clients. I appreciate that the dough starts with a convenient hot roll mix.

—Elizabeth Area, Stillwater, Oklahoma

1 package (16 ounces) hot roll mix
1 cup strawberry jam
1/2 cup finely chopped dried apricots
1/4 cup chopped walnuts
1 tablespoon butter, melted
2 teaspoons sugar

Prepare hot roll mix according to package directions. While dough is resting, combine the jam, apricots and walnuts in a bowl. Turn dough onto a lightly floured surface; roll into a 14-in. x 9-in. rectangle. Place on a greased foil-lined baking sheet.

Spread filling down center third of rectangle. On each long side, cut 1-in.-wide strips about 2-1/2 in. into center. Starting at one end, fold alternating strips at an angle across filling. Pinch ends to seal. Cover and let rise until doubled, about 30 minutes. Brush braid with butter and sprinkle with sugar. Bake at 350° for 25-30 minutes or until golden brown. Cool on a wire rack. **Yield:** 10-12 servings.

Crumb-Topped Blueberry Muffins

(Pictured on page 165)

For years I've searched for the perfect blueberry muffins without success.
Then I came up with this winning recipe.
—Helen Woronik, Salem, Connecticut

4 cups all-purpose flour
1 cup sugar
6 teaspoons baking powder
1/2 teaspoon salt
1 cup cold butter
2 eggs, lightly beaten
1-1/3 cups milk
2 teaspoons grated orange peel
2 teaspoons almond extract
1 teaspoon vanilla extract
2 cups fresh blueberries
TOPPING:
1/4 cup sugar
3 tablespoons all-purpose flour
1/4 teaspoon ground cinnamon
2 tablespoons cold butter

In a bowl, combine the flour, sugar, baking powder and salt. Cut in butter until mixture resembles coarse crumbs. Combine the eggs, milk, orange peel and extracts; stir into crumb mixture just until moistened. Gently fold in blueberries (batter will be stiff). Fill paper-lined or greased muffin cups two-thirds full.

In a bowl, combine the sugar, flour and cinnamon. Cut in butter until mixture resembles coarse crumbs. Sprinkle about 1 teaspoonful over each muffin. Bake at 375° for 20-25 minutes or until a toothpick comes out clean. Cool for 5 minutes before removing from pans to wire racks. **Yield:** 2 dozen.

BAKE BIGGER BLUEBERRY MUFFINS

CRUMB-TOPPED Blueberry Muffins (above) can also be baked in one dozen jumbo-size muffin cups. Bake at 375° for 25-30 minutes or until a toothpick comes out clean.

Sweet Cream Biscuits

People are surprised that these three-ingredient biscuits have such wonderful homemade flavor.
—Dee Saron, Spring Valley, California

2 cups biscuit/baking mix
2/3 cup heavy whipping cream
2 tablespoons sugar

In a bowl, combine the biscuit mix, cream and sugar; stir just until moistened. Turn onto a lightly floured surface; knead 8-10 times. Pat or roll out to 1/2-in. thickness; cut with a floured 2-1/2-in. biscuit cutter. Place 2 in. apart on a lightly greased baking sheet. Bake at 450° for 10-12 minutes or until golden brown. Remove to a wire rack. Serve warm. **Yield:** 1 dozen.

Paska Easter Bread

(Pictured at right)

Paska is a traditional Easter bread prepared with lots of eggs, making it much richer than ordinary sweet breads. The beautifully braided top will earn you many compliments.
— Millie Cherniwchan
Smoky Lake, Alberta

   2 packages (1/4 ounce *each*)
      active dry yeast
   1 teaspoon plus 1/3 cup sugar,
      divided
   4 cups warm water (110° to
      115°), *divided*
   1 cup nonfat dry milk powder
13-1/2 to 14-1/2 cups all-purpose
      flour, *divided*
   6 eggs, beaten
   1/2 cup butter, melted
   1 tablespoon salt
EGG GLAZE:
   1 egg
   2 tablespoons water

In a large mixing bowl, dissolve yeast and 1 teaspoon sugar in 1 cup warm water. Let stand for 5 minutes. Add remaining water. Beat in the milk powder and 5 cups flour until smooth. Cover and let rise in a warm place until bubbly, about 20 minutes. Add eggs, butter, salt and remaining sugar; mix well. Stir in enough remaining flour to form a soft dough. Turn onto a floured surface; knead until smooth and elastic, about 8-10 minutes. Place in a greased bowl, turning once to grease top. Cover and let rise in a warm place until doubled, about 1 hour.

Punch dough down. Turn onto a lightly floured surface; divide in half and set one portion aside. Divide remaining portion in half; press each portion into a well-greased 10-in. springform pan. Divide reserved dough into six balls. Shape each ball into a 30-in. rope; make two braids of three ropes each. Place a braid around the edge of each pan, forming a circle. Trim ends of braids, reserving dough scraps. Pinch ends of braids to seal. Shape scraps into two long thin ropes; form into rosettes or crosses. Place one decoration in the center of each loaf. Cover and let rise until doubled, about 1 hour.

In a small bowl, beat egg and water; brush over dough. Bake at 350° for 50-60 minutes or until golden brown. Remove from pans to wire racks to cool. **Yield:** 2 loaves.

Cream Cheese Bundles

A cream cheese center provides a pleasant surprise when folks bite into these rich bundles.
—Maxine Cenker, Weirton, West Virginia

5-1/2 cups all-purpose flour
1/2 cup sugar
2 packages (1/4 ounce *each*)
  quick-rise yeast
1/2 teaspoon salt
1 cup water
1/2 cup butter
3 eggs
FILLING:
1 package (8 ounces) cream
  cheese, softened
1 egg
1/4 cup sugar
1/2 teaspoon vanilla extract
TOPPING:
2 tablespoons butter, melted
1-1/2 cups confectioners' sugar
2 to 3 tablespoons milk
1/2 teaspoon vanilla extract
1/3 cup finely chopped pecans,
  toasted

In a large mixing bowl, combine 3 cups flour, sugar, yeast and salt. In a saucepan, heat water and butter to 120°-130°; stir into dry ingredients. Beat in eggs until smooth. Stir in enough remaining flour to form a soft dough. Turn onto a floured surface; knead until smooth and elastic, about 6-8 minutes. Cover and let rest for 10 minutes.

Meanwhile, in a small mixing bowl, combine the filling ingredients; beat until smooth. Roll out dough to a 21-in. x 14-in. rectangle, about 1/4 in. thick. Let rest for 5 minutes. Cut into 3-1/2-in. squares. Spoon 1 tablespoon of filling onto each square. Bring corners together over filling; pinch seams to seal. Place seam side down in greased muffin cups. Cover and let rise until doubled, about 1-1/2 hours.

Bake at 375° for 15-20 minutes or until golden brown. Remove from pans to wire racks to cool. Brush with butter. In a small bowl, combine the confectioners' sugar, milk and vanilla until smooth; drizzle over bundles. Sprinkle with pecans. Refrigerate leftovers. **Yield:** 2 dozen.

Dilly Cheese Ring

As a stay-at-home mom with three children, I don't have time for a lot of involved cooking.
This delicious bread goes together in a flash thanks to a biscuit mix.
—Peggy-Jo Thompson, Lebanon, Tennessee

3 cups biscuit/baking mix
1-1/2 cups (6 ounces) shredded
  cheddar cheese
1 tablespoon sugar
1/2 to 1 teaspoon dill weed
1/2 teaspoon ground mustard
1 egg, lightly beaten
1-1/4 cups milk
1 tablespoon vegetable oil

In a large bowl, combine the first five ingredients. In a small bowl, combine the egg, milk and oil. Stir into dry ingredients just until moistened. Pour into a greased 10-in. fluted tube pan. Bake at 350° for 35-40 minutes or until a toothpick inserted near the center comes out clean. Cool for 10 minutes before removing from pan to a wire rack. **Yield:** 1 loaf.

Chocolate-Hazelnut Swirl Bread

(Pictured at right)

Homemade breads are my favorite goodies to give. After delivering these lovley loaves to friends and family one Christmas, people kept asking me for the recipe. I was happy to share it!
—Nancy Tafoya, Fort Collins, Colorado

1/2 cup butter, softened
　1 cup sugar
　2 eggs
　1 teaspoon almond extract
　1 teaspoon vanilla extract
　2 cups all-purpose flour
　1 teaspoon baking powder
　1 teaspoon baking soda
1/4 teaspoon salt
　1 cup (8 ounces) sour cream
TOPPING:
1/3 cup finely chopped hazelnuts
1/3 cup miniature semisweet
　　chocolate chips
　3 tablespoons sugar
3/4 teaspoon ground cinnamon

In a mixing bowl, cream butter and sugar. Add eggs, one at a time, beating well after each addition. Beat in extracts. Combine the flour, baking powder, baking soda and salt; add to the creamed mixture alternately with sour cream.

Pour half of the batter into a greased 9-in. x 5-in. x 3-in. loaf pan. Combine topping ingredients; sprinkle two-thirds over the batter. Top with the remaining batter. Sprinkle with remaining topping; press down lightly. Bake at 350° for 60-70 minutes or until a toothpick inserted near the center comes out clean. Cool for 10 minutes before removing from pan to a wire rack. **Yield:** 1 loaf.

HISTORY OF HOT CROSS BUNS

IF YOU PASS a pan of hot cross buns around your dinner table this Easter, enlighten guests with this bit of history.

English immigrants brought to America the recipe for these traditional Easter buns dotted with raisins and currants. A cross is cut into the top before baking, then piped with frosting when baked and cooled.

Apricot Pecan Bread

*Enjoy slices of this fruit and nut quick bread alongside breakfast or
as a snack any time of day. One loaf won't last long!*
—Beatrice Pratten, Canton, Illinois

2 cups all-purpose flour
3/4 cup sugar
1/2 teaspoon baking soda
1/2 teaspoon salt
1/4 teaspoon baking powder
1 egg, lightly beaten
1 cup orange juice
3 tablespoons butter, melted
1 cup chopped pecans
1/2 cup finely chopped dried
   apricots

In a large bowl, combine the flour, sugar, baking soda, salt, and baking powder. In another bowl, combine the egg, orange juice and butter. Stir into the dry ingredients just until moistened. Fold in the pecans and apricots.

Pour into a greased 9-in. x 5-in. x 3-in. loaf pan. Bake at 325° for 50-60 minutes or until a toothpick inserted near the center comes out clean. Cool for 10 minutes before removing from pan to a wire rack. **Yield:** 1 loaf.

Caraway Rye Rolls

*These mild-flavored rolls appeal to folks of every age and pair well with a variety of menus.
I sometimes shape the dough into loaves for sandwiches.*
—Sue Stitzel, Craig, Colorado

2 cups rye flour
1/4 cup sugar
2 packages (1/4 ounce *each*)
   active dry yeast
1 tablespoon salt
2 to 3 teaspoons fennel seed
2 teaspoons caraway seeds
3-1/2 to 4-1/2 cups all-purpose flour
2-1/2 cups water
3 tablespoons shortening

In a large mixing bowl, combine the rye flour, sugar, yeast, salt, fennel seed, caraway seeds and 2 cups all-purpose flour. In a saucepan, heat water and shortening to 120°-130°. Add to the dry ingredients; beat just until moistened. Beat on medium speed for 3 minutes. Stir in enough remaining flour to form a firm dough. Turn onto a floured surface; knead until smooth and elastic, about 6-8 minutes. Place in a greased bowl, turning once to grease top. Cover and let rise in a warm place until doubled, about 1 hour.

Punch dough down. Turn onto a lightly floured surface; divide into six portions. Divide each portion into 10 pieces; shape each piece into a ball. Place three balls in each greased muffin cup. Cover and let rise until doubled, about 30 minutes. Bake at 375° for 15-20 minutes or until golden brown. Cool for 5 minutes before removing from pans to wire racks. **Yield:** 20 rolls.

Herbed Onion Focaccia

(Pictured at right)

This recipe makes three savory flat breads, but don't be surprised to see them all disappear from your dinner table!
—Melanie Eddy, Manhattan, Kansas

1 tablespoon active dry yeast
1-1/2 cups warm water (110° to 115°), *divided*
1 teaspoon sugar
6 tablespoons olive oil, *divided*
2 teaspoons salt
4 to 4-1/2 cups all-purpose flour
3 tablespoons finely chopped green onions
1-1/2 teaspoons minced fresh rosemary *or* 1/2 teaspoon dried rosemary, crushed
1-1/2 teaspoons small fresh sage leaves *or* 1/2 teaspoon rubbed sage
1-1/2 teaspoons minced fresh oregano *or* 1/2 teaspoon dried oregano
Seasoned olive oil *or* additional olive oil, optional

In a large mixing bowl, dissolve yeast in 1/2 cup warm water. Add sugar; let stand for 5 minutes. Add 4 tablespoons oil, salt, 2 cups flour and remaining water. Beat until smooth. Stir in enough remaining flour to form a soft dough. Turn onto a floured surface; knead until smooth and elastic, about 6-8 minutes. Place in a greased bowl, turning once to grease top. Cover and let rise in a warm place until doubled, about 1 hour.

Punch dough down. Divide into three portions. Cover and let rest for 10 minutes. Shape each portion into an 8-in. circle; place on greased baking sheets. Cover and let rise until doubled, about 30 minutes. Using the end of a wooden spoon handle, make several 1/4-in. indentations in each loaf. Brush with remaining oil. Sprinkle with green onions, rosemary, sage and oregano. Bake at 400° for 20-25 minutes or until golden brown. Remove to wire racks. Serve with olive oil for dipping if desired. **Yield:** 3 loaves.

SPECIAL *Celebrations*

Occasions throughout the year call for special gatherings
with relatives and friends. Start the year off with a bang
by celebrating the Chinese New Year! Come February 14,
treat your sweetie to a fireside Valentine's Day dinner.
If winter blues make you want to hibernate, treat your
child to a teddy bear birthday party instead.
Soak up the sunshine with a Memorial Day get-together,
beach picnic or gathering in the garden.
Then in autumn, quarterback a winning tailgate party!

Chinese New Celebration

THE CHRISTMAS tree has been taken down and the party hats from New Year's Eve are packed away. But don't let the winter blues take over. Instead, usher in the Chinese New Year!

In 2005, the Chinese New Year begins on February 9 and is celebrated with cultural traditions as well as the culinary delights featured here.

Kick off this fun feast with authentic dishes such as Asian Spring Rolls (including a peanut dipping sauce!) and Chinese-Style Pork Tenderloin.

Oriental Tossed Salad, Stir-Fried Lemon Chicken, Almond Tea and plenty of steamed white rice complete the Asian-inspired menu. (Recipes shown at right.)

From the Orient
(Clockwise from top)

Oriental Tossed Salad (p. 178)

Stir-Fried Lemon Chicken (p. 182)

Chinese-Style Pork Tenderloin (p. 182)

Asian Spring Rolls (p. 180)

Almond Tea (p. 178)

Oriental Tossed Salad

(Pictured on page 177)

*Cubed cooked chicken marinates overnight in a sweet and salty sauce, giving
every bite great flavor. Fried wonton strips add fun crunch to this main-dish salad.*
—*Jennifer Pate, Kingman, Arizona*

1/4 cup soy sauce
1 teaspoon sugar
2 cups cubed cooked chicken
Oil for deep-fat frying
12 wonton wrappers, cut into
   thin strips
1 large bunch green leaf lettuce,
   chopped (about 12 cups)
10 large fresh mushrooms, thinly
   sliced
4 green onions, chopped
DRESSING:
1/2 cup vegetable oil
1/3 cup white vinegar
1/4 cup sugar
1 tablespoon soy sauce
1 teaspoon salt
1/2 teaspoon pepper

In a large resealable plastic bag, combine the soy sauce and sugar. Add chicken; seal bag and turn to coat. Refrigerate overnight.

Just before serving, in an electric skillet or deep-fat fryer, heat oil to 375°. Fry wonton strips for 1-2 minutes or until golden brown. Drain on paper towels. In a large salad bowl, combine the lettuce, mushrooms and onions. Add the wonton strips and chicken with any remaining soy sauce mixture.

In a jar with a tight-fitting lid, combine the dressing ingredients; shake well. Drizzle 1/2 to 3/4 cup over salad; toss to coat. Save remaining dressing for another use. **Yield:** 15 servings.

Almond Tea

(Pictured on page 176)

*Almond extract gives traditional tea a tasty twist.
Serve cupfuls alongside an Oriental-theme meal or with an assortment of desserts.*
—*Dixie Terry, Marion, Illinois*

4 cups hot water
1/2 cup sugar
2 tablespoons instant tea
1 tablespoon lemon juice
3/4 to 1 teaspoon almond extract
1/4 teaspoon vanilla extract

In a large saucepan, bring the water and sugar to a boil; cook and stir until sugar is dissolved. Remove from the heat; stir in the tea, lemon juice and extracts. **Yield:** 4-5 servings.

Egg Rolls

(Pictured at right)

This recipe is truly a family favorite. My husband, Doug, makes them often for family meals and my sister serves them every Tuesday night at the restaurant she owns. Feel free to use hot sausage if you and your family like food with a little more kick.
— *Donna Frandsen, Cohasset, Minnesota*

3/4 **pound bulk pork sausage**
2 **cups coleslaw mix**
1 **can (8 ounces) sliced water chestnuts, drained**
1/4 **cup chopped green onions**
3 **tablespoons soy sauce**
1 **teaspoon garlic powder**
1/2 **teaspoon ground ginger**
1/8 **teaspoon salt**
1/8 **teaspoon pepper**
1 **package (16 ounces) egg roll wrappers***
1 **egg, beaten**
Oil for deep-fat frying
Sweet-and-sour sauce

In a large nonstick skillet, cook the sausage over medium heat until no longer pink; drain well. Stir in the coleslaw mix, water chestnuts, onions, soy sauce, garlic powder, ginger, salt and pepper. Saute until cabbage is crisp-tender.

Position an egg roll wrapper with one point toward you. Place about 1/4 cup sausage mixture in the center. Fold bottom corner over filling; fold sides toward center over filling. Roll toward the remaining point. Moisten top corner with beaten egg; press to seal. Repeat with remaining wrappers and filling.

In an electric skillet or deep-fat fryer, heat oil to 375°. Fry egg rolls, a few at a time, for 1-2 minutes on each side or until golden brown. Drain on paper towels. Serve with sweet-and-sour sauce. **Yield:** 14 egg rolls.

WELCOME IN YEAR OF THE ROOSTER!

THE CHINESE CALENDAR is based on a 60-year lunar calendar, which is composed of five 12-year cycles. Each of the 12 years is represented by an animal. It's believed that the animal ruling in the year you are born affects your personality.

In 2005, the celebrations for the Year of the Rooster begin on February 9 (when the new moon appears) and continue until the next full moon 15 days later.

People born in the Year of the Rooster are said to be observant and loyal. They also are conscious of appearance and like to be noticed and flattered.

Asian Spring Rolls

(Pictured on page 176)

The peanut dipping sauce is slightly spicy but really complements these traditional vegetable-filled spring rolls. They take some time to prepare but are well worth it!
—*Nirvana Harris, Mundelein, Illinois*

3 tablespoons lime juice
1 tablespoon hoisin sauce
1 teaspoon sugar
1 teaspoon salt
3 ounces uncooked vermicelli rice noodles
1 large carrot, grated
1 medium cucumber, peeled, seeded and julienned
1 medium jalapeno pepper, seeded and chopped
1/3 cup chopped dry roasted peanuts
8 spring roll wrappers *or* rice papers (8 inches)
1/2 cup loosely packed fresh cilantro
PEANUT SAUCE:
2 garlic cloves, minced
1/2 to 1 teaspoon crushed red pepper flakes
2 teaspoons vegetable oil
1/4 cup hoisin sauce
1/4 cup creamy peanut butter
2 tablespoons tomato paste
1/2 cup hot water

In a small bowl, combine the lime juice, hoisin sauce and sugar; set aside. In a large saucepan, bring 2 qts. water and salt to a boil. Add noodles; cook for 2-3 minutes or until tender. Drain and rinse with cold water. Transfer to a bowl and toss with 2 tablespoons reserved lime juice mixture; set aside. In another bowl, combine the carrot, cucumber, jalapeno and peanuts. Toss with the remaining lime juice mixture; set aside.

Soak spring roll wrappers in cool water for 5 minutes. Carefully separate and place on a flat surface. Top each with several cilantro leaves. Place 1/4 cup carrot mixture and 1/4 cup noodles down the center of each wrapper to within 1-1/2 in. of ends. Fold both ends over filling; fold one long side over the filling, then carefully roll up tightly. Place seam side down on serving plate. Cover with damp paper towels until serving.

In a small saucepan, cook garlic and pepper flakes in oil for 2 minutes. Add the remaining sauce ingredients; cook and stir until combined and thickened. Serve with spring rolls. **Yield:** 8 spring rolls (1 cup sauce).

Editor's Note: Vermicelli rice noodles and spring roll wrappers can be found in the ethnic section of most large grocery stores or Chinese grocery stores. When cutting or seeding hot peppers, use rubber or plastic gloves to protect your hands. Avoid touching your face.

Fortune Cookies

(Pictured at right)

Our home is often filled with family and friends, so I'm always cooking up something. I created this recipe when I was looking for a treat to surprise my husband.
—*Susan Bettinger*
Battle Creek, Michigan

3 tablespoons butter, softened
3 tablespoons sugar
1 egg white
1/2 teaspoon vanilla extract
1/3 cup all-purpose flour

Write fortunes on small strips of paper (3-1/2 in. x 1/4 in.); set aside. Line a baking sheet with parchment paper. Draw two 3-1/2-in.-circles on paper; set aside. In a small mixing bowl, beat the butter, sugar, egg white and vanilla. Add flour; mix well. Spread 1 tablespoon batter over each circle. Bake at 400° for 5-6 minutes or until lightly browned.

Slide parchment paper onto a work surface. Cover one cookie with a kitchen towel. Place a fortune in the center of the other cookie; loosen cookie from parchment paper with a thin spatula. Fold cookie in half over fortune strip so the edges meet; hold edges together for 3 seconds. Place center of cookie over the rim of a glass; gently press ends down to bend cookie in middle. Cool for 1 minute before removing to a wire rack. Repeat with second cookie. If cookies become too cool to fold, return to oven to soften for 1 minute. Repeat with remaining batter and fortunes. **Yield:** 10 cookies.

FORMING FORTUNE COOKIES

1. Spread 1 tablespoon batter over each 3-1/2-in. circle on a parchment paper-lined baking sheet. Bake as directed.

2. Slide parchment paper onto a work surface. Cover one cookie with a kitchen towel. Place a fortune in the center of the other cookie; loosen cookie from parchment paper with a thin spatula. Fold cookie in half over fortune strip so the edges meet; hold edges together for 3 seconds.

3. Place cookie over the rim of a glass; gently press ends down. Cool for 1 minute before removing to a wire rack.

Chinese-Style Pork Tenderloin

(Pictured on page 176)

Our Test Kitchen home economists share this recipe for a main course with authentic Asian flair.

2 pork tenderloins (1 pound *each*)
1 teaspoon red liquid food coloring
1/2 teaspoon seasoned salt
1/4 cup pineapple juice
1/4 cup sherry *or* chicken broth
1/4 cup honey
2 tablespoons soy sauce
1 teaspoon minced fresh gingerroot

Brush pork with food coloring and sprinkle with seasoned salt. Place on a rack in a shallow roasting pan. Bake, uncovered, at 425° for 30-35 minutes or until a meat thermometer reads 160°.

In a saucepan, combine the pineapple juice, sherry or broth, honey, soy sauce and ginger. Bring to a boil; simmer, uncovered, for 5 minutes. Thicken if desired. Thinly slice pork; serve with pineapple sauce. **Yield:** 6-8 servings.

Stir-Fried Lemon Chicken

(Pictured on page 177)

Stir-fry is such a terrific entree to serve guests because the main ingredients can be cut up and refrigerated in advance. This recipe created in our Test Kitchen has wonderful lemon flavor.

2 teaspoons cornstarch
1/4 teaspoon plus 1/8 teaspoon ground ginger, *divided*
4 teaspoons soy sauce
1 tablespoon sherry *or* chicken broth
1 tablespoon lemon juice
1-1/2 pounds boneless skinless chicken breasts, cut into 1/2-inch strips
1-1/2 teaspoons grated lemon peel
6 tablespoons vegetable oil, *divided*
1-1/4 cups uncooked long grain rice
2-1/2 cups chicken broth
1/4 teaspoon salt
1/8 teaspoon pepper

1 medium sweet red pepper, cut into 1/4-inch strips
1 medium green pepper, cut into 1/4-inch strips
2 green onions, sliced

In a large bowl, combine the cornstarch and 1/4 teaspoon ginger. Stir in the soy sauce, sherry or broth and lemon juice until smooth. Add the chicken and lemon peel; toss to coat. Refrigerate for 30 minutes.

Heat 2 tablespoons oil in a large saucepan over medium-high heat. Add the rice; cook and stir for 5 minutes or until rice begins to brown. Add the broth, salt, pepper and remaining ginger. Bring to a boil. Reduce heat; cover and cook for 20 minutes or until rice is tender.

In a large skillet or wok, stir-fry peppers in 2 tablespoons oil until crisp-tender. Remove from the skillet and keep warm. In the same pan, cook chicken mixture in remaining oil until chicken juices run clear. Stir in peppers and onions. Serve with rice. **Yield:** 4 servings.

Chinese New Year Table

(Pictured at right)

WHEN setting the table for a Chinese New Year party, make it festive with some time-honored decorations.

In China, the color red represents fire (which drives away bad luck) and prosperity. So use red dishes, table linens and paper lanterns.

Oranges and tangerines are symbols of abundant happiness. Scatter them on the dinner table and send some home with guests.

On the first day of the New Year, it's customary for people of Chinese origin to give children little red envelopes (called lai see), which are filled with money. These filled packets are meant to bring good luck.

No Asian-inspired meal is complete without Fortune Cookies. (See the recipe on page 181.) In the photo above, we created a party favor by putting a Fortune Cookie in a small decorative mesh bag and setting it on top of a plate.

As the finishing touches, we added a napkin folded like a fan (see instructions below) and a set of chopsticks.

FAN NAPKIN FOLD

A FAN napkin fold perfectly plays upon the theme of a Chinese New Year meal. This fold works best with a stiff napkin that holds a crease. Begin by placing a square napkin on a flat surface. Fold two opposite side edges in so that they meet in the center, making a rectangle.

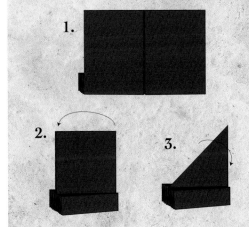

1. Starting at one short end, fold the napkin into 1-inch accordion pleats, stopping about 4 inches from the opposite end. Make sure the fold of the last pleat is at the bottom edge and all the pleats are underneath.

2. Fold the napkin in half lengthwise so half of the pleats are now on top.

3. Fold the upper left corner down and tuck it behind the center pleat, forming a triangle. Release and let the pleats fan out. Adjust folds and back triangle as needed so the fan stands upright.

Fireside Valentine's
Day Dinner

INSTEAD of making reservations and heading to a restaurant for a mediocre meal on Valentine's Day, invite your one and only to a flavorful fireside supper at home!

You'll only have eyes for each other…until you catch a glimpse of Orange-Glazed Cornish Hens! These big birds feature a special seasoned stuffing and finger-licking-good citrus glaze.

You'll both fancy Raspberry Spinach Salad, which pairs berries, sugared almonds and a slightly sweet dressing.

Then show heartfelt affection for each other by sharing succulent Miniature Spiced Chocolate Cakes topped with hot fudge sauce. (All recipes shown at right.)

TABLE FOR TWO

Orange-Glazed Cornish Hens (p. 186)

Raspberry Spinach Salad (p. 188)

Miniature Spiced
Chocolate Cakes (p. 187)

Wild Rice Cheese Soup

The addition of chopped apple, beer and Gouda cheese makes this version of wild rice soup extra special.
—*Christine Paulton, Phelps, Wisconsin*

2 tablespoons finely chopped onion
2 tablespoons butter
1-1/4 cups chicken broth
1 cup chopped peeled apple
1/2 cup beer *or* additional chicken broth
1/2 cup cooked wild rice
1/4 teaspoon white pepper
8 ounces Gouda cheese, shredded

4 teaspoons all-purpose flour
2/3 cup half-and-half cream

In a saucepan, saute onion in butter until tender. Add the broth, apple, beer or additional broth, wild rice and pepper; bring to a boil. Reduce heat; simmer, uncovered, for 10 minutes.

In a bowl, combine cheese and flour; gradually add to soup. Bring to a boil, stirring constantly. Reduce heat to low; stir in cream. Cook for 2-3 minutes or until heated through. **Yield:** 4 servings.

Orange-Glazed Cornish Hens

(Pictured on pages 184 and 185)

When I make these succulent stuffed Cornish hens, my husband's only complaint is that he gets full before he's ready to quit eating!
—*Cathy Broker, Meridian, Idaho*

3 bacon strips, diced
1/2 cup finely shredded carrot
1/4 cup chopped onion
1-1/2 cups unseasoned stuffing cubes
2 tablespoons minced fresh parsley
1/4 teaspoon dried savory
Dash pepper
1/4 teaspoon plus 1/2 teaspoon chicken bouillon granules, *divided*
2 tablespoons hot water
2 Cornish game hens (22 ounces *each*)
1 tablespoon vegetable oil
1/4 cup white wine *or* apple juice

2 tablespoons plus 2/3 cup orange juice, *divided*
1 tablespoon butter
1 tablespoon brown sugar
1-1/2 teaspoons cornstarch

In a small skillet, cook bacon over medium heat until crisp. Remove with a slotted spoon to paper towels. In the drippings, saute carrot and onion until tender; transfer to a large bowl. Stir in the stuffing cubes, parsley, savory, pepper and bacon.

Dissolve 1/4 teaspoon bouillon in hot water; pour over stuffing mixture and gently toss to moisten. Spoon into hens. Tie legs of each hen together; turn wings under backs. Place on a greased rack in a roasting pan. Lightly brush hens with oil; loosely cover with foil. Bake at 375° for 30 minutes.

Meanwhile, in a saucepan, combine the wine or apple juice, 2 tablespoons orange juice and butter. Bring to a boil; remove from the heat. Set aside 1/4 cup for sauce and keep warm. Brush remaining glaze over hens. Bake 40-50 minutes longer or until meat juices run clear and a meat thermometer inserted into stuffing reads 165°, brushing every 15 minutes with glaze.

For sauce, in a small saucepan, combine the brown sugar, cornstarch, and remaining bouillon and orange juice until smooth. Stir in reserved glaze. Bring to a boil; cook and stir for 1-2 minutes or until thickened. Serve with hens. **Yield:** 2 servings.

Miniature Spiced Chocolate Cakes

(Pictured at right and on page 185)

In keeping with chocolate's association with Valentine's Day, our home economists created these individual chocolate cakes. Set out two forks and share this dessert with the one you love!

  2/3 cup butter
    7 ounces German sweet
      chocolate
  1/2 teaspoon ground cardamom
  1/2 teaspoon ground cinnamon
  1/8 teaspoon white pepper
  1/8 teaspoon ground cloves
    3 eggs
    3 egg yolks
  1/2 teaspoon rum extract
  1/2 teaspoon vanilla extract
1-1/2 cups confectioners' sugar
  1/2 cup all-purpose flour
Additional confectioners' sugar
Hot fudge ice cream topping,
    warmed

In a heavy saucepan over low heat, melt the butter, chocolate, cardamom, cinnamon, pepper and cloves; stir until smooth. Remove from the heat; cool for 5 minutes. In a bowl, whisk the eggs, yolks and extracts. Whisk in confectioners' sugar until smooth and blended. Whisk in chocolate mixture. Add flour; whisk until blended.

Pour into four generously greased 6-oz. souffle dishes or custard cups to within 1/4 in. of the top. Place on a baking sheet. Bake at 425° for 15-17 minutes or until a thermometer inserted near the center reads 160°.

Cool on a wire rack for 5 minutes. Remove cakes from dishes to dessert plates. Dust with confectioners' sugar and drizzle with fudge topping. Serve immediately. **Yield:** 4 servings.

Raspberry Spinach Salad

(Pictured on pages 184 and 185)

Sugared almonds provide fun crunch in this slightly sweet spinach salad.
You can easily double the recipe when entertaining a larger group.
—Lauri Mills, Mississauga, Ontario

2-1/4 teaspoons sugar
   2 tablespoons slivered almonds
   5 cups fresh baby spinach
1/2 cup fresh raspberries
DRESSING:
   2 tablespoons vegetable oil
   1 tablespoon raspberry vinegar
   1 tablespoon sugar
3/4 teaspoon poppy seeds
1/2 teaspoon finely chopped
   onion
1/4 teaspoon Worcestershire
   sauce
Dash paprika

In a small heavy skillet, melt sugar over medium heat, stirring constantly. Add almonds; stir to coat. Spread on foil to cool; break apart. In a salad bowl, gently toss the spinach and raspberries.

In a jar with a tight-fitting lid, combine the dressing ingredients; shake well. Pour over salad. Sprinkle with sugared almonds; toss to coat. **Yield:** 4 servings.

Mediterranean Shrimp and Pasta

When our appetites are hearty, I double this dish. The shrimp and pasta are tossed in a light sauce.
—Charolette Westfall, Houston, Texas

   4 ounces uncooked linguine
   3 green onions, thinly sliced
   2 garlic cloves, minced
   2 tablespoons olive oil
1/2 cup sliced fresh mushrooms
   3 plum tomatoes, chopped
   1 jar (6 ounces) marinated
   artichoke hearts, drained
1/4 cup white wine *or* chicken
   broth
   1 teaspoon Italian seasoning
1/4 teaspoon salt
1/8 teaspoon dried rosemary,
   crushed

1/8 teaspoon pepper
1/2 pound medium shrimp, peeled and deveined
Grated Parmesan cheese, optional

Cook linguine according to package directions. Meanwhile, in a skillet, saute onions and garlic in oil until tender. Add mushrooms and tomatoes; cook and stir for 3 minutes. Stir in the artichoke hearts, wine or broth, Italian seasoning, salt, rosemary and pepper. Bring to a boil. Reduce heat; simmer, uncovered, for 5 minutes or until mixture reaches desired thickness.

Add shrimp; cook and stir for 3 minutes or until shrimp turn pink. Drain linguine; top with shrimp mixture and toss to coat. Sprinkle with Parmesan cheese if desired. **Yield:** 2 servings.

Chocolate Cherry Heart

(Pictured at right)

My family enjoys this dessert so much that I make it throughout the year by simply using the pie pastry circles. Packaged products make it a snap to prepare.
—Jackie Hannahs, Fountain, Michigan

1 package (15 ounces) refrigerated pie pastry
2 teaspoons all-purpose flour
1 egg white, beaten
1/4 cup ground almonds
2 tablespoons sugar
1 package (8 ounces) cream cheese, softened
1 cup confectioners' sugar
1/4 to 1/2 teaspoon almond extract
1/2 cup heavy whipping cream
1 jar (16 ounces) hot fudge ice cream topping
2 cans (21 ounces *each*) cherry pie filling

Let pastry stand at room temperature for 15-20 minutes. Unfold pastry and place each circle on an ungreased baking sheet. Sprinkle each with 1 teaspoon flour; turn over. Using a 9-in. paper heart pattern, cut out a heart from each circle. Prick pastries all over with a fork. Brush with egg white. Combine almonds and sugar; sprinkle over pastries. Bake at 450° for 7-9 minutes or until lightly browned. Carefully slide crusts onto wire racks to cool.

In a mixing bowl, combine the cream cheese, confectioners' sugar and almond extract; beat until smooth. Add cream; beat until thickened.

Place one crust on a serving plate; spread with half of the fudge topping. Carefully spread with half of the cream cheese mixture; top with half of the cherry pie filling. Top with remaining crust, fudge topping and cream cheese mixture. Spoon remaining cherry pie filling to within 1 in. of edges. Chill until set. Refrigerate leftovers. **Yield:** 6-8 servings.

Orange Fantasy Fudge

Orange and chocolate team up in this full-flavored fudge. My daughter, Melissa,
created the recipe one day when experimenting in the kitchen.
—Marie Bickel, LaConner, Washington

1-1/2 teaspoons plus 1/2 cup butter, softened, *divided*
1-1/2 cups sugar
1 can (5 ounces) evaporated milk
2 cups (12 ounces) semisweet chocolate chips
1 jar (7 ounces) marshmallow creme
3 teaspoons orange extract
1 teaspoon vanilla extract

Line a 9-in. square pan with foil; grease the foil with 1-1/2 teaspoons butter and set aside. In a heavy saucepan, combine the sugar, milk and remaining butter. Cook and stir over medium heat until sugar is dissolved. Bring to a rapid boil; boil for 5 minutes, stirring constantly.

Reduce heat to low; stir in chocolate chips and marshmallow creme until melted and blended. Remove from the heat; stir in extracts. Pour into prepared pan. Refrigerate overnight or until firm.

Using foil, lift fudge out of pan; carefully peel off foil. Cut fudge into 1-in. squares. Store in the refrigerator. **Yield:** 2-1/4 pounds.

Crab-Stuffed Mushrooms

When my brother arrives at family gatherings, the first thing he asks
is whether or not I brought this appetizer!
—Kelly English, Cogan Station, Pennsylvania

3 tablespoons butter, *divided*
1 tablespoon all-purpose flour
1/2 cup milk
2 slices bread, crusts removed and cubed
1-1/2 teaspoons Worcestershire sauce
1 teaspoon dried minced onion
1/2 cup mayonnaise
1 tablespoon lemon juice
1/2 teaspoon salt
1/8 teaspoon pepper
48 whole medium mushrooms
3 cans (6 ounces *each*) crabmeat, drained, flaked and cartilage removed
Paprika

In a large saucepan, melt 1 tablespoon butter. Stir in flour until smooth. Gradually stir in milk. Bring to a boil over medium heat; cook and stir for 2 minutes or until thickened. Reduce heat; stir in the bread cubes, Worcestershire sauce and onion. Remove from the heat; cool to room temperature. Stir in mayonnaise, lemon juice, salt and pepper; set aside.

Remove and chop the mushroom stems; set caps aside. In a skillet, saute chopped mushrooms and crab in the remaining butter. Using a slotted spoon, transfer to the sauce. Stuff 1 tablespoonful into each mushroom cap. Place on a greased baking sheet; sprinkle with paprika. Bake at 400° for 25-30 minutes or until mushrooms are tender. **Yield:** 4 dozen.

Heartthrob Cookies

(Pictured at right)

I've made these peppermint-flavored cookies for Valentine's Day as well as wedding receptions. I especially like that they don't require frosting.
—*Luella Dirks, Emelle, Alabama*

2 cups butter-flavored
   shortening
2 cups sugar
2 eggs
2 teaspoons vanilla extract
1/4 to 1/2 teaspoon peppermint
   extract
4 cups all-purpose flour
1 teaspoon baking powder
1/4 teaspoon salt
15 drops red food coloring
Red decorating gel

In a large mixing bowl, cream shortening and sugar. Add eggs, one at a time, beating well after each addition. Beat in extracts. Combine the flour, baking powder and salt; gradually add to the creamed mixture. Divide dough in half. Tint one portion pink; leave remaining dough white. Cover and refrigerate for 1 hour or until easy to handle.

On a floured surface, roll out each portion of dough to 1/4-in. thickness. Cut out hearts with a small heart-shaped cookie cutter dipped in flour.

For Heart-to-Heart Cookies: On an ungreased baking sheet, arrange hearts in groups of three in a straight line with sides of hearts touching. Bake at 375° for 8-10 minutes or until edges are lightly browned. Remove to wire racks to cool. Pipe Valentine phrases on cookies.

For Valentine Wreaths: On an ungreased baking sheet, arrange alternating colors of six small hearts in a circle with sides of hearts touching. Bake at 375° for 8-10 minutes or until edges are lightly browned. Remove to wire racks to cool. Pipe Valentine phrases on cookies. **Yield:** about 5-1/2 dozen (depending on size).

Almond French Toast Hearts

I like to surprise my family at breakfast by having heart-shaped French toast on the table.
Confectioners' sugar, strawberries and almond butter tastefully top off each bite.
—Donna Cline, Pensacola, Florida

6 slices bread
2 eggs
1/4 cup milk
1-1/2 teaspoons almond extract,
  divided
2 tablespoons plus 1 cup butter,
  divided
3 tablespoons confectioners'
  sugar
Additional confectioners' sugar
Sliced fresh strawberries

Cut out bread slices with a 3-3/4-in. heart-shaped cookie cutter; discard trimmings. In a shallow bowl, combine the eggs, milk and 1/2 teaspoon almond extract. Dip bread on both sides in egg mixture. In a large skillet, melt 2 tablespoons butter. Fry bread hearts until golden brown on both sides.

For almond butter, in a small mixing bowl, combine confectioners' sugar and remaining butter and extract; mix well. Sprinkle French toast with additional confectioners' sugar. Serve with almond butter and strawberries. **Yield:** 3 servings.

CRUSTS MAKE GREAT CROUTONS

INSTEAD of throwing away the trimmed bread pieces when making Almond French Toast Hearts, use them to make salad croutons!

Cube the bread trimmings and place on a baking pan. Drizzle with melted butter. Season with garlic powder and seasoned salt; toss to coat. Bake at 350° until lightly browned. Turn off the oven and let dry.

Coffee House Slush

Coffee drinks are all the rage these days. This slush rivals any from a gourmet coffee shop.
—Shannon Wade, Kansas City, Kansas

6 cups strong brewed coffee
2 cups sugar
2 quarts milk
1 quart half-and-half cream
4 teaspoons vanilla extract
Whipped cream

In a 5-qt. freezer container, stir coffee and sugar until sugar is dissolved. Stir in the milk, cream and vanilla. Cover and freeze overnight. To serve, thaw in the refrigerator for 8-10 hours or until slushy. Spoon into glasses; garnish with whipped cream. **Yield:** 5 quarts.

Romantic Table for Two

(Pictured at right)

CREATE a cozy atmosphere when making a special meal on Valentine's Day. Begin by draping the table in an elegant cloth with white and red hues. Place a lovely Heart-Shaped Napkin (instructions below) on top of each dinner plate.

Then add some ambiance by creating Rose Candleholders. Here's how:

Cut the stem off of a large rose, making sure the bottom is even. Use your fingers to fully open the rose. If necessary, remove some center petals so there's a small open area in the middle.

Place a tea light candle in a clear tea light holder; set inside the rose. Place the Rose Candleholder on a small saucer or candle base. To prevent wilting, make these flower candleholders just before sitting down to dinner.

HEART-SHAPED NAPKIN

1. Place a square napkin on a flat surface. Fold two opposite side edges in so that they meet in the center, making a rectangle.

2. Fold the rectangle in half lengthwise. Rotate the napkin so that the single fold is on the bottom.

3. With your finger in the center of the rectangle, bring up one end of the napkin until it touches your finger.

4. Bring up the other end so that the two ends touch and a point is formed on the bottom.

5. Tuck under the two upper corners to create a heart shape.

Teddy Bear Birthday Party

KIDS of all ages are crazy about teddy bears. So surprise your little one on their birthday with a fun-filled party centered on those furry friends!

Dessert is a bare necessity for kids. Your own bear cubs will be keen on the tasty assortment pictured at right.

To make tiny tummies growl with delight, have adorable Brown Bear Cake take center stage at the table.

Honey Snack Mix and Bear Claw Cookies fit the bill for energetic kids who crave on-the-go munchies that won't slow them down.

On the following pages, you'll find more main courses, appetizers and sides dishes just right for teddy-bear-loving tykes!

BIRTHDAY BASH

Brown Bear Cake (p. 196)

Honey Snack Mix (p. 199)

Bear Claw Cookies (p. 197)

TEDDY BEAR BIRTHDAY PARTY PLANNER

HOSTING a child's birthday party at home doesn't have to be a bear! Here are some tips to make your teddy bear party a success:

- Purchase teddy bear invitations. Or make your own by using festive paper and a bear or honey pot cookie cutter.
- On the invitations, encourage guests to bring along their favorite teddy bear or other stuffed animal.
- Plan on having the party last for 1-1/2 to 2 hours. Make it clear on the invitation if lunch or just dessert will be served so parents can feed their kids accordingly beforehand.

- Kids love to be involved, so have them help with the invitations, whether it be addressing them, stuffing them or simply putting them in the mailbox.
- For the party, set up two tables...one for the kids and one for their furry friends.
- Don't forget decorations like balloons, party hats and streamers.
- Get the party going with a bear-related game. (See page 200 for *Grrr*eat Teddy Bear Party Games!)
- For party favors, hand out treat bags filled with Honey Snack Mix (page 199) or gummy bears.

Brown Bear Cake

(Pictured on page 195)

Homemade chocolate frosting dresses up a boxed cake mix in this cute cake from our Test Kitchen home economists.

2 packages (18-1/4 ounces *each*) chocolate cake mix
4 ounces cream cheese, softened
1 tablespoon butter, softened
4 cups confectioners' sugar
1/3 cup baking cocoa
1/4 cup milk
3 cups flaked coconut, *divided*
Brown gel food coloring
5 chocolate-covered peppermint patties
16 brown milk chocolate M&M's
2 dark chocolate kisses
5 pieces red shoestring licorice

Prepare cake mixes according to package directions. Pour 3 cups batter into a greased and floured 2-qt. round baking dish. Pour 1-1/2 cups batter into a greased and floured 1-qt. ovenproof bowl. Using remaining batter, fill six greased jumbo muffin cups and four greased regular muffin cups two-thirds full.

Bake cupcakes for 18-20 minutes and cakes for 40-45 minutes at 350° or until a toothpick inserted near the center comes out clean. Cool cupcakes for 5 minutes and cakes for 10 minutes before removing from pans to wire racks to cool completely.

Level the top of the cakes, four jumbo cupcakes and two regular cupcakes. (Save the remaining cupcakes for another use.) Place large cake, top side down, on an 18-in. x 12-in. covered board. For teddy bear's head, place the small cake, top side down, above large cake. Position jumbo cupcakes, cut side up, for arms and legs. Place regular cupcakes on top of head for ears.

In a large mixing bowl, beat the cream cheese and butter until smooth. Add the confectioners' sugar, cocoa and milk;

beat until smooth. Frost tops and sides of cakes and cupcakes. Tint 2-1/4 cups coconut dark brown; tint remaining coconut light brown.

Sprinkle dark brown coconut over arms and legs. Leaving a 4-in. circle in center of bear's body, sprinkle dark brown coconut in a 1-in. circle around edge of cake. Sprinkle dark brown coconut in a 1/2-in. circle around edges of the head and ears. Press dark brown coconut into the sides of the body, head and ears. Sprinkle light brown coconut over the middle of the body, head and ears.

Position one peppermint patty on face for nose. Place one peppermint patty and four M&M's on each paw. Insert chocolate kisses point side down for eyes. Cut one licorice piece into two 2-in. strips; shape to form a mouth. Cut two licorice pieces into a 7-in. strip; place around neck. Shape the remaining licorice into a bow; place below neck. Store in the refrigerator. **Yield:** 18-20 servings.

Bear Claw Cookies

(Pictured at right and on page 195)

Kids can help add the "claws" to our Test Kitchen's clever cookies. Don't be surprised if they swipe a sample before party guests arrive!

  1 cup butter, softened
1-1/2 cups sugar
  2 eggs
  2 teaspoons vanilla extract
  2 cups all-purpose flour
2/3 cup baking cocoa
3/4 teaspoon baking soda
1/2 teaspoon salt
2-1/2 cups sweetened puffed wheat
      cereal
  3 tablespoons semisweet
      chocolate chips, melted
  2 tablespoons slivered almonds

In a mixing bowl, cream butter and sugar. Add eggs, one at a time, beating well after each addition. Beat in vanilla. Combine the flour, cocoa, baking soda and salt; gradually add to creamed mixture. Stir in cereal. Cover and refrigerate for 1 hour or until easy to handle.

Roll into 1-in. balls. Place 2 in. apart on ungreased baking sheets. Flatten with a glass dipped in sugar. Bake at 350° for 9-11 minutes or until edges are firm. Remove to wire racks to cool completely.

Place melted chocolate in a pastry bag or resealable plastic bag; cut a small hole in corner of bag. For bear claws, pipe three small dabs of chocolate on each cookie; top each with an almond. **Yield:** 3 dozen.

Delicious Chicken Dippers

Our home economists coated chicken strips with a slightly sweet sauce before rolling them in a seasoned crumb mixture. Teriyaki sauce complements apricot preserves and honey.

3/4 cup apricot preserves
1/3 cup honey
2 tablespoons teriyaki sauce
1-1/2 teaspoons lemon juice
1-1/2 pounds boneless skinless
    chicken breasts, cut into
    1-inch strips
1-1/2 cups crushed sesame crackers
    (about 38 crackers)
1/2 teaspoon ground ginger
1/4 teaspoon salt

In a bowl, combine the preserves, honey, teriyaki sauce and lemon juice. Set aside 1/2 cup to serve as a dipping sauce. Add chicken to remaining mixture and stir to coat. Let stand for 15 minutes.

In a large resealable plastic bag, combine the cracker crumbs, ginger and salt. With tongs, add chicken in batches to crumb mixture; shake to coat. Place in a single layer on greased baking sheets. Bake at 450° for 9-11 minutes or until juices run clear, turning once. Serve with reserved sauce. **Yield:** 6 servings.

Rainbow Gelatin Salad

This seven-layer gelatin salad will elicit oohs and aahs from all of your guests. It's well worth the time it takes to prepare.
— Dianna Badgett, St. Maries, Idaho

7 packages (3 ounces *each*)
    assorted flavored gelatin
4-1/2 cups boiling water, *divided*
4-1/2 cups cold water, *divided*
1 can (12 ounces) evaporated
    milk, chilled, *divided*

In a bowl, dissolve one package of gelatin in 3/4 cup boiling water. Stir in 3/4 cup cold water. Pour into a 13-in. x 9-in. x 2-in. dish coated with nonstick cooking spray; refrigerate until firm, about 1 hour.

Dissolve a second package of gelatin in 1/2 cup boiling water. Stir in 1/2 cup cold water and 1/2 cup milk. Spoon over the first layer. Chill until firm.

Repeat five times, alternating plain gelatin with creamy gelatin. Chill until each layer is firm before adding the next layer. Refrigerate overnight. Cut into squares. **Yield:** 16-20 servings.

Editor's Note: This salad takes time to prepare since each layer must be set before the next layer is added.

Swiss Swirl Ice Cream Cake

(Pictured at right)

With cake rolls, ice cream and hot fudge, this dessert suits anyone with a sweet tooth. Family and friends get a kick out of this treat's fun appearance.
—*Danielle Hales, Baltimore, Maryland*

10 to 12 Swiss Cake Rolls*
2 pints vanilla ice cream, softened
3/4 cup hot fudge ice cream topping
2 pints chocolate ice cream, softened

Line a 2-qt. bowl with plastic wrap. Cut each cake roll into eight slices; place in prepared bowl, completely covering the bottom and sides. Cover and freeze for at least 20 minutes or until cake is firm.

Spread vanilla ice cream over cake. Cover and freeze for at least 1 hour. Spread with fudge topping. Freeze for at least 1 hour. Spread with chocolate ice cream. Cover and freeze for up to 2 months. Just before serving, remove from the freezer and invert onto a serving plate. Remove bowl and plastic wrap. Cut into wedges. **Yield:** 12-14 servings.

***Editor's Note:** This recipe was tested with Little Debbie Swiss Cake Rolls.

Honey Snack Mix

(Pictured on page 195)

Little cubs can't resist gobbling up the crackers, cereal, raisins and candy in this sweet snack mix created in our Test Kitchen.

1 package (10 ounces) honey-flavored bear-shaped graham crackers (about 4 cups)
3 cups Honeycomb cereal

1-1/2 cups Reese's Pieces
1 cup chocolate-covered raisins

In a large bowl, combine all ingredients. Store in an airtight container. **Yield:** 9 cups.

Teddy Bear Sandwiches

A bear shape is cut out of the top bread slice revealing a special peanut butter filling in these cute sandwiches from our Test Kitchen. Make them ahead or have party guests assemble the sandwiches to their liking.

1-1/3 cups peanut butter
1/4 cup honey
16 slices bread
2 medium bananas, thinly sliced
   or 1/2 cup strawberry jam
24 raisins

In a bowl, combine peanut butter and honey. Spread over eight slices of bread; top with bananas or spread with jam. Using a 4-in. teddy bear cookie cutter, cut a bear shape in the center of the remaining slices of bread; remove centers and save for another use. Place cutout bread over peanut butter. Arrange three raisins on each for eyes and nose. **Yield:** 8 sandwiches.

Peanut Butter Cheese Ball

It's easy to encourage children to eat an apple a day when this creamy peanut butter spread is served with it! I've made this cheese ball for many occasions, and it's always well received.
— Tessie Hughes, Marion, Virginia

1 package (8 ounces) cream cheese, softened
1-1/2 cups peanut butter
1/2 cup confectioners' sugar
1 teaspoon vanilla extract
3/4 cup chopped peanuts
Apple slices

In a small mixing bowl, beat cream cheese until light. Add the peanut butter, confectioners' sugar and vanilla; beat until smooth. Shape into a ball; roll in peanuts. Wrap in plastic wrap. Refrigerate until serving. Serve with apples. **Yield:** 2-1/2 cups.

GRRREAT TEDDY BEAR PARTY GAMES!

KIDS are always game for a little fun like these teddy bear-related ideas:

- **Pin the Bow Tie on the Bear.** Cut out a bear from brown construction paper and bow ties from red paper. Use bandanas for blindfolds. See which guest comes closest to taping their bow tie onto the bear's neck.
- **Honey Pot Guessing Game.** Fill a jar with yellow and black jelly beans (to look like bees). The child whose guess is closest to the actual amount wins and takes the jelly bean-filled jar home.
- **Pass the Teddy Bear.** Purchase an inexpensive stuffed bear. Have the kids sit in a circle. As the music plays, have them pass the bear around the circle. When the music stops, the child holding the bear bows out. The last one remaining wins the bear.

Raspberry Fruit Dip

(Pictured at right)

A cool, creamy raspberry dip enhances the naturally sweet flavor of fruit.
—Dolores Ann Thorp
Mechanicstown, Ohio

1 cup fresh *or* frozen
  unsweetened raspberries,
  thawed
1 package (8 ounces) cream
  cheese, softened
2 tablespoons sugar
Assorted fresh fruit

Place raspberries in a blender or small food processor; cover and process until pureed. Strain to remove seeds. In a small mixing bowl, beat cream cheese and sugar until smooth. Add raspberry puree; beat until well blended. Cover and refrigerate until serving. Serve with fruit. **Yield:** 1-1/2 cups.

Bacon Cheddar Dip

Give this recipe a try if you're looking for a deliciously different dip to serve with crackers, potato chips or vegetables. Ranch salad dressing adds a little zest.
—Kathy Westendorf, Westgate, Iowa

2 cups (16 ounces) sour cream
1 cup (4 ounces) finely
  shredded cheddar cheese
1 envelope ranch salad dressing
  mix
2 to 4 bacon strips, cooked and
  crumbled
Crackers, potato chips *or* fresh
  vegetables

In a bowl, combine the sour cream, cheddar cheese, salad dressing mix and bacon. Cover and refrigerate for at least 1 hour. Serve with crackers, chips or vegetables. **Yield:** 2-1/2 cups.

Memorial Day Get-Together

IT'S TEMPTING to treat Memorial Day simply as the unofficial start of summer.

But when you gather with family and friends over this long weekend, take time to remember those who lost their lives defending our country.

One way to pay tribute is by planning a picnic with an all-American meal.

Topped with Sweet Brown Mustard and Pepper Onion Saute, Grilled Seasoned Bratwurst will shine in this stars-and-stripes menu.

Instead of making an ordinary green salad, display Tomato Zucchini Salad on a pretty platter.

Guests will be in their glory when you tap into Lemon Chiffon Blueberry Dessert. (All recipes shown at right.)

PATRIOTIC PICNIC
(Clockwise from bottom)

Tomato Zucchini Salad (p. 206)

Grilled Seasoned Bratwurst with
Sweet Brown Mustard (p. 204)

Pepper Onion Saute (p. 204)

Lemon Chiffon
Blueberry Dessert (p. 205)

Grilled Seasoned Bratwurst

(Pictured on page 202)

Whether you're hosting a picnic at home or at a park, our Test Kitchen home economists suggest cooking the bratwurst on the stovetop first. Then you can quickly brown them on the grill.

8 uncooked bratwurst links
3 cans (12 ounces *each*) beer *or* nonalcoholic beer
1 large onion, halved and sliced
2 tablespoons fennel seed
8 bratwurst sandwich buns, split

Place the bratwurst in a large saucepan or Dutch oven; add the beer, onion and fennel. Bring to a boil. Reduce heat; cover and simmer for 8-10 minutes or until meat is no longer pink. Drain and discard beer mixture.

Grill bratwurst, covered, over indirect medium heat for 7-8 minutes or until browned. Serve on buns. **Yield:** 8 servings.

Sweet Brown Mustard

(Pictured on page 203)

This versatile sweet and slightly spicy mustard goes well with a variety of meats.
—Rhonda Holloway, Port Richey, Florida

1 can (14 ounces) sweetened condensed milk
1 cup spicy brown mustard
2 tablespoons prepared horseradish
2 tablespoons Worcestershire sauce

In a small bowl, combine all of the ingredients until smooth. Cover and store in the refrigerator for up to 2 weeks. **Yield:** 2-1/3 cups.

Pepper Onion Saute

(Pictured on page 203)

Dress up brats and burgers with this colorful condiment that combines sweet onions and red peppers.
—Pati Fried, Oakland, California

2 large onions, sliced
1/2 teaspoon Italian seasoning
2 tablespoons olive oil
2 large sweet red peppers, julienned

In a large skillet, saute onions and Italian seasoning in oil until tender. Add peppers. Saute until onions begin to brown. **Yield:** 8-10 servings.

Lemon Chiffon Blueberry Dessert

(Pictured at right and on page 203)

This cool and creamy no-bake dessert is perfect for hot summer days. I sometimes replace raspberries for half of the blueberries to make it look more patriotic.
—Jodie Cederquist, Muskegon, Michigan

1-1/2 cups graham cracker crumbs (about 24 squares)
1-1/3 cups sugar, *divided*
1/2 cup butter, melted
1-1/2 cups fresh blueberries, *divided*
1 package (3 ounces) lemon gelatin
1 cup boiling water
2 packages (one 8 ounces, one 3 ounces) cream cheese, softened
1 teaspoon vanilla extract
1 carton (16 ounces) frozen whipped topping, thawed

In a small bowl, combine the cracker crumbs, 1/3 cup sugar and butter. Set aside 2 tablespoons for topping. Press the remaining crumb mixture into a 13-in. x 9-in. x 2-in. dish. Sprinkle with 1 cup blueberries.

In a small bowl, dissolve gelatin in boiling water; cool. In a large mixing bowl, beat cream cheese and remaining sugar. Add vanilla; mix well. Slowly add dissolved gelatin. Fold in whipped topping. Spread over blueberries. Sprinkle with reserved crumb mixture and remaining blueberries. Cover and refrigerate for 3 hours or until set. Refrigerate leftovers. **Yield:** 12-15 servings.

Tomato Zucchini Salad

(Pictured on page 202)

If making this pretty vegetable salad for a potluck, make sure you use
a platter with raised sides to prevent it from spilling when transporting it.
—*Charlotte Bryont, Greensburg, Kentucky*

4 medium zucchini, cut into
    1/4-inch slices
3 medium tomatoes, cut into
    1/4-inch slices
1/3 cup vegetable oil
3 tablespoons white vinegar
1-1/2 teaspoons lemon juice
1 teaspoon sugar
1/2 teaspoon salt
1/2 teaspoon ground mustard
1/2 teaspoon dried oregano
1/4 teaspoon coarsely ground
    pepper
Pitted ripe olives

Place 1 in. of water and zucchini in a skillet; bring to a boil. Reduce heat; cover and simmer for 2-3 minutes or until crisp-tender. Drain and pat dry. Arrange zucchini and tomatoes in alternating circles on a serving platter.

In a jar with a tight-fitting lid, combine the oil, vinegar, lemon juice, sugar, salt, mustard, oregano and pepper; shake well. Drizzle over zucchini and tomatoes. Cover and refrigerate for at least 2 hours. Place olives in center of vegetables. **Yield:** 6 servings.

SUMMER SQUASH SECRETS

SUMMER SQUASH have edible thin skins and soft seeds. Zucchini, pattypan and crookneck are the most common varieties.

Choose firm summer squash with brightly colored skin that's free from spots and bruises. Generally, the smaller the squash, the more tender it will be. Refrigerate summer squash in a plastic bag for up to 5 days.

Before using, wash squash and trim both ends. If using sliced summer squash in salads or stir-fries, blot dry with a paper towel.

One pound summer squash equals about 3 medium or 2-1/2 cups chopped.

Memorable Dill Dip

It's nice to rely on a classic recipe like this when hosting a get-together.
—*Bonnie Davis, Easton, Pennsylvania*

1 cup (8 ounces) sour cream
1 cup mayonnaise
1 tablespoon dried minced onion
1 tablespoon dried parsley flakes
1 tablespoon dill weed
1/4 teaspoon celery salt
1/4 teaspoon garlic powder
1/4 teaspoon coarsely ground pepper
1/8 teaspoon sugar
Assorted fresh vegetables

In a bowl, combine the first nine ingredients. Cover and refrigerate overnight. Serve with vegetables. **Yield:** 2 cups.

Vegetable Shrimp Salad

(Pictured at right)

With shrimp, asparagus and a blend of peppers, this refreshing salad is not only delicious but pleasing to the eye as well!
—Elizabeth Rivera Ortiz
Jayuya, Puerto Rico

1 cup uncooked long grain rice
1/4 pound fresh asparagus, cut into 1-inch pieces
3/4 pound cooked medium shrimp, peeled and deveined
2 jars (7-1/2 ounces *each*) marinated artichoke hearts, drained
1/4 pound fresh snow peas, cut into 1-inch pieces
1/2 cup *each* julienned sweet red, yellow and green pepper
4 green onions, thinly sliced
1 celery rib, sliced
1/4 cup olive oil
3 tablespoons lemon juice
1 tablespoon minced fresh parsley
1 tablespoon soy sauce
1/2 teaspoon lemon-pepper seasoning
Salt and pepper to taste

Cook rice according to package directions; drain and rinse with cold water. Place in a large serving bowl; cool. Place the asparagus in a small saucepan; add a small amount of water. Bring to a boil; cook for 3 minutes. Drain and rinse with cold water.

Add the asparagus, shrimp, artichokes, snow peas, peppers, onions and celery to the rice. In a small bowl, whisk the oil, lemon juice, parsley, soy sauce, lemon-pepper, salt and pepper. Pour over shrimp mixture and toss gently. Chill until serving. **Yield:** 6 servings.

Confetti Guacamole

Whenever I make this colorful guacamole for summer get-togethers,
I'm sure to double the recipe because one batch just isn't enough!
—Cindy Colley, Othello, Washington

2 medium ripe avocados, peeled
1 cup frozen corn, thawed
1 cup canned black beans,
   rinsed and drained
1 medium tomato, peeled,
   seeded and diced
1/4 cup lemon juice
1 tablespoon chopped green
   onion
1 jalapeno pepper, seeded and
   chopped*
1/2 to 1 teaspoon minced garlic
1/2 teaspoon salt
Corn *or* tortilla chips

In a bowl, mash the avocados. Gently stir in the corn, beans, tomato, lemon juice, onion, jalapeno, garlic and salt. Serve immediately with chips. **Yield:** 3-1/2 cups.

   *Editor's Note: When cutting or seeding hot peppers, use rubber or plastic gloves to protect your hands. Avoid touching your face.

SEEDING A JALAPENO PEPPER

TO REDUCE the heat of jalapenos and other hot peppers, cut the peppers in half; remove and discard the seeds and membranes. If you like very spicy foods, add the seeds to the dish you're making instead of discarding them.

Ham 'n' Swiss Potato Salad

With red potatoes, ham, swiss cheese and olives, this potato salad stands out from any others.
I submitted the recipe to our kitchen at work, and now it's on the cafeteria menu!
—Jauneen Hosking, Greenfield, Wisconsin

3 pounds unpeeled small red
   potatoes, cooked and sliced
1/2 pound Swiss cheese, cut into
   1/2-inch cubes
1-1/2 cups mayonnaise
1 teaspoon salt
1 teaspoon minced chives
1/4 teaspoon white pepper
1/4 teaspoon cayenne pepper

1/2 cup cubed fully cooked ham
1 can (2-1/4 ounces) sliced ripe olives, drained

In a large bowl, combine the potatoes and cheese. In a small bowl, combine the mayonnaise, salt, chives, white pepper and cayenne; pour over potato mixture and toss gently to coat. Gently fold in the ham and olives. Cover and chill for 4 hours or until serving. **Yield:** 12 servings.

Antipasto-Stuffed Baguettes

(Pictured at right)

These Italian-style sandwiches can be served as an appetizer or as a light lunch. A homemade olive paste makes every bite delicious.
—Dianne Holmgren, Prescott, Arizona

  1 **can (2-1/4 ounces) sliced ripe olives, drained**
  2 **tablespoons olive oil**
  1 **teaspoon lemon juice**
  1 **garlic clove, minced**
1/8 **teaspoon *each* dried basil, thyme, marjoram and rosemary, crushed**
  2 **French bread baguettes (8 ounces *each*)**
  1 **package (4 ounces) crumbled feta cheese**
1/4 **pound thinly sliced Genoa salami**
  1 **cup packed fresh baby spinach**
  1 **jar (7-1/4 ounces) roasted red peppers, drained and chopped**
  1 **can (14 ounces) water-packed artichoke hearts, drained and chopped**

In a blender or food processor, combine the olives, oil, lemon juice, garlic and herbs; cover and process until olives are chopped. Set aside 1/3 cup olive mixture (refrigerate remaining mixture for another use).

Cut the top third off each baguette; carefully hollow out bottoms, leaving a 1/4-in. shell (discard removed bread or save for another use). Spread olive mixture in the bottom of each loaf. Sprinkle with feta cheese. Fold salami slices in half and place over cheese. Top with the spinach, red peppers and artichokes, pressing down as necessary. Replace bread tops. Wrap loaves tightly in foil. Refrigerate for at least 3 hours or overnight.

Serve cold, or place foil-wrapped loaves on a baking sheet and bake at 350° for 20-25 minutes or until heated through. Cut into slices; secure with a toothpick. **Yield:** 3 dozen.

Editor's Note: 1/3 cup purchased tapenade (olive paste) may be substituted for the olive mixture.

Peanut Butter Oatmeal Cookies

*These soft cookies are a favorite of relatives and friends. When I double the recipe
and take them to work, they always disappear.*
—Kristi Christianson, East Grand Forks, Minnesota

1 jar (12 ounces) peanut butter
1/2 cup butter, softened
1 cup plus 2 tablespoons packed
   brown sugar
1 cup sugar
3 eggs
2 teaspoons baking soda
3/4 teaspoon vanilla extract
3/4 teaspoon corn syrup
4-1/2 cups quick-cooking oats
1 cup (6 ounces) miniature
   semisweet chocolate chips
1/2 cup English toffee bits *or*
   almond brickle chips

In a large mixing bowl, cream the peanut butter, butter and sugars. Add eggs, one at a time, beating well after each addition. Beat in baking soda, vanilla and corn syrup. Stir in the oats, chips and toffee bits.

Drop by rounded tablespoonfuls 2 in. apart onto greased baking sheets. Bake at 350° for 10-12 minutes or until lightly browned. Cool for 1 minute before removing to wire racks. **Yield:** about 6-1/2 dozen.

Editor's Note: Reduced-fat or generic brands of peanut butter are not recommended for this recipe. This recipe does not use flour.

Bacon-Wrapped Beef Patties

*My family loves these spruced-up hamburgers all year long.
Bacon flavors the meat and adds a tasty twist.*
—Jody Bahler, Wolcott, Indiana

1 cup (4 ounces) shredded
   cheddar cheese
2/3 cup chopped onion
1/4 cup ketchup
2 eggs, lightly beaten
3 tablespoons Worcestershire
   sauce
2 tablespoons grated Parmesan
   cheese
1 teaspoon seasoned salt
1/4 teaspoon pepper
2 pounds ground beef
10 bacon strips
10 hamburger buns, split, optional

In a bowl, combine the first eight ingredients. Crumble beef over mixture and mix well. Shape into ten 3/4-in.-thick patties. Wrap each patty with a bacon strip; secure with toothpicks.

Grill patties, uncovered, over medium heat for 5-6 minutes on each side or until juices run clear and a meat thermometer reads 160°. Serve on buns if desired. **Yield:** 10 servings.

Banana Split Ice Cream

(Pictured at right)

Summer celebrations with my family aren't complete until I dish out tasty homemade ice cream. This recipe from my mom is a favorite.
—Kara Cook, Elk Ridge, Utah

3/4 cup plus 2 tablespoons sugar
1 cup water
1 cup milk
2 cups miniature marshmallows
4 teaspoons lemon juice
1 can (8 ounces) crushed
  pineapple, undrained
2 medium ripe bananas, finely
  chopped
1/2 cup chopped maraschino
  cherries, drained and patted
  dry
1 cup heavy whipping cream,
  whipped
Chocolate syrup

In a heavy saucepan, bring the sugar, water and milk to a boil. Reduce heat; cook until sugar is dissolved. Add marshmallows and stir until melted. Remove from the heat; cool for 15 minutes. Stir in lemon juice. Cover and refrigerate for 8 hours or overnight.

Stir in the pineapple, bananas and cherries. Fold in whipped cream. Fill cylinder of ice cream freezer two-thirds full; freeze according to manufacturer's directions. Refrigerate remaining mixture until ready to freeze. Allow to ripen in ice cream freezer or firm up in the refrigerator freezer for 2-4 hours before serving. Serve with chocolate syrup. **Yield:** 1-1/2 quarts.

REMEMBERING THE MEANING OF MEMORIAL DAY

ALTHOUGH Memorial Day has simply come to symbolize the start of summer for many people, its true purpose is to honor the men and women who lost their lives while serving our country.

Here are a few ways you can observe the real meaning of Memorial Day with your family:

- Take time to explain the meaning of Memorial Day to children or grandchildren.

- Proudly fly the American flag.
- Take your family to a Memorial Day parade in your community.
- Place a donation in an American Legion kettle and get a red poppy for your lapel.
- Make a point of attending a ceremony at the local war memorial.
- Stop by a local cemetery and place flags on the graves of fallen soldiers.

Plan a Picnic at the Beach

WHEN YOU pack your picnic basket and head to the beach this summer, skip the standard sandwiches and whet your appetite with some seaside sensations!

Because it can be served cold as well as warm, Oven-Fried Picnic Chicken is a hearty take-along entree that's great for get-togethers all season long.

Beat the summer heat with a cold soup such as Shrimp Gazpacho, featuring the fresh flavors of shrimp, tomatoes, cucumbers and more.

When having fun in the sun, it's best to skip chocolate desserts that can melt. Instead, make a batch of crowd-pleasing Almond-Coconut Lemon Bars. (All recipes shown at right.)

WATERFRONT FARE
(Clockwise from top right)

Almond-Coconut Lemon Bars (p. 214)

Shrimp Gazpacho (p. 215)

Oven-Fried Picnic Chicken (p. 214)

Almond-Coconut Lemon Bars

(Pictured on page 213)

*Our Test Kitchen home economists give traditional lemon bars
a tasty twist with the addition of almonds and coconut.*

1-1/2 cups all-purpose flour
  1/2 cup confectioners' sugar
  1/3 cup blanched almonds, toasted
    1 teaspoon grated lemon peel
  3/4 cup cold butter, cubed
FILLING:
    3 eggs
1-1/2 cups sugar
  1/2 cup flaked coconut, chopped
  1/4 cup lemon juice
    3 tablespoons all-purpose flour
    1 teaspoon grated lemon peel
  1/2 teaspoon baking powder
Confectioners' sugar

In a food processor, combine the flour, confectioners' sugar, almonds and lemon peel; cover and process until nuts are finely chopped. Add butter; pulse just until mixture is crumbly. Press into a greased 13-in. x 9-in. x 2-in. baking dish. Bake at 350° for 20 minutes.

  Meanwhile, in a bowl, whisk eggs, sugar, coconut, lemon juice, flour, lemon peel and baking powder; pour over the hot crust. Bake for 20-25 minutes or until light golden brown. Cool on a wire rack. Dust with confectioners' sugar. Cut into squares. **Yield:** 3-4 dozen.

Oven-Fried Picnic Chicken

(Pictured on page 212)

*My great-grandson Austin eats only chicken, so it appears on the menu at every family gathering.
This version, which marinates chicken in lemonade, is among his favorites.*
—Anneliese Deising, Plymouth, Michigan

  1 can (12 ounces) frozen
    lemonade concentrate,
    thawed
  1 broiler/fryer chicken (3 to 4
    pounds), cut up
1/2 cup plus 2 tablespoons
    all-purpose flour
1-1/2 teaspoons salt
  1/2 teaspoon pepper
  1 cup vegetable oil
  2 tablespoons butter, melted

Refrigerate 1/4 cup lemonade concentrate for basting. Pour remaining concentrate into a large resealable plastic bag; add chicken. Seal bag and turn to coat; refrigerate for 4 hours, turning occasionally.

  Drain and discard marinade from chicken. In a large resealable plastic bag, combine the flour, salt and pepper. Add chicken, a few pieces at a time, and shake to coat. In a large skillet, brown chicken in oil for 1-1/2 to 2 minutes on each side or until golden brown.

  Place chicken on a rack in a shallow roasting pan. Brush with butter. Bake, uncovered, at 350° for 50-55 minutes or until juices run clear, basting with reserved lemonade concentrate every 15 minutes. Serve warm or cold. **Yield:** 4-6 servings.

Shrimp Gazpacho

(Pictured at right and on page 213)

This refreshing tomato-based soup from our Test Kitchen features shrimp, cucumber and avocados.

6 cups spicy V8 juice
2 cups cold water
1 pound cooked medium shrimp, peeled and deveined
2 medium tomatoes, seeded and diced
1 medium cucumber, seeded and diced
2 medium ripe avocados, diced
1/2 cup lime juice
1/2 cup minced fresh cilantro
1/2 teaspoon salt
1/4 to 1/2 teaspoon hot pepper sauce

In a large bowl, combine all ingredients. Cover and refrigerate for 1 hour. Serve cold. **Yield:** 12 servings (about 3 quarts).

Editor's Note: This recipe is best served the same day it's made.

PLASTIC CUPS SERVE AS SOUP BOWLS!

WHEN hosting an informal gathering like a beach picnic, keep the dinnerware casual as well. For example, serve Shrimp Gazpacho in disposable plastic drinking cups along with plastic spoons, as shown in the photo above.

Disposable plastic serving dishes are easy to transport and can be tossed away when finished, leaving you with fewer things to pack up at the end of the day.

Simple Citrus Punch

There's no doubt this refreshing beverage will quench your summertime thirst!
—Irene Kusler, Eureka, South Dakota

1 can (12 ounces) frozen limeade concentrate, thawed
3/4 cup lemonade concentrate
2 cups water
1/4 cup sugar, optional
2 liters ginger ale, chilled
Ice cubes

In a large punch bowl, combine the limeade and lemonade concentrates. Stir in water and sugar if desired. Stir in the ginger ale. Serve immediately over ice. **Yield:** about 3 quarts.

Peppery Grilled Steaks

Coarsely ground pepper adds the perfect amount of spice to flank steaks.
We enjoy this grilled entree year-round.
—*Lynn McAllister, Mt. Ulla, North Carolina*

1/4 cup red wine vinegar
1/4 cup olive oil
1/4 cup Dijon mustard
　4 garlic cloves, minced
　2 green onions, chopped
　4 teaspoons coarsely ground
　　pepper
　1 teaspoon dried thyme
　1 teaspoon dried rosemary,
　　crushed
1/2 teaspoon salt
　3 beef flank steaks (about 1
　　pound *each*)

In a large resealable plastic bag, combine the vinegar, oil, mustard, garlic, onions, pepper, thyme, rosemary and salt; add steaks. Seal bag and turn to coat; refrigerate for 8 hours or overnight.

　Drain and discard marinade. Grill steaks, covered, over medium heat for 6-10 minutes on each side or until meat reaches desired doneness (for rare, a meat thermometer should read 140°; medium, 160°; well-done, 170°). **Yield:** 10-12 servings.

Vegetable Barley Salad

I often serve this salad as an entree on summer nights when it's too hot to eat a heavy meal.
The recipe makes a big batch, which is terrific for taking to potlucks.
—*Patricia Lewandowski, Warwick, Massachusetts*

　4 cups water
　2 cups uncooked medium pearl
　　barley
　2 cups fresh broccoli florets
　2 cups diced carrots
　1 cup halved cherry *or* grape
　　tomatoes
1/2 cup chopped green onions
1/2 cup julienned sweet red *or*
　　green pepper
1/4 cup sunflower kernels
1/2 cup lemon juice
1/2 cup olive oil
1/4 cup white wine vinegar
　2 teaspoons grated lemon peel
　2 garlic cloves, peeled
1/2 teaspoon salt

1/4 to 1/2 teaspoon pepper
　1 tablespoon grated Parmesan cheese

In a large saucepan, bring water to a boil. Add the barley. Reduce heat; cover and cook for 30-35 minutes or until tender. Rinse with cold water; drain well.

　Place broccoli and carrots in a steamer basket. Place in a saucepan over 1 in. of water; bring to a boil. Cover and steam for 3-4 minutes or until crisp-tender. Rinse with cold water; drain.

　In a large salad bowl, combine the barley, broccoli and carrots, tomatoes, onions, red pepper and sunflower kernels. In a blender, combine the lemon juice, oil, vinegar, lemon peel, garlic, salt and pepper; cover and process until combined. Pour over barley mixture and stir to coat. Refrigerate for at least 1 hour. Just before serving, sprinkle with Parmesan cheese. **Yield:** 14 servings.

Crab-Salad Jumbo Shells

(Pictured at right)

I received this recipe from a friend and adjusted the ingredients to suit my family's tastes. It's a fun and flavorful way to serve crab salad.
—JoAnne Anderson, Knoxville, Iowa

30 jumbo pasta shells
1 cup finely chopped fresh
   broccoli florets
1 garlic clove, minced
2 packages (8 ounces *each*)
   imitation crabmeat, chopped
1 cup (8 ounces) sour cream
1/2 cup mayonnaise
1/4 cup finely shredded carrot
1/4 cup diced seeded peeled
   cucumber
1 tablespoon chopped green
   onion
1 teaspoon dill weed

Cook pasta according to package directions; rinse in cold water and drain well. In a microwave-safe bowl, combine the broccoli and garlic. Cover and microwave on high for 1 minute or until crisp-tender. Transfer to a large bowl; stir in the remaining ingredients. Stuff into pasta shells. Cover and refrigerate overnight. **Yield:** 30 stuffed shells.

Family Traditions

Every summer we head to North Carolina's Outer Banks for a week-long vacation with my husband's family. To prevent chaos in the kitchen of our rented beach house, we've developed a schedule where each family cooks dinner one night, while another family cleans up. We've had fun sampling a variety of foods!
—Diana Leskauskas
Chatham, New Jersey

Chicken-Spinach Pasta Salad

*Hot summer nights call for cool salads such as this. I created the recipe by accident
one day when tossing together whatever ingredients I had on hand.*
—Diane Weiss, Royal Oak, Michigan

1-3/4 cups uncooked small pasta
    shells
  4 cups baby spinach
2-1/2 cups julienned cooked chicken
  1/2 cup crumbled blue cheese
  1/4 cup pine nuts
DRESSING:
  1 tablespoon water
  1 tablespoon lemon juice
  1 tablespoon white balsamic
    vinegar
  1 tablespoon vegetable oil
  1 tablespoon minced chives
  1/2 teaspoon Dijon mustard
  1/4 teaspoon dried basil
Dash *each* garlic powder and
  cayenne pepper

Cook pasta according to package directions; rinse in cold water and drain well. In a large bowl, gently toss the pasta, spinach, chicken, blue cheese and pine nuts. In a small bowl, whisk the dressing ingredients. Drizzle over salad and toss to coat. Serve immediately. **Yield:** 6-8 servings.

Al Fresco Watermelon Salad

*This unique onion and watermelon salad makes appearances at many family gatherings
in summer. The savory seasonings complement every bite of sweet melon.*
—Lorraine Wilson, Woodsfield, Ohio

  4 cups cubed seeded watermelon
  1 medium sweet onion,
    quartered and thinly sliced
  2 tablespoons minced fresh basil
  1/4 cup balsamic vinegar
Salt and pepper to taste

In a large bowl, combine the watermelon, onion and basil. Drizzle with vinegar; toss gently. Add salt and pepper. Refrigerate for up to 1 hour. Serve with a slotted spoon. **Yield:** 4-6 servings.

ARE YOU SWEET ON ONIONS?

FOR the best flavor, make Al Fresco Watermelon Salad (above) with sweet onions, such as Vidalia, Walla Walla or Bermuda.

Hazelnut Madeleine Cookies

(Pictured at right)

As an appropriate dessert for a beach picnic, our home economists came up with these cookies, which bake in a shell-shaped Madeleine pan.

1/2 cup whole hazelnuts, toasted
1 tablespoon confectioners' sugar
1 tablespoon plus 1/2 cup butter, *divided*
2 tablespoons plus 1 cup all-purpose flour, *divided*
2 eggs, *separated*
2/3 cup sugar
1/4 teaspoon vanilla extract
1 teaspoon baking powder
1/8 teaspoon salt
Additional confectioners' sugar, optional

In a food processor, combine the hazelnuts and confectioners' sugar; cover and process until nuts are finely chopped. Set aside. Melt 1 tablespoon butter. Brush two Madeleine pans with butter. Dust with 2 tablespoons flour; tap pans to remove excess flour and set aside. Place remaining butter in a saucepan. Melt over low heat for 4-5 minutes or until a light amber color; set aside to cool.

In a large mixing bowl, beat egg yolks and sugar until thick and a pale lemon color. Stir in melted butter and vanilla. Combine the baking powder, salt and remaining flour; stir into butter mixture just until combined. In a small mixing bowl, beat egg whites on high speed until stiff peaks form; fold into batter. Gently fold in reserved nut mixture.

With a tablespoon, fill prepared pans two-thirds full. Bake at 325° for 18-20 minutes or until golden brown. Cool for 2 minutes before inverting pans onto wire racks to remove cookies. Cool completely. Lightly dust with additional confectioners' sugar if desired. **Yield:** 2 dozen.

Editor's Note: Madeleine pans can be ordered from Sweet Celebrations. Call 1-800/328-6722 or visit their Web site, *www.sweetc.com*. They are also available from Williams-Sonoma. Call 1-877/812-6235 or visit their Web site, *www.williams-sonoma.com*.

MAKING MADELEINE COOKIES

BRUSH Madeleine pans with melted butter. Dust with flour; tap pans to remove excess. Fill pans two-thirds full with batter; bake as directed.

Pineapple Mango Salsa

This fruit salsa served with tortilla chips is great for summer barbecues.
It also can be served alongside fish and chicken entrees.
—Mary Gloede, Lakewood, Wisconsin

1 cup chopped peeled mango
1 cup pineapple tidbits
1/2 cup diced sweet red pepper
1 plum tomato, seeded and
    chopped
3 tablespoons minced fresh
    cilantro
2 green onions, sliced
2 tablespoons lime juice
1 tablespoon lemon juice
1 jalapeno pepper, finely
    chopped*
Tortilla chips

In a bowl, combine the first nine ingredients. Cover and refrigerate for 1 hour or until chilled. Serve with tortilla chips. **Yield:** 2-2/3 cups.

    *Editor's Note: When cutting or seeding hot peppers, use rubber or plastic gloves to protect your hands. Avoid touching your face.

NIFTY NATURAL PAPER WEIGHT

SPEND any time at the beach and you know it can get pretty breezy! To stop a gust of wind from blowing away paper plates and napkins, create a paper weight from an ordinary rock, as shown in the photo at right and on page 212.

Chicken Salad Croissants

Fresh dill is the secret to the success of these cold sandwiches.
I like to use miniature croissants when serving them as an appetizer.
—Jessie Yates, Monette, Arkansas

3 cups diced grilled chicken
1 can (11 ounces) mandarin
    oranges, drained and halved
1 cup halved seedless red
    grapes
2 celery ribs, finely chopped
1/2 cup mayonnaise
1/4 cup sunflower kernels

2 tablespoons minced fresh dill *or* 2 teaspoons dill
    weed
7 croissants *or* 21 miniature croissants, split

In a bowl, combine the first seven ingredients. Spoon onto croissants; replace tops. If using large croissants, cut into thirds. Serve immediately. **Yield:** 21 servings.

Homemade Sand Castles

(Pictured above)

*These cute sand castles remain intact indefinitely. You can use them as
a table topper at home or take them to the beach for a picnic table centerpiece.*

1/3 cup all-purpose flour
2 tablespoons sugar
1 cup cold water
6 cups moist sand
**Sand castle molds of various shapes
and sizes**
Nautical rope, rocks and seashells

In a saucepan, combine flour and sugar. Gradually add cold water; mix well. Cook and stir over low heat until mixture thickens to pudding consistency.

Place sand in a large pail; stir in flour mixture. When cool to the touch, mix together with your hands, adding more water if needed so that sand holds its shape. Firmly pack into molds. Invert on a flat surface; remove molds.

Let dry completely before handling. Depending on the humidity, this may take a few days.

To create a centerpiece, weave rope between the sand castles; fill in with sand, rocks and seashells.

Editor's Note: The sand mixture will keep for weeks when stored in an airtight container.

MAKING HOMEMADE SAND CASTLES

1. Stir the warm flour mixture into the sand. When cool to the touch, mix together with your hands.

2. Firmly pack sand mixture into sand castle molds.

3. Unmold onto a flat surface. Let stand until completely dry.

SPECIAL Celebrations

Ladies' Luncheon in the Garden

AT THE HEIGHT of summer, it's fun to incorporate fresh herbs and edible flowers into every aspect of your cooking.

Celebrate the fabulous flavors of this all-too-short season by hosting a glorious garden party for a few friends.

Start by setting up a table in the backyard to catch a cool breeze through the trees.

As guests arrive, welcome them around back for a refreshing beverage like Peachy Lemonade.

Soak up every second of summer as you nibble on Herbed Shrimp Appetizer and a selection of fresh breads topped with Garlic Basil Butter. (All recipes shown at right.)

This chapter also features a selection of entrees, side dishes and desserts that showcase the summer's freshest flavors.

Garden Party

Peachy Lemonade (p. 227)

Herbed Shrimp Appetizer (p. 225)

Garlic Basil Butter (p. 229)

Thyme 'n' Thyme Again Salad Dressing

You just can't beat the flavor of fresh herbs. For a little extra zest,
I sometimes use lemon or caraway thyme.
—Barbara Balazs, Huntington Beach, California

1/3 cup olive oil
1/4 cup red wine vinegar
1/4 cup crumbled feta cheese
2 tablespoons minced fresh thyme
1 tablespoon minced fresh oregano
1 tablespoon minced fresh marjoram
1 tablespoon Dijon mustard
1 garlic clove, minced
1-1/2 to 2 teaspoons sugar
1/4 teaspoon white pepper
1/8 teaspoon salt
Mixed salad greens

In a jar with a tight-fitting lid, combine the first 11 ingredients. Shake well just before serving over salad greens. Store in the refrigerator. **Yield:** 1 cup.

Lemon Balm Bread

This moist quick bread tastes best the day after it's made.
Lemon balm is a lovely addition to both the batter and glaze.
—Connie Yeagley, Cleona, Pennsylvania

1/2 cup butter, softened
1 cup sugar
1/4 cup finely chopped lemon balm leaves
2 eggs
1-1/2 cups all-purpose flour
1-1/2 teaspoons baking powder
1/4 teaspoon salt
1/2 cup milk
1/4 cup chopped walnuts, optional
1 tablespoon grated lemon peel
GLAZE:
1/3 cup sugar
2 tablespoons water
1 tablespoon lemon juice
2 tablespoons finely chopped lemon balm leaves

In a large mixing bowl, cream the butter, sugar and lemon balm. Add eggs, one at a time, beating well after each addition. Combine the flour, baking powder and salt; add to creamed mixture alternately with milk. Stir in walnuts if desired and lemon peel. Pour into a greased 8-in. x 4-in. x 2-in. loaf pan. Bake at 350° for 50-60 minutes or until a toothpick comes out clean.

In a small bowl, whisk the sugar, water and lemon juice; stir in lemon balm. Spoon over warm bread while still in pan. Cool for 10 minutes before removing from pan to a wire rack to cool completely. **Yield:** 1 loaf.

Herbed Shrimp Appetizer

(Pictured at right and on page 223)

As guests arrive at your garden party, encourage them to sample these marinated shrimp from our Test Kitchen. Herbs, lime juice and red peppers give them great flavor.

3/4 cup olive oil
1/3 cup lime juice
1/3 cup diced sweet red pepper
1/3 cup diced sweet onion
3 garlic cloves, minced
4 teaspoons minced chives
2 teaspoons minced fresh tarragon
2 teaspoons snipped fresh dill
1-1/2 pounds cooked large shrimp, peeled and deveined
Nasturtiums, calendula, rosemary, dill sprigs and flat leaf parsley

In a bowl, combine the first eight ingredients. Place the shrimp in a large resealable plastic bag; add herb mixture. Seal bag and toss to coat. Refrigerate for at least 4 hours. With a slotted spoon, transfer shrimp to a serving bowl. Garnish with flowers and herbs. **Yield:** about 4 dozen.

HOW TO COOK RAW SHRIMP

TO COOK raw shrimp in water, add 1 pound shrimp (with or without shells) and 1 teaspoon salt to 3 quarts boiling water. Reduce heat and simmer, uncovered, for 1 to 3 minutes or until the shrimp turns pink.

Watch closely to avoid overcooking. The meat of uncooked shrimp will turn from translucent when raw to pink and opaque when cooked. Drain immediately.

Pesto Chicken

These pesto-filled chicken rolls-ups from our Test Kitchen can be served warm
as an entree or cooled and sliced for an elegant appetizer.

1 cup loosely packed fresh basil
   leaves
1/4 cup minced fresh parsley
1/4 cup grated Parmesan cheese
1/4 cup olive oil
1 tablespoon pine nuts
1 to 2 garlic cloves
4 boneless skinless chicken
   breast halves
1/2 teaspoon salt
1/4 teaspoon pepper
2 tablespoons butter, melted

For pesto, combine the first six ingredients in a blender; cover and process until blended. Flatten chicken to 1/4-in. thickness; sprinkle with salt and pepper. Spread each with 2 tablespoons pesto to within 1/2 in. of the edges. Roll up jelly-roll style, starting with a short side; secure with a toothpick or small metal skewer.

Place chicken in a greased 11-in. x 7-in. x 2-in. baking dish; brush with butter. Bake, uncovered, at 375° for 30 to 35 minutes or until chicken juices run clear. Remove toothpicks or skewers. Serve warm as a main course.

For an appetizer, cool for 15 minutes, then refrigerate until chilled. Cut cold chicken into 1/2-in. slices. **Yield:** 4 main course or 12-16 appetizer servings.

Dandelion Potato Salad

Friends and family will love the crunchy produce in this tasty potato salad.
Dandelion leaves are a deliciously different addition in spring.
—*Florence Tice, Rushville, Indiana*

4 hard-cooked eggs
1-1/3 cups water
1-1/2 teaspoons salt, *divided*
4 cups cubed peeled potatoes
1/2 cup sugar
4 teaspoons all-purpose flour
1/2 cup white vinegar
1 teaspoon prepared mustard
1-1/2 cups diced onions
1/4 cup mayonnaise
3/4 teaspoon celery salt
1/4 teaspoon garlic powder
1/4 teaspoon pepper
1/2 cup chopped green pepper
1/2 cup chopped sweet red pepper
1/2 cup sweet pickle relish

1 to 1-1/2 cups snipped dandelion *or* spinach leaves
Paprika

Peel eggs. Chop three eggs and slice one for garnish; set aside. In a saucepan, bring water and 1 teaspoon salt to a boil over medium heat. Add potatoes. Cook until tender. Meanwhile, in another saucepan, combine sugar, flour, vinegar and mustard until smooth. Bring to a boil; cook and stir for 2 minutes or until thickened. Add onions; cook 2 minutes longer. Drain potatoes; add onion mixture.

In a small bowl, combine the mayonnaise, celery salt, garlic powder, pepper and remaining salt. Add to the potato mixture; toss to coat. Stir in the chopped eggs, green and red peppers, pickle relish and dandelion leaves. Cover and refrigerate until serving. Garnish with sliced egg; sprinkle with paprika. **Yield:** 10-12 servings.

Peachy Lemonade

(Pictured at right and on page 223)

Our home economists perk up plain lemonade with peach nectar. Frozen peach slices serve as clever ice cubes that keep this beverage cool without diluting the flavor.

2 quarts lemonade
2 cans (5-1/2 ounces *each*) peach *or* apricot nectar
1 cup frozen peach slices
Fresh mint sprigs, snapdragons and lemon balm

In a 3-qt. glass pitcher, combine the lemonade and nectar; refrigerate until chilled. Just before serving, stir the lemonade mixture; add frozen peach slices. Place mint sprigs along the sides of the pitcher and float the flowers on top of the lemonade. **Yield:** about 2-1/2 quarts.

BEADED BEVERAGE COVERS

ALONG with summer's beautiful weather come pesky bugs and bees! Discourage these uninvited guests from sampling your Peachy Lemonade by making Beaded Beverage Covers (as shown above).

Purchase small square cloth doilies. To create weights, string beads onto a threaded needle and sew them onto each corner of the doily.

Have these beaded doilies on the table so that guests can keep their beverages covered.

Marigold Cheese Dip

Have a backyard bed of marigolds? Share some with guests the next time you entertain by adding them to a cream cheese dip. It's a surprisingly delicious appetizer.
—Dixie Terry, Marion, Illinois

1 package (8 ounces) cream
   cheese, softened
1 cup (8 ounces) sour cream
1/4 teaspoon vanilla extract
1/4 to 1/2 teaspoon salt
1/4 teaspoon coarsely ground
   pepper
1 teaspoon minced chives
1 teaspoon minced fresh savory
1 teaspoon minced fresh
   marigold petals
Assorted crackers

In a small mixing bowl, beat the cream cheese, sour cream, vanilla, salt and pepper until smooth. Stir in the chives, savory and marigold petals. Cover and refrigerate for at least 1 hour. Serve with crackers. **Yield:** 2 cups.

Asparagus Soup with Herbs

The fresh flavor of herbs shines through in this special soup. Because it calls for frozen asparagus, you can make it any time of year.
—Bev Smith, Ferndale, Washington

1 large onion, chopped
2 garlic cloves, minced
2 tablespoons olive oil
2 cans (14-1/2 ounces *each*)
   chicken broth
1 cup minced fresh parsley
1 large carrot, cut into 1-inch
   pieces
5 fresh basil leaves, minced
1 to 2 teaspoons minced fresh
   tarragon
1/2 teaspoon salt
1/4 teaspoon pepper
Dash cayenne pepper

1 package (10 ounces) frozen asparagus spears,
   thawed
Sour cream and chopped tomatoes, optional

In a large saucepan, saute onion and garlic in oil until tender. Stir in the broth, parsley, carrot, basil, tarragon, salt, pepper and cayenne. Cut asparagus into 1-in. pieces; set tips aside. Add asparagus pieces to saucepan. Bring to a boil. Reduce heat; cover and simmer for 20 minutes or until vegetables are tender. Cool slightly.

Puree soup in batches in a blender. Return to the saucepan. Stir in asparagus tips; cook for 5 minutes or until crisp-tender. Garnish with sour cream and tomatoes if desired. **Yield:** 4 servings.

Garlic Basil Butter

(Pictured at right and on page 223)

Instead of serving plain butter alongside an assortment of fresh breads, prepare this herb-laden whipped butter from our home economists.

1/2 cup butter, softened
  4 teaspoons minced fresh basil
1-1/2 teaspoons minced fresh parsley
1/2 teaspoon garlic powder
Fresh sage and thyme

In a small mixing bowl, combine the butter, basil, parsley and garlic powder. Beat on medium-low speed until mixture is combined. Garnish with sage and thyme. **Yield:** 1/2 cup.

Mint Salad Dressing

Fresh mint is a popular perennial herb that will grow in almost any soil. Here it stars in a special salad dressing.
—Suzanne McKinley, Lyons, Georgia

1/2 cup sugar
1/4 cup water
  1 tablespoon minced fresh mint leaves
1/2 cup olive oil
  4 teaspoons lemon juice
  1 teaspoon salt
1/2 teaspoon paprika
Mixed salad greens

In a saucepan, combine the sugar, water and mint. Simmer for 1-2 minutes or until sugar is dissolved. Remove from the heat; cover and let stand for 1 hour. Strain and discard mint.

Place olive oil in a small bowl; whisk in mint syrup. Whisk in lemon juice, salt and paprika. Drizzle over salad greens. **Yield:** 3/4 cup.

Rose Petal Sorbet

(Pictured at right)

Hot summer days call for a refreshing sorbet.
This recipe from our Test Kitchen combines pleasing citrus and floral flavors.

2 cups red *or* pink rose petals
2-1/4 cups sugar, *divided*
4 cups water
6 medium juice oranges
6 to 14 drops red food coloring,
   optional

With kitchen scissors, cut off the white portion at the stem end of each rose petal. With a mortar and pestle or in a food processor, mash or process petals into a paste, gradually adding 1/4 cup sugar. In a saucepan, bring water to a boil. Stir in remaining sugar until dissolved. Stir in the rose paste. Boil, without stirring, for 10 minutes. Remove from the heat; cool for at least 1 hour.

Strain, reserving rose syrup. Discard rose pulp. Squeeze the juice from the oranges and strain; discard pulp and seeds. Add 2-2/3 cups orange juice and food coloring if desired to the rose syrup. Transfer to a freezer container; cover and freeze for at least 8 hours or until firm. **Yield:** 10 servings.

Parmesan Salmon Fillets

Our home economists top pan-fried salmon with a salsa-like compote for a colorful summer entree.
If you can't find lovage leaves, use celery leaves instead.

TOMATO LOVAGE COMPOTE:
2 large tomatoes, seeded and
   chopped
1/2 cup finely chopped red onion
1/3 cup minced lovage *or* celery
   leaves
1/4 cup lemon juice
1/4 cup olive oil
1 tablespoon grated lemon peel
1/2 teaspoon salt
1/2 teaspoon hot pepper sauce
SALMON:
1 egg
2 tablespoons milk

1 cup dry bread crumbs
1/2 cup grated Parmesan cheese
4 salmon fillets (6 ounces *each*)
3 tablespoons vegetable oil

In a large bowl, gently toss the compote ingredients. Cover and let stand at room temperature for 1 hour.

In a shallow bowl, whisk the egg and milk. In another shallow bowl, combine bread crumbs and Parmesan cheese. Pat salmon dry with paper towels. Dip in milk mixture, then coat with crumb mixture. In a large nonstick skillet, cook the salmon in oil over medium-high heat until fish flakes easily with a fork, turning once. Serve with compote. **Yield:** 4 servings.

Citrus-Scented Geranium Cookies

(Pictured at right)

Geraniums are one of my favorite flowers. Not only are they beautiful garden accents, but they can enhance any culinary dish. Any scented geranium leaf can be used in this cookie recipe.
—Emma Marshall, Savannah, Georgia

1 cup butter, softened
1-1/2 cups confectioners' sugar
1 egg
2 tablespoons finely chopped lemon-, lime- *or* orange-scented geranium leaves
1 tablespoon lemon juice
1 teaspoon vanilla extract
1/8 teaspoon almond extract
2-1/2 cups all-purpose flour
1 teaspoon baking soda
1 teaspoon cream of tartar

LEMON GLAZE:
1 cup confectioners' sugar
2 teaspoons lemon juice
2 to 3 teaspoons water
1/4 teaspoon vanilla extract

In a large mixing bowl, cream butter and confectioners' sugar. Beat in the egg, geranium leaves, lemon juice and extracts. Combine the flour, baking soda and cream of tartar; gradually add to creamed mixture. Cover and refrigerate for 2 hours or until easy to handle.

Divide dough in half. On a lightly floured surface, roll out each portion to 1/4-in. thickness. Cut with a 2-in. cookie cutter dipped in sugar. Place 2 in. apart on greased baking sheets. Bake at 375° for 9-10 minutes or until edges are lightly browned. Remove to wire racks to cool. In a small bowl, combine glaze ingredients. Brush over cooled cookies. **Yield:** 3 dozen.

Watercress Dip

This dip developed in our Test Kitchen is similar to mock guacamole.
A bit of horseradish gives it some zip.

1 tablespoon lemon juice
1 tablespoon prepared
  horseradish
1 garlic clove, minced
1/2 teaspoon salt
1/4 teaspoon white pepper
1 bunch watercress, trimmed
  (about 6 cups)

4 green onions, cut into fourths
1 package (8 ounces) cream cheese, cubed
Tortilla chips

In a food processor or blender, combine the first seven ingredients. Cover and process until finely chopped. Add cream cheese; process until creamy and blended. Refrigerate until serving. Serve with chips. **Yield:** 1-3/4 cups.

Penne with Edible Flowers

Our home economists color a flavorful side dish with pretty purple chive blossoms and
the petals of edible flowers. Serve this hot pasta dish with a variety of entrees.

1 package (1 pound) penne *or*
  medium tube pasta
3 garlic cloves, minced
3 tablespoons olive oil
1 cup oil-packed sun-dried
  tomatoes, drained and thinly
  sliced
1/4 cup minced fresh parsley
6 chive blossoms, broken into
  florets
3 tablespoons minced fresh
  chives
1 cup assorted edible flower
  petals

Cook pasta according to package directions. Meanwhile, in a small skillet, saute garlic in oil for 1 minute. Drain pasta. In a large bowl, toss the pasta, garlic, tomatoes, parsley, chive blossoms, chives and flowers. Serve immediately. **Yield:** 10-12 servings.

COOKING WITH EDIBLE FLOWERS

SEVERAL recipes in the chapter call for edible fresh flowers. Make sure to properly identify flowers before picking and use *only* the petals or blossoms (not the stems, leaves, pistil or stamen). Double-check that they're edible and have not been treated with chemicals. (If you're unsure if a flower is edible, check with your local poison control center.)

Types of edible flowers include calendula, chrysanthemum, common wild violet, dandelion, daylily, dianthus, edible orchid, fuchsia, impatiens, lilac, marigold, nasturtium, pansy, rose, snapdragon and scented geranium.

Daylily Salad

(Pictured at right)

Daylily buds add color to this creative salad. The flavor is a cross between lettuce and cabbage.
—Janice Graves, Blountsville, Alabama

2 cups daylily buds (about 50 buds), sliced
1 cup torn lettuce
1/2 medium cucumber, sliced
1 medium tomato, diced
2 celery ribs, sliced
1/4 cup shredded red cabbage
3 radishes, sliced
Salad dressing of your choice

In a large salad bowl, combine the daylily buds, lettuce, cucumber, tomato, celery, cabbage and radishes. Serve with dressing. **Yield:** 4-6 servings.

Nasturtium Spread

I love to graze on nasturtiums and cherry tomatoes while working in my garden. These pretty flowers taste as good as they look!
—Sonya Anthony, Mt. Auburn, Illinois

1 package (8 ounces) cream cheese, softened
1/4 cup chopped nasturtium flowers
1/4 cup prepared horseradish
Crackers *or* snack rye bread

In a small mixing bowl, beat the cream cheese, nasturtium flowers and horseradish until well blended. Serve with crackers or bread. **Yield:** 1-1/2 cups.

Avocado Pineapple Salsa

This colorful salsa developed by our home economists features the leaves of lovage, which is an aromatic perennial herb. Sweet pineapple balances perfectly with tart lime.

1 fresh pineapple, peeled and diced
1 medium ripe avocado, peeled and diced
1/3 cup finely chopped red onion
5 lovage *or* celery leaves, finely chopped
1 jalapeno pepper, seeded and chopped*
3 tablespoons lime juice
1 teaspoon grated lime peel
1/4 teaspoon salt
Tortilla chips

In a bowl, combine the first eight ingredients. Cover and refrigerate for at least 30 minutes before serving. Serve with tortilla chips. **Yield:** 5 cups.

*Editor's Note: When cutting or seeding hot peppers, use rubber or plastic gloves to protect your hands. Avoid touching your face.

Strawberry Vinegar

If you're looking for a fun and flavorful way to enjoy juicy strawberries, try this vinegar from our Test Kitchen. Use it to make the Creamy Strawberry Salad Dressing on the opposite page.

2 pints fresh strawberries, halved
2 cups cider vinegar
2 tablespoons sugar

In a large saucepan, combine strawberries and vinegar; let stand for 1 hour. Add sugar; bring to a boil. Reduce heat; cover and simmer for 10 minutes. Cool. Strain through a double layer of cheesecloth; do not press fruit. Let stand for 1 hour. Store in a sterilized jar in a cool dark place. **Yield:** 2-1/2 cups.

FRESH STRAWBERRY FACTS

LOOK for brightly colored, plump and fragrant strawberries with the green hulls intact. Avoid any that are soft, shriveled or moldy.

Wash berries before removing hulls.
One pint of strawberries yields 1-1/2 to 2 cups sliced.

Chair-Back Herb Bouquet

(Pictured at right)

NOT ONLY can fresh herbs flavor a variety of foods, they can provide a fabulous fragrance as well!

At your garden party, consider attaching easy Herb Bouquets to the backs of the guests' chairs.

First, tie onto the back of each chair a napkin that coordinates with your tablecloth.

For the Herb Bouquets, gather an assortment of fresh herbs, such as mint, sage and thyme. Tie with a ribbon and tuck into the knot of the napkin.

These aromatic bouquets can also serve as party favors.

Creamy Strawberry Salad Dressing

My family can't resist a sweet spinach and strawberry salad topped with this lovely dressing. Every bite smacks of summer.
—Kimberly Klindworth, Olathe, Kansas

1 cup sliced fresh strawberries
1/2 cup orange juice
2 tablespoons Strawberry Vinegar (recipe on opposite page) *or* raspberry vinegar
2 tablespoons olive oil
4 teaspoons honey
1/4 teaspoon salt
Baby spinach, red onion rings, orange segments, toasted sliced almonds and additional fresh strawberries

In a blender, combine the first six ingredients. Cover and process until pureed. Refrigerate until serving. In a salad bowl or on individual salad plates, combine the spinach, onion, orange, almonds and additional strawberries. Serve with dressing. **Yield:** 1-1/2 cups.

Take Time Out to Tailgate

IS IT up to you to tackle the task of cooking a meal that your husband and his buddies can take to the big game this fall?

There's no need to fumble around the kitchen if you turn to this make-ahead menu!

Jumbo Greek Sub is just the sandwich for satisfying hearty appetites. Pass the platter and watch slices disappear!

For a side dish that's teeming with colorful produce and winning flavor, you can't go wrong with a cool Dressed-Up Vegetable Salad.

Then score extra points with the guys by packing a big batch of Chocolate Mint Delights. (All recipes shown at right.)

OUTDOOR EATING
(Top to bottom)

Chocolate Mint Delights (p. 239)

Dressed-Up Vegetable Salad (p. 240)

Jumbo Greek Sub (p. 238)

Jumbo Greek Sub

(Pictured on page 237)

It's nice to make just one sandwich that generously feeds six people.
This meal from our Test Kitchen is easy to transport to a tailgate party or potluck.

2 **boneless skinless chicken breast halves (6 ounces** *each***)**
1 **cup olive oil vinaigrette salad dressing,** *divided*
1 **tablespoon olive oil**
1 **loaf (1 pound) unsliced Italian bread**
1/4 **cup crumbled basil and tomato-flavored feta** *or* **plain feta cheese**
1/4 **cup sliced ripe olives**
1 **jar (7-1/4 ounces) roasted red peppers, drained**
15 **to 20 cucumber slices (1/8 inch thick)**

Flatten chicken to 1/4-in. thickness. Place in a large resealable plastic bag. Add 3/4 cup salad dressing; seal and turn to coat. Refrigerate for 3 hours.

Drain and discard marinade. In a skillet, cook chicken in oil for 5 minutes on each side or until juices run clear. Cool. Cut the top third off the loaf of bread. Carefully hollow out top and bottom, leaving a 1/2-in. shell (discard removed bread or save for another use). Brush remaining salad dressing on cut sides of bread. Sprinkle feta and olives in bottom half of bread. Top with chicken, red peppers and cucumber. Replace bread top. Wrap tightly in plastic wrap; refrigerate for at least 2 hours. **Yield:** 6-8 servings.

Grilled Glazed Drummies

My family prefers these mild-tasting chicken wings more than the
traditional hot wings. They are great for any gathering.
—Laura Mahaffey, Annapolis, Maryland

1 **cup ketchup**
1/3 **cup soy sauce**
4 **teaspoons honey**
3/4 **teaspoon ground ginger**
1/2 **teaspoon garlic powder**
3 **pounds chicken drumettes (about 24)**

In a bowl, combine the ketchup, soy sauce, honey, ginger and garlic powder; mix well. Pour 1 cup marinade into a large resealable plastic bag; add the chicken. Seal bag and turn to coat; refrigerate for at least 4 hours or overnight. Cover and refrigerate remaining marinade for basting.

Drain and discard marinade from chicken. Grill chicken, covered, over medium heat for 5 minutes. Turn and baste with reserved marinade. Grill 10-15 minutes longer or until juices run clear, turning and basting occasionally. **Yield:** 2 dozen.

Chocolate Mint Delights

(Pictured at right and on page 237)

I tuck a chocolate-covered peppermint patty into every one of these rich cookies. The drizzle on top adds a nice touch. I revised a brownie recipe to create these take-along treats.
—Heather Sandberg
Waukesha, Wisconsin

  1 **cup butter, softened**
  1 **cup sugar**
  1 **egg**
  1 **teaspoon vanilla extract**
1-3/4 **cups all-purpose flour**
  1/2 **cup baking cocoa**
1-1/2 **teaspoons baking powder**
  1/4 **teaspoon salt**
 24 **bite-size chocolate-covered**
    peppermint patties
ICING:
 18 **bite-size chocolate-covered**
    peppermint patties
4-1/2 **teaspoons butter**

In a mixing bowl, cream butter and sugar. Beat in egg and vanilla. Combine the flour, cocoa, baking powder and salt; gradually add to creamed mixture. Cover and refrigerate for 30 minutes or until easy to handle. Shape dough into two 6-in. rolls; wrap each in plastic wrap. Refrigerate for 2 hours or until firm.

Unwrap dough and cut into 1/4-in. slices. Place one slice on waxed paper; top with a peppermint patty and a second dough slice. Press edges of dough together to completely cover the peppermint patty. Repeat.

Place 2 in. apart on ungreased baking sheets. Bake at 325° for 11-13 minutes or until set, watching carefully. Cool for 5 minutes before removing to wire racks. For icing, in a microwave, melt peppermint patties and butter; stir until smooth. Drizzle over cookies. **Yield:** 2 dozen.

Editor's Note: This recipe was tested with Pearson's Mint Patties.

Country Ribs with Ginger Sauce

This recipe comes from my church kitchen. It's appeared on many menus through the years because the ribs have such mass appeal.
—Evangeline Jones, Standfordville, New York

3 pounds boneless country-style pork ribs
1/4 cup sugar
1/2 teaspoon salt
1/2 cup soy sauce
1/2 cup ketchup
3 tablespoons brown sugar
2 teaspoons minced fresh gingerroot

Sprinkle ribs with sugar and salt; rub into both sides of meat. Refrigerate for 2 hours. In a small bowl, combine the soy sauce, ketchup, brown sugar and ginger. Spoon half of the sauce over both sides of ribs; refrigerate for 1 hour. Set remaining sauce aside for basting.

Place ribs on a greased rack in a 15-in. x 10-in. x 1-in. baking pan. Bake at 450° for 15 minutes; drain. Reduce heat to 350°; bake 1-1/2 hours longer or until meat is tender, basting with remaining sauce every 15 minutes. **Yield:** 8-12 servings.

Dressed-Up Vegetable Salad

(Pictured on page 237)

If taking our Test Kitchen's marinated veggie salad to a picnic, simply place it in a covered plastic container and pop it into your cooler for easy transporting.

2 cups fresh broccoli florets
1 medium sweet yellow pepper, cut into 1-inch pieces
1 medium sweet orange pepper, cut into 1-inch pieces
1/2 medium red onion, cut into 1/4-inch wedges
1 cup halved cherry tomatoes
DRESSING:
6 tablespoons olive oil
3 tablespoons red wine vinegar
1-1/2 teaspoons Dijon mustard
2 to 3 garlic cloves, minced
1 teaspoon dried oregano
3/4 teaspoon sugar
1/4 teaspoon salt
1/8 teaspoon pepper

In a salad bowl, combine the vegetables. In a jar with a tight-fitting lid, combine the dressing ingredients; shake well. Drizzle over vegetables and toss to coat. Cover and refrigerate for at least 1 hour. Toss before serving. **Yield:** 8 servings.

BUYING AND STORING BROCCOLI

BROCCOLI comes from the Latin word brachium, which means branch or arm.

When purchasing broccoli, look for bunches that have a deep green color, tightly closed buds and crisp leaves. Store in a resealable plastic bag in the refrigerator for up to 4 days. Wash just before using.

One pound of broccoli yields about 2 cups florets.

Chip 'n' Dip Burgers

(Pictured at right)

French onion dip and potato chips top these special hamburgers. They're so delicious, no other toppings are needed!
— Diane Hixon, Niceville, Florida

1-1/2 cups crushed potato chips, *divided*
1-1/2 cups French onion dip, *divided*
1/4 cup dill pickle relish
1-1/2 pounds ground beef
    6 hamburger buns, toasted

In a bowl, combine half of the potato chips and half of the dip; add relish. Crumble beef over the mixture and mix well. Shape into six patties. Grill, covered, over medium heat for 6 minutes on each side or until meat is no longer pink. Serve on buns; top with remaining chips and dip. **Yield:** 6 servings.

Stuffed Gouda Spread

I have fun experimenting with different cheeses in my cooking.
I don't know a busy who doesn't appreciate make-ahead appetizers like this!
—Sally Halfaker, St. Charles, Missouri

    1 package (7 ounces) Gouda
        cheese
1/4 cup beer *or* nonalcoholic beer
    2 tablespoons butter, cubed
    1 teaspoon Dijon mustard
1-1/2 teaspoons snipped fresh dill
    or 1/2 teaspoon dill weed
Crackers *or* pretzels

Carefully slice off the top of the waxed coating on the cheese round. Scoop out the cheese; set waxed shell aside. Place cheese in a food processor. Add the beer, butter and mustard; cover and process until smooth. Stir in dill. Spoon into the reserved shell. Refrigerate until serving. Serve with crackers or pretzels. **Yield:** 1-1/3 cups.

Hearty Party Meatballs

This flavorful, filling appetizer is similar to Swedish meatballs.
They always disappear when I make them for parties.
—*Sue Graham, Kansas City, Missouri*

4 bacon strips, diced
2 teaspoons beef bouillon
   granules
2 cups boiling water
1 egg
1/4 cup dry bread crumbs
3/4 teaspoon salt, *divided*
Dash pepper
1 pound lean ground beef
2 medium onions, sliced and
   separated into rings
1/4 cup all-purpose flour
1 can (12 ounces) beer *or* 1-1/2
   cups beef broth
2 teaspoons brown sugar
2 teaspoons white vinegar
1/2 teaspoon dried thyme
1/4 to 1/2 teaspoon browning
   sauce, optional

In a small skillet, cook bacon over medium heat until crisp; remove to paper towels. Drain, reserving drippings. In a small bowl, dissolve bouillon in boiling water. In a large bowl, combine the egg, 1/4 cup of bouillon, bread crumbs, 1/4 teaspoon salt and pepper. Crumble beef over mixture and mix well. Shape into 1-in. balls.

In a large skillet, brown meatballs in 1 tablespoon of reserved bacon drippings; drain. With a slotted spoon, transfer to a greased 11-in. x 7-in. x 2-in. baking dish. In the same skillet, saute onions until tender; drain. Place over meatballs.

In a saucepan, combine flour and 2 tablespoons of reserved drippings until smooth. Gradually stir in beer or broth and remaining bouillon. Add the brown sugar, vinegar, thyme and remaining salt. Bring to a boil; cook and stir for 2 minutes or until thickened. Stir in browning sauce if desired. Pour over meatballs. Cover and bake at 350° for 40-45 minutes or until meat is no longer pink. Sprinkle with bacon. **Yield:** 2 dozen.

Oatmeal Pecan Bars

These chewy bars took first place in the bar cookie division at our county fair in 2001.
Topping them with a coconut-pecan frosting is a tasty twist.
—*Leslie Duncan, Hayden, Idaho*

2 cups all-purpose flour
2 cups old-fashioned oats
1-1/2 cups packed brown sugar
1 teaspoon baking soda
1 cup cold butter
1 can (15 ounces) coconut
   pecan frosting
1 cup (6 ounces) semisweet
   chocolate chips
1/2 cup chopped pecans

In a large bowl, combine the flour, oats, brown sugar and baking soda. Cut in butter until mixture resembles coarse crumbs. Set aside 2 cups for topping. Press remaining crumb mixture into a greased 15-in. x 10-in. x 1-in. baking pan. Bake at 350° for 8-10 minutes or until set.

In a microwave-safe bowl, heat frosting for 30-45 seconds or until softened; stir well. Spread over crust. Sprinkle with chocolate chips and pecans. Top with reserved crumb mixture. Bake for 14-18 minutes or until frosting is bubbly and top is golden brown. Cool completely on a wire rack; cut into squares. **Yield:** 40 servings.

Black Bean Dip

(Pictured at right)

With black beans, avocados, corn, peppers and cilantro, this family-favorite bean dip has lots of flavor and texture. This dip came about when I was experimenting with a similar recipe one day.
—Cheryl Anderson, Lincolnville, Maine

2 medium ripe avocados, peeled and diced
2 tablespoons lime juice
1 can (15-1/4 ounces) whole kernel corn, drained
1 can (15 ounces) black beans, rinsed and drained
1 medium sweet red pepper, chopped
6 green onions, chopped
2 tablespoons minced fresh cilantro
3 garlic cloves, minced
2 tablespoons olive oil
1 teaspoon red wine vinegar
1/2 teaspoon salt
1/4 teaspoon pepper
Tortilla chips

In a bowl, combine avocados and lime juice; let stand for 10 minutes. In a large bowl, combine the corn, beans, red pepper, onions, cilantro and garlic. In a small bowl, whisk the oil, vinegar, salt and pepper. Drizzle over corn mixture; toss to coat. Gently fold in the avocado mixture. Cover and refrigerate for at least 2 hours or until chilled. Serve with tortilla chips. **Yield:** 4-1/2 cups.

CUTTING KERNELS FROM CORNCOBS

WHEN making Black Bean Dip (above), you can use 1-3/4 cups fresh corn kernels instead of canned corn.

To cut kernels from a corncob, stand one end of the cob on a cutting board. Starting at the top, run a sharp knife down the cob, cutting deeply to remove whole kernels.

One medium cob yields about 1/2 cup kernels.

Zesty Smoked Links

These flavorful sausages prepared in a slow cooker are great when entertaining.
Men in the family can't resist these basic but good snacks.
—*Jackie Boothman, La Grande, Oregon*

1 **bottle (12 ounces) chili sauce**
1 **cup grape jelly**
2 **tablespoons lemon juice**
2 **packages (1 pound *each*)**
   miniature smoked sausage
   links *and/or* hot dogs

In a large skillet, combine chili sauce, jelly and lemon juice; cook over medium-low heat until jelly is melted. Stir in sausages. Reduce heat; cover and cook for 30 minutes or until heated through, stirring occasionally. Serve immediately or keep warm in a slow cooker. **Yield:** about 32 servings.

GREAT TIPS FOR TAILGATING

YOU'RE guaranteed a successful tailgate party with these winning helpful hints:

- Keep the menu simple. Guests aren't expecting a seven-course meal at this kind of casual get-together. Three to four home-made dishes should be the maximum. Fill in with purchased items like chips and dip if necessary.
- When selecting foods, look for ones that are easy to eat while standing up or sitting in a lawn chair. Also, dishes made without perishable ingredients (such as mayonnaise) travel best. Rely on foods that can be made ahead and brought to the event or that can be cooked there on the grill. When transporting, remember to keep hot foods hot and cold foods cold.
- If you're feeling ambitious, handle all the food yourself and divide the cost among the group. Or assign a food item to each person attending.
- To get an early start in the morning, pack the car the night before with nonperishable food, chairs and tables. Don't forget supplies like a blanket or tablecloth to spread over the tailgate and a variety of paper products (plates, napkins, utensils, paper towels, trash bags, resealable plastic bags, etc.).
- True tailgaters proudly show their support of the team, so dress in team colors or jerseys!
- Just before heading out, pack the food and beverage coolers. Covered plastic containers work great for all kinds of food because they prevent leaks and won't break during transport.
- When you get to the parking lot, fly a team banner so other tailgaters in your group can find you. Or keep in contact with cell phones.
- Plan on eating at least 45 minutes before the game starts. This gives you time to clean up and pack things away.
- Before heading into the game, make note of your parking location so you're not lost in a sea of cars afterward.
- Instead of fighting traffic jams when the game is over, linger in the parking lot for an hour or so. Rehash the highlights of the game over a snack or dessert.

Sweet 'n' Salty Snack Mix

(Pictured at right)

When my children were growing up, they enjoyed making—and eating!—this snack mix, especially on Halloween. Now my grandchildren love it as well.
—Ann Brown, Bolivar, Missouri

2-1/2 quarts popped popcorn
2 cups salted peanuts
2 cups miniature pretzels
2 cups raisins
1 cup plain M&M's
1 cup candy corn
1/2 cup sunflower kernels

In a large bowl, combine all of the ingredients; mix well. Store in an airtight container. **Yield:** about 4 quarts.

Sub Salad

salami, ham, pepperoni and cheeses make this hearty salad a favorite of hungry folks. I sometimes serve this in a bread bowl.
—Dana Pletz, Wilmington, Delaware

8 ounces hard salami, diced
8 ounces fully cooked ham, diced
8 ounces pepperoni, diced
4 ounces provolone cheese, diced
4 ounces American cheese, diced
2 medium tomatoes, chopped
1 medium red onion, chopped
1/2 cup mayonnaise
1 tablespoon olive oil
1/2 teaspoon garlic salt
1/4 teaspoon dried oregano
French bread slices

In a 2-1/2-qt. glass serving bowl, combine the first seven ingredients. In a small bowl, combine the mayonnaise, oil, garlic salt and oregano. Pour over meat mixture and toss to coat. Cover and refrigerate until serving. Serve with French bread. **Yield:** 8-10 servings.

REFERENCE INDEX

Use this index as a guide to the many helpful hints, food facts, decorating ideas and step-by-step instructions throughout the book.

GENERAL RECIPE INDEX

This handy index lists every recipe by food category, major ingredient and/or cooking method.

ALPHABETICAL INDEX

Refer to this index for a complete alphabetical listing of all recipes in this book.